PLAS

PITT
LATIN
AMERICAN
SERIES

BLACK
LABOR
ON A
WHITE
CANAL

BLACK LABOR
ON A WHITE CANAL

PANAMA, 1904–1981

Michael L. Conniff

University of Pittsburgh Press

Published by the University of Pittsburgh Press, Pittsburgh, Pa. 15260
Copyright © 1985, University of Pittsburgh Press
Feffer and Simons, Inc., London

Library of Congress Cataloging in Publication Data

Conniff, Michael L.
  Black labor on a white canal.

  Bibliography: p. 211.
  Includes index.
  1. Blacks—Panama—History—20th century. 2. Panama
—Race relations. 3. Labor policy—United States—
History—20th century.   4. Labor policy—Canal Zone—
History—20th century.   I. Title.
F1577.B55C67 1985   305.8'96'072875   84-21970
ISBN 0-8229-3509-0

To George W. Westerman

Contents

Tables and Figures

Preface

THREE PRINCIPAL GROUPS worked together to build the Panama Canal: North Americans, Panamanians, and West Indians. When they finished, they created a microsociety in the ten-mile-wide Zone to run the canal. From the very beginning, the canal was a body of water surrounded by controversy, partly because of the large number of West Indians who stayed on after their canal work was completed. American managers exploited them in a regime I call a third-country labor system. Panamanians labeled them undesirable immigrants and tried to send them away. Many did leave Panama during hard times, moving to other parts of Latin America or to the United States. The majority remained as an unwanted minority and built a defensive subculture to cope with American racism and exploitation, as well as Panamanian chauvinism.

The story of the West Indians in Panama is moving toward a satisfactory ending. The U.S. government has gradually reduced racism and exploitation and in 1977 concluded a treaty with Panama providing for the latter's eventual ownership of the canal. Descendants of the West Indian immigrants are treated fairly under its terms—neither as a disadvantaged minority nor as a protected group. They share the same benefits and responsibilities as their Latin Panamanian compatriots. Many Panamanians have recognized the faults of their earlier rejection of the West Indian community and are dealing with the resultant problems of prejudice and discrimination. The treaty still has years to run and Panama must continue to combat racism, but both processes are moving in complementary and humane directions.

[xiii]

Telling the story of the West Indians in Panama required some special treatment. I tried to understand and represent as fairly as possible the viewpoints of the three groups. This necessitated research in Washington, D.C., and London, where bureaucrats made decisions about the canal and the laborers. I relied heavily on the canal administration files for the U.S. side, and on interviews and newspapers for the Panamanian and West Indian positions. The discussion moves chronologically, dealing with successive generations of West Indians. The scenes shift between the Antilles, the canal, Panama City, and Washington. I hope that this organization can be followed easily and avoids favoring one point of view over another.

Since most documentation came from primary materials, I provide an essay on sources and selected bibliography. Out of the thousands of titles about the Panama Canal and race relations, I list only those that deal specifically with the West Indians in Panama. I have kept notes as succinct as possible, by using *passim* for runs of correspondence in a single file and by citing newspaper articles by date only. To save space, I have combined multiple references in a single note covering an entire paragraph. Even though many documents appear in several different files, I provide only one location. An experienced researcher can easily find all of the material cited in the notes. As for style, I have retained British spelling in quotations but have modernized capitalization throughout. After some concerted attempts, I gave up trying to calculate precise numbers of migrants and permanent settlers. Immigration data are hopelessly flawed, and Panamanian censuses stopped tabulating race after 1940. The figures provided are my best guesses after juggling the numbers cited by various official sources.

Many people helped in the preparation of this book, and several merit special thanks. In the early stages, David McCullough and Tom Holloway gave warm encouragement. In field research, I was helped by Pandora Aleman, Harold Caroll, and the staff of the Diablo Records Center; Patrice Brown of the Suitland, Maryland, Records Center; Paul Saxton, Teresita de Appin, and the International Communication Agency staff in Panama; Arilla Kourany, Farrell Brody, and Nan Chong; and from Olive Senior in Kingston and Velma Newton in Bridgetown. Several colleagues have shared notes and ideas along the way. John Major, who is writing a book on U.S.-Panamanian relations, has been a comrade-in-arms. Carol Rodrigues played an important part while I was in Panama. Bon Richardson, Alda Harper, Alberto Smith, and Eunice Mason provided guidance. Audley Webster, Alfred Osborne, Ed Gaskin, and Leroy Gittens were especially helpful interviewees. In the end, however, it was George Westerman who contributed the most to this book by sharing his experiences, clippings, and papers. The book is dedicated to him.

Preface

The Fulbright-Hayes program, Tinker Foundation, American Philosophical Society, and Research Allocations Committee of the University of New Mexico gave me generous support. Renee Gaffan and Sharon O'Brien kindly word-processed the book. My warmest appreciation goes to all who contributed to its completion.

BLACK
LABOR
ON A
WHITE
CANAL

1

Introduction

TWO SUBJECTS dominate this book. The first is the settlement of over 100,000 black West Indians in the small Central American republic of Panama. Many of these people were hired as the unskilled work force for the isthmian canal that the United States began to build in 1904. The second is U.S. labor policy on the canal from that date until the United States began to relinquish its control over the waterway by the Carter-Torrijos Treaty of 1977. Each in turn forms part of a larger concern. The West Indian experience in Panama has been a microcosm of the African diaspora in which blacks have been scattered abroad by the forces of slavery, poverty, and white supremacy. Canal labor policy was likewise a key element in the colonial relationship between the American colossus and its tiny Panamanian client-state. *Black Labor on a White Canal* traces the history of the West Indian predicament on the isthmus under both American and Panamanian masters. The climax came when West Indians and Panamanians began to come to terms with one another and when Washington acknowledged that its prized outpost at the crossroads of the Americas was an anachronism in a largely decolonized world.

The Caribbean migrations to Panama had begun in the early nineteenth century and increased during periods of railroad and canal construction. About 5,000 went to work on the Panama Railroad between 1850 and 1855. Then as many as 50,000 went there during the abortive French canal project of 1880–1889. Most returned to the islands, but some remained in Panama to farm, start businesses, raise families, or wait for the next big undertaking. Colón, at the Caribbean terminus of

[3]

the railroad, became one more link in the chain of West Indian settlements along the north coast of Central America.

Migration during the American construction period became a tidal wave, bringing approximately 150,000 persons in the decade 1904–1914. Most did not plan to stay. Eventually, though, tens of thousands remained because the islands offered few opportunities that could compete with the pay and benefits available in Panama. The West Indians settled, married, had children, and became the largest immigrant group in the sparsely populated country.[1]

Panamanians at first viewed the West Indians as a necessary inconvenience for completing the canal, but by the 1920s latent chauvinism flared into a campaign to deport the immigrants. Competition for canal jobs, racial aversion, and anger over the rising cost of living fueled the agitation. The rejection reached a peak in 1941, when a new constitution took citizenship away from many who were born there, and several laws severely restricted the rights of the entire black community. These events belied the Latin Americans' claims of racial tolerance.

The immigrants banded together and created a defensive subculture. British West Indian schools, businesses, and associations multiplied, and black immigrants looked to the Canal Zone for protection. Their leaders requested U.S. citizenship, opportunities to migrate to the United States, or a chance to settle on vacant Zone land. Failing this, they began collaborating with Latin Panamanian politicians who promised to protect them from deportation.[2]

Panamanians believed that, short of deportation, the only way to accommodate so many foreigners was through assimilation: they should give up their own culture and adopt that of Panama. This meant renouncing British nationality, hispanicizing their names, speaking Spanish, marrying Latin spouses, converting to Catholicism, and ending ties with the islands. Many thousands, caught in the crossfire of Panamanian chauvinism and American discrimination in the 1930s and 1940s, took this route.

West Indian community leaders, however, argued that they should not have to give up their cultural traditions in order to be accepted. Those traditions helped them in canal employment. Many schools and businesses in Panama needed their English language and cross-cultural skills. To be absorbed piecemeal by giving up all of their traditions amounted to cultural extinction. Rather, some argued, Panamanians had to respect their contribution to the nation and accept them as equals before blending of cultures could proceed. This process of pluralist accommodation without suppression of immigrant traditions will be called *integration* throughout this book.[3]

Canal managers from the United States took advantage of the cheap labor and distance from Washington to create a life of relative luxury for employees who were U.S. citizens. They divided the work force into two

[4]

payrolls, skilled and unskilled, termed the *gold* and *silver rolls*. This system, examined in greater detail below, put U.S. citizens on the gold roll and provided salaries at least 25 percent higher than those for comparable jobs in the United States. In addition, gold employees enjoyed free housing, utilities, schools, and medical care, and had liberal leaves and vacations. Their combined wages and benefits amounted to double what was paid in the United States from the 1920s to the 1950s. Canal policy accentuated the privileged status of U.S. employees by denying these benefits to noncitizen employees, those on the silver roll.

Silver workers outnumbered gold by four or five to one. Only half lived in the Canal Zone, in inferior housing for which they paid modest rent. Zone life was regimented and segregated. Virtually all facilities existed in duplicate, one set for gold (or white) employees, another for silver. Americans did not admit that they practiced Jim Crow segregation because it was not permitted under the U.S. Constitution. Rather, they used the gold-silver system to disguise it. For their part, silver workers had difficulty fighting segregation because they were not citizens.[4]

The canal labor regime was not simply a dual or split one, because it formed part of the Panamanian and even the overall Caribbean economy. I have chosen to call it a third-country labor system, because nationals from beyond the two primary countries—Panama and the United States—provided the bulk of the work force. This allowed canal management to hold wages down with abundant imported labor and to provoke competition between the immigrants and local workers. This rivalry, by hindering interaction between the two groups, impeded integration as well.[5]

As unfair as the third-country labor system seems in hindsight, it did not differ greatly from practices then current around the world. Most of the East Indians and Chinese indentured workers in the European empires were in fact third-country nationals employed by colonial companies.[6] Had the canal labor system been reformed after the 1920s, the damage done to the West Indians and to U.S.-Panamanian relations would have been limited. Canal administrators certainly had such an opportunity after 1921, when a special board recommended raising the silver wages to equal those received by beginning gold workers and replacing many of the latter. They had another chance in 1936, when the U.S. secretary of state signed a note promising equality of opportunity and treatment in labor relations. The first generation of Panamanians of West Indian descent came of age in the 1930s and could have qualified for these equality provisions.

A number of circumstances, however, enabled canal administrators to perpetuate the third-country labor system beyond the 1950s. Costs were a factor, especially during the Depression and World War II. Panama's restrictive policies on citizenship, moreover, put the West Indian descendants' status in doubt and thereby reinforced the exploitative system. Many canal officials gave hiring preference to the members of the next generation, out of a sense of responsibility to the community that the canal had engendered. Security also favored the status quo, because a weak and dependent labor force could not afford to be disloyal.

Thus in the years of depression and war, canal managers decided not to phase out the third-country labor system. Still, the exploitative situation might have been rectified in the late 1940s without lasting consequences. Two other attendant decisions, however, rendered the status quo reprehensible and made the system nearly impossible to reform later. First, racism and segregation continued to characterize labor relations and reinforced the third-country system. By the 1950s, the Canal Zone fell behind the District of Columbia in racial improvements, allowing critics to make damaging comparisons with the U.S. South. Second, Zone administrators gave little support to the "colored" schools (as those for nonwhites were called) on the assumption that the rising generation would be fit only for manual labor. This condemned the majority to inferior education and limited job opportunities after World War II. Lack of instruction in Spanish and Panamanian culture, which might have facilitated West Indian acceptance in Panama, created a generation of Canal Zone citizens out of touch with their adopted homeland. Such policies, hard to square with the official presentation of the American way of life, complicated U.S.-Panamanian relations until the 1980s.

Change did come to the Canal Zone, of course, and it proved more traumatic because of entrenched labor distinctions, segregation, and educational neglect. After World War II Panama rescinded laws against the West Indian community and began to attack discrimination in jobs and public facilities in the Zone. By this time most non-U.S. employees were Panamanian descendants of West Indians, so the system evolved into a dual or split one based on nationality. Washington, embarrassed by unfair labor and racial practices there, put on pressure to merge the two rolls and end segregation. Canal officials went on the defensive and subverted the intent of studies, orders, and even laws. From the 1950s on they retreated gradually, giving up peripheral advantages but protecting the heartland of U.S. privilege. Only when President Johnson (followed by Nixon, Ford, and Carter) decided to replace the 1903 treaty did the very bases of the Zonian way of life begin to erode.[7]

The treaty of 1977 and the Panama Canal Act of 1979 provide for a transition from U.S. to Panamanian operation of the canal and for Panamanian ownership after the year 2000. For better or worse, the United States is liquidating its colonialist role in the Canal Zone. In order to accomplish this transition, the dual wage system and racial discrimination had to be eliminated. Some descendants of the West Indians raised doubts about Panama's intentions toward them, fearing that they would lose their jobs, homes, and cultural identity. The treaty and act contained safeguards against such abuses, but some persons have unquestionably suffered.

[6]

Nevertheless, an expected exodus of noncitizen canal employees to the United States (provided for in the act) has not materialized. The treaty framers anticipated an exodus because they realized the noncitizen employees would be transferred to lower-paid jobs or would be terminated and that the benefits of living in the Zone would end. A similar decline in living standards following the 1955 treaty provoked a large migration of West Indian descendants to the United States. This reinforced some Panamanians' conviction that the emigrants were not loyal to their adopted country. The exodus also deprived the West Indian community of leaders in all fields, a brain drain. Thus officials expected a similar phenomenon after the 1977 treaty. In fact, the U.S. consulate received only about 11 percent of the anticipated requests for visas under the act.

Not only the brain drain but also the unsettled period of the diaspora itself had all but ended for the West Indian community in Panama by 1977. Integration was not complete in the 1970s, but a dialogue between Panamanian and West Indian intellectuals had defined and explored most aspects of the question. Racial tolerance after the treaty stood at an all-time high.

Therefore my investigation reveals great improvements in the two major problems in Panama: racism and exploitative labor practices. Most of the West Indian community have found homes in Panama and have achieved some degree of integration or social assimilation. Canal labor policies toward the West Indians became less discriminatory and eventually approximated a single wage scale for all employees. Appraisal of the larger problems—the cultural integration and U.S.-Panamanian relations—must await the conclusion of the 1977 treaty in the year 2000. Yet there, too, most indications are positive.

Race Relations

This book also compares race relations across several societies. Americans applied their own racial definitions to the heterogeneous population of Panama and segregated it into the gold and silver rolls of the Canal Zone. Most West Indians were familiar with racial discrimination in the British colonies, although it took different forms. Finally, the Panamanians, who had hitherto not been particularly concerned with racial distinctions, were forced to deal with a vast influx of black people after construction began on the canal. The confrontation of different racial ideologies and their evolution over time provides a continuing theme for this narrative.

That North Americans should replicate the Jim Crow racial system in the Canal Zone was not inevitable. First, most canal employees came from the North, where segregation had been mild before 1904. Second, the West Indian blacks to whom they applied Jim Crow laws bore little resemblance to the blacks in the southern United States. Perhaps the

[7]

Americans, thrown into a confusing racial and cultural setting, wished to minimize contact with people unlike themselves. Yet, as in the States, race distinctions clashed with their democratic ethic and with the Constitution as well.

Gold-silver segregation, rationalized as local custom, accomplished the isolation of whites from blacks the Americans apparently desired. The southerners among canal managers helped mold the system into a replica of Jim Crow. Northerners, as one observer noted, readily learned to hate blacks. A high level of racial antagonism prevailed, exacerbated by the hardships of the construction camp setting. Whites treated blacks harshly, and white children learned to bully black children. Disparities in living conditions convinced the next generation of whites that they were superior to blacks. Only then—in the 1930s—did whites display the benevolent paternalism toward blacks with which southerners justified their superior status. The fact that silver workers were not U.S. citizens, however, kept Zonian paternalism on a formal level. As the descendants of West Indians became integrated into Panamanian society, formality between the races stiffened and benevolence waned. The simple racial model of the early gold-silver system became obsolete.

Because racist attitudes were becoming less acceptable in the United States, Zonians needed to buttress the gold-silver division with other justifications. At various times they cited differences of nationality, tropical climate, customs, and physiology as further reasons for the segregation of workers. Their racial ideology became so rigid that they could not relinquish it when pressured to do so by the evolution of U.S. civil rights laws and developments in U.S.-Panamanian affairs. Thus, the race and labor policies of the Canal Zone, locked into position early in the century, had to be broken by American, West Indian, and Panamanian reformers. The gold-silver system went from being an anomaly to an embarrassment to an obstacle in the path of U.S. foreign policy.

West Indians brought a different concept of race relations from the islands. Slavery had ended in the British, French, and Danish possessions between 1838 and 1848, and two full generations of free blacks had arisen before the American canal era. Few of the islands had prospered, but the freedmen and their descendants had developed a sense of independence and personal dignity. British subjects in particular came to prize their connection with the greatest nation on earth. Most had become peasant farmers and artisans.

British colonial methods of dealing with freedmen included cooptation of light-skinned blacks, inflating local pride, and cajolery. Talented mulattoes had early on been absorbed into the bureaucracies and small professional strata and helped keep the black majority in line. This intermediate group served as a buffer to reduce friction and unpleasantness between the tiny white elite and the black masses.[8]

Some Jewish, Spanish, Portuguese, and Middle Eastern families

[8]

that had become racially mixed nonetheless identified with the colonial elite and reinforced the system of white rule. These were the so-called white West Indians discussed in chapter 4. By doling out favors and privileges to these two groups, the British could continue to run the islands without excessive administrative costs.

The British also built up localist feelings and promoted rivalry among the islands in order to prevent the formation of pan-Caribbean sentiments that might lead to an anticolonialist movement. Inhabitants of each island were taught that they were better than those of other islands. After several generations of such peaceful rivalry, the West Indians found it hard to get along with one another. Second-generation immigrants in Panama formed benevolent societies by island of origin and preferred to marry persons from the same island. One man who had worked in Bocas del Toro before moving to the Canal Zone said, "There is no sense putting so many different races together—Jamaicans and Bims [Barbadians] and Martiniques in the same room. It is not right." A number of authors cited this interisland jealousy as an obstacle to black solidarity.[9]

Finally, the British elite developed new labor techniques that circumvented the West Indians' natural desire for freedom from supervision. One observer claimed, "It is really only Englishmen that can manage coloured labor. . . . The West Indian Negro has been subjected to kindness and strict justice . . . tempered with a little wit or sarcasm."[10] Sugar planters began buying cane from peasant producers and gradually induced dependence upon cash income that bound the blacks to the mills. Others experimented with sharecropping to produce the same result. Most other forms of manual labor came to be done on a piece basis. Planters used black rather than white foremen and observed rules scrupulously to build a mystique of fairness. They thus imbued artisans with pride in their work and in the larger enterprise of making the island economies productive.

The West Indian labor system ultimately relied on cajolery, flattery, and tokenism, and could not endure. Pay and productivity remained extremely low throughout the postemancipation Caribbean. Tens of thousands of black workers voted with their feet by migrating to Central America and other parts. Occasionally so many left that crops at home were endangered. Then planters (assisted by the British Colonial Office) would import indentured workers from India and the Middle East to cover the labor shortages. While initially expensive, this solution created an effective third-country labor system with a divided and powerless work force. Trinidad and Guyana became segmented societies of this kind and remain divided even today.

The British themselves knew that the native labor system was a sham, though they rarely admitted it. Most also concealed their disdain toward their West Indian subjects. They realized that the islands could never prosper and had to export able-bodied men in order to survive. Therefore, with feigned benevolence, they encouraged their subjects to emigrate. Occasionally their true feelings came out. One Foreign Office functionary wrote on the cover of a note from Panama, "The petitioners, who are probably niggers, seem to think that 'British protection' means an alteration of the laws of Panama to suit them."[11] A few years later Governor Olivier of Jamaica inspected the Canal Zone and found:

> The episode [building the canal] has been educational both for West Indians as workers and for Americans as employers of coloured labor. The desultory Jamaican has been forced to conform to the conditions under which alone highly organized industry can be carried on. . . . The methods and manners of white United States foremen in dealing with Negroes have been very wholesomely civilized.

The governor assumed that the West Indians would remain along the north coast of Central America indefinitely, turning the region into an informal part of the British Empire. He did not expect them to return to the islands.[12]

Following a 1920 West Indian strike against the canal, a visiting white Jamaican observed that the workers were "still the 'white man's burden' and it will be hundreds of years before they cease to be."[13] Eventually the British would give up these unprofitable dependencies in the Caribbean anyway. The British were just as racist as the Americans, but they were more skillful in concealing it and in knowing where their long-term interests lay.

The West Indians themselves rarely knew how the British really felt about them. As a result they saw British racial and colonial policy as very different from American treatment of blacks, and they tended to idealize this view after being in the Canal Zone.[14] They remembered with nostalgia the island societies and the peculiar tolerance they had enjoyed. This romanticization of British colonial treatment caused many first- and second-generation immigrants to remain loyal to the British Empire and its symbols. This had two effects: it made West Indians more demanding of racial equality in the Canal Zone, yet naive in their expectations. For example, many were satisfied when canal officials acted with paternalism reminiscent of the British. They lost touch with rising black nationalism and labor militancy elsewhere. These innovations had to be introduced in Panama by Marcus Garvey in the 1920s, the National Association for the Advancement of Colored People in the 1940s, and black American leaders in the 1950s.

Second, the West Indians' attachment to British colonial racial practices made it difficult for them to get along with the Panamanians, who saw West Indians as subservient and obsequious, willing to be "trampled under foot by the gringos." Panamanians also doubted their sincerity in wanting naturalization. Thus British race relations had a negative effect on the accommodation of West Indians to their new home in Panama.

Panamanian attitudes toward blacks formed the third element in the complex racial equation of the canal. Before 1903, when Panama was part of Colombia, race was a minor factor in the affairs of Panama. The elite, descended from Spanish colonists, prided themselves on racial purity but accepted nonwhites as necessary in politics and business. Some elite families, moreover, had branches of mulattoes or mestizos who enjoyed social acceptance. Among the middle and lower classes, miscegenation had produced a highly mixed population, especially in the cities. Indeed, Colombians called Panama their black province. Two mulattoes had been governors in the province, several held management positions with the Panama Railroad, and one owned the country's leading newspaper.[15]

Panamanians, like most Latin Americans, had a racial ideology quite distinct from the Anglo-Saxon one. They relied on somatic indicators to distinguish among the races and possessed a wide spectrum of designations. They had inherited from colonial times an ethic (not always practiced) of interracial harmony that discouraged segregation. This tradition had been strengthened during the Enlightenment and following independence from Spain. In addition, Panamanians were less exposed to the racist biological theories popular in Europe around the turn of the century and thus had little intellectual basis for racism. So for these reasons, Panamanian social thought was largely integrationist with regard to race.

After the United States began building the canal, however, Panama's elite displayed some of the race prejudices that had been latent earlier. They realized that North Americans preferred to deal with whites, so they gradually adopted a policy favoring whites in high government posts and in the diplomatic corps. In the early years the Americans reinforced this preference by favoring the Conservative party (largely made up of white families) over the Liberals, which included many mixed-bloods. Then, when the canal laid off thousands of workers after construction ended, jobs became scarcer, and hard times set in, especially after 1920. Some labor leaders and politicians began to blame the West Indians, and soon anti-immigrant sentiment laced with racism spread throughout the general public. People called them *chombos* (niggers) and other derogatory names and made jokes about negroid features. The easygoing tolerance of racially diverse people disappeared.

However, Panamanian racism never took on the harsh, rigid character of Zone segregation. Rejection of the West Indians arose out of economic frustration, and it fed on cultural differences as well. Race provided an easy way to identify the scapegoats but was not the principal cause of animosity. Most Panamanians did not experience physical revulsion toward blacks from the same social level. Race would rarely influence personal dealings. No law restricted West Indians' civil rights solely because of race. Prejudices could be overcome by those with talent, money, good looks, or other personal qualities. Therefore, racial barriers in Panama were weak.

After the peak of chauvinism in the early 1940s, Panamanian racism attenuated rapidly. By the end of the decade a North American specialist described it as more a cultural than a racial prejudice. He feared that Panamanians might eventually adopt a less flexible position, however, rejecting negroid characteristics per se, as Americans did.[16] That prediction was not borne out, due to the rise in integrationist sentiment in the United States and to the adversarial relationship between the two countries.

How did the three traditions of race relations interact? The very existence of different ideologies and behavior hindered the acceptance of West Indians in Panama, because an entirely new generation of leaders had to grow to maturity before compromises became possible. When that occurred, West Indian descendants and Panamanians allied against Canal Zone practices. To its credit, the United States government also opposed Zone racism.

Some Panamanians insisted that the country did not know race prejudice until exposed to the U.S. system. In this view, Panamanians learned prejudice from the Americans but then rejected it as unnatural. Racism was an aberration. The record does not support this interpretation, however, because the white Panamanian elite had collaborated with the Zonians to keep the racially mixed masses in a subservient position. The apexes of the two social pyramids leaned toward each other and formed a bond. The racial policies that flowed from that arrangement soon permeated both societies. Only when the Panamanian elite saw their interests as antithetical to those of the Zone elite and broke the bond did rivalry for the allegiance of the nonwhite majority begin. Panama, with a more humane tradition and a larger stake in the outcome, prevailed over the Zonians. Again to the credit of the United States, its government chose the winning side.

The West Indian Subculture

The emergence of a distinctive West Indian subculture in Panama provides another underlying theme for this book. Any immigrant group retains its culture for a time. The length depends upon the difficulties of assimilation and integration and the security afforded by the new homeland. Through the 1920s, Jamaicans, Barbadians, Martinicans, and others, formed their associations and maintained island traditions. Ethnic, religious, and language differences kept them separate. If necessary, they could all work together, as during the 1920 strike. But when Panamanians branded them as undesirables in 1926 and began threatening deportation, the West Indians coalesced into a defensive unity. The common danger overcame their differences. Broader-based pressure groups arose, the West Indian weekly *Panama Tribune* began publication, local schools were founded, and a new subculture was born.

The unique West Indian subculture borrowed from a variety of traditions: British, Caribbean, North American, and Panamanian. However, this synthesis was only fleeting, because too many contradictory elements were hastily thrown together. Its guardedness discouraged creative interaction among the parts, so when the danger passed in the 1950s, it gradually disintegrated. This subculture was above all a response to Panamanian chauvinism and to American mistreatment.

Schools became beacons that guided the Canal Zone's West Indians through the stormy 1930s and 1940s. Canal administrators neglected the education of black children born and raised in the Zone, allowing West Indian teachers in the all-black segregated schools to create a philosophy and curriculum tailored to the black community's needs. Alfred Osborne stood out as a leader in the so-called colored schools. The son of a Canal Zone principal, Osborne completed high school and college in Chicago and became a naturalized U.S. citizen. Upon his return to the Canal Zone in the 1930s, he conducted a normal school in which he developed a curriculum guide and trained thirty-seven of the brightest first-generation black Panamanians to be teachers. After 1945 this cadre of leaders took over the Zone colored schools, unions, churches, and social clubs. They took an integrationist philosophy from the classroom and disseminated it throughout the community.[17]

The tenets of West Indian integrationism included: (1) incorporation of the best of British, American, and Panamanian cultures into their own; (2) loyalty to Panama as citizens; (3) using opportunities for individual and group advancement in the United States; and (4) nonviolent and nonradical means of promoting the interests of the community. This philosophy guided the first-generation blacks in the Canal Zone and tended to undermine the West Indian subculture that formed in the 1930s. As they gained acceptance beyond the Zone in Panama itself, the defensive solidarity of the 1930s and 1940s became unnecessary and even a hindrance to integration.

The man who did the most to define and to carry out this philosophy was George Westerman, newspaperman, diplomat, and intellectual leader of first-generation Panamanians of West Indian descent. This study relies heavily on his writings and interpretations.[18]

Panamanian schools also played an important role in the integration of West Indian immigrant children. Some Canal Zone West Indians, recognizing the need to establish ties with Latin Panamanian society, sent their children to school in Panama to learn Spanish, local history and customs, and how to get along socially. By the 1940s the University of Panama played a similar role for black youths from the Canal Zone. Panamanian Schools provided a medium for two-way exchanges between the host and immigrant societies, outside the restrictive atmosphere of the Zone and free of Panamanian politics.

Education and Zone schools receive considerable attention in this study, because they provide a means for tracing the evolution of the

West Indian subculture. They reveal how West Indian adults defined and passed on to the next generation their own identity and that which they hoped their descendants would assume. Education meant so much to the black community because at times it was the only part of their lives they controlled.

This study covers some eighty years of history and hence touches on several generations of West Indians. Without imputing theoretical value to the concept, I have used generational analysis to synthesize the socio-cultural attributes of different age groups through time. I also use it to trace their relations with the changing world around them. Generations provide a shorthand for discussing the collective experience of thousands of people. Generations act and are acted upon, and the result is social history. Table 1 identifies the five generations discussed in this book.

The first- and second-generation immigrants moved back and forth between the islands and Panama to satisfy labor demands. They identified closely with British traditions and planned to retire on the islands or to use their earnings (called Panama money) to start small businesses there. As the decades passed, however, they became increasingly dependent upon Panama. The islands' economies languished, while that of the isthmus boomed. Even during layoffs and hard times, they could live better in Panama that at home. Those men who decided to stay sent for their wives and children or chose spouses from among the single women who had migrated to Panama. The decision to stay, often arrived at reluctantly and under duress, was made tens of thousands of times.

The children of immigrants and those who were naturalized became first-generation Panamanians. This book is primarily about them and

Table 1. Generations of West Indians in Panama

	Arrived/Born	*Citizenship*
Immigrants		
First Generation	1880–1903	British, French, and some Panamanian by
Second Generation	1904–1920	naturalization
Panamanians		
First Generation	1904–1928	Panamanian at birth; some dual citizenship (British/Panamanian)
Second Generation	1928–1961	Panamanian upon 21st birthday except from 1941 to 1945
Third Generation	1961–	Panamanian at birth; some dual citizenship (U.S./Panamanian)

their children. Chapter 4 picks up this generational analysis in the period following construction of the canal. The citizenship issue proved complex and controversial, for it symbolized the very role the new community would play in Panama. The details of this legal and social integration of first-generation black Panamanians provide another theme for the narrative.

To summarize, *Black Labor on a White Canal* will deal primarily with the massive influx of West Indians to Panama and their subsequent accommodation in the Canal Zone and adjacent cities of Panamá and Colón. Canal employment played the dominant role in the process, for most West Indians worked in the Zone and decided to stay because of good canal wages. Their attachment to the canal, however, hindered their adjustment to the Latin American society in which they would eventually remain. The canal employed West Indians and their children as a third-country labor force to depress wages and maximize control over workers. This system used race as a dividing wedge between West Indians and Hispanic Panamanians. Because of this, Panamanians at first opposed the permanent settlement of West Indians in their country. After the Second World War, however, Panamanians began to accept the immigrants and their children. By the 1950s the canal way of life was on the defensive, attacked simultaneously by Hispanic and West Indian Panamanians and by various agencies of the U.S. government.

2

West Indians in Panama Before 1903

WHEN U.S. OFFICIALS decided to recruit West Indians to work on the canal, they knew the group had already proved itself capable of heavy physical labor in the tropics. The diaspora had first taken West Indian blacks to the north coast of Panama in the 1820s, and several large construction projects soon brought more immigrants. By the 1890s West Indians had settled all along the Mosquito Coast and were concentrated in the region soon to be used for the U.S. canal. Nineteenth-century racial, ethnic, national, and labor relations would condition the West Indian experience in the later American era.

In the 1820s several British planters from San Andrés and Providence Island homesteaded with their slaves in the region of Bocas del Toro, on Panama's northwest coast, then under Colombian rule. The government of recently independent Colombia had imposed unreasonable taxes on their sugar operations, but planters in Bocas escaped such imposts. They were joined by a few Jamaican and North American whites. The settlement in Bocas remained small, subsisting on fishing, slash-and-burn agriculture, and forest gathering. West Indian peddlers traveling by mule and canoe traded with the Guaymi Indians and eventually taught them English and converted them to Protestantism. West Indians migrated to and from Bocas and other coastal towns by means of trading and fishing schooners.[1]

Emancipation in the British West Indies in 1838 freed over half a million slaves, transforming the islands' societies and economies. Most freedmen preferred not to do plantation work, and the sugar industries

gradually declined. Blacks in Jamaica and the Windwards took up farming in the hills or moved to towns and cities to find jobs. On the smaller
islands, migration became a way of life. The white colonial elite and
mulatto middle classes managed to reconstruct the social hierarchy so
that blacks remained at the bottom. In such a precarious position, black
freedmen had to take any jobs that appeared, including those abroad.
Thus began the trans-Caribbean migration phase of the diaspora.[2]

The California gold rush rekindled interest in a modern transportation route across Central America and spurred larger migrations. Two
crossings were developed, Vanderbilt's steamship and stage line in Nicaragua and the New York–based Panama Railroad. Both enterprises used
imported labor, largely Jamaican. Some 5,000 eventually worked on the
Panama line. These projects proved that West Indian blacks resisted
tropical diseases better than other workers and that they were available in
large numbers due to the islands' depressed economies.[3]

Caribbean migrations resumed in the 1880s as a result of two developments, the French canal project and the spread of banana cultivation. By then steamships visited the islands regularly, and far more
islanders took jobs abroad. The first French company employed over
50,000 West Indians during its unsuccessful bid to cut a seaway across
the isthmus, and its successor, the Compagnie Nouvelle, kept a skele-
ton work force until 1904 to protect its concession. The French period
marked a quantum leap in Caribbean migration, and it established patterns followed by the next generation of immigrants. Jamaicans moved
to Panama by schooner or ship, according to labor supply and demand.
They also took trips back home, to the consternation of French
officials.[4] After the collapse of the first company, many West Indians
stayed in Central America, moving on to Costa Rica, Guatemala, or
even Mexico.

Banana cultivation also proved a boon to the region's economy after
the 1880s, expanding commercial agriculture and inducing thousands
more to migrate. Jamaica itself exported bananas, but soon U.S. and
British companies opened up larger plantations on the Caribbean coast of
Central America. Bananas, then, reinforced the movement of laborers
from the islands to the mainland. By the early twentieth century, the
United Fruit Company operated a string of banana ports, including
Puerto Limón (Costa Rica) and Bocas del Toro. Limón had attracted
thousands of Jamaicans during the days when Minor C. Keith built a
railroad to the highlands. In this way, the few isolated West Indian
settlements of mid-century became thriving export centers.

In addition to West Indians, hundreds of whites of various nationalities came to supervise banana operations. The fruit companies provided
their white personnel with special housing and other facilities not available to the black workers. Most also established a dual wage system
favorable to their managerial staff.[5] This "tropical labor" system, fol-

lowed by the Panama Railroad as well, served as the pattern for what became the third-country system of the Canal Zone a decade later. The U.S. canal, then, was not built in a vacuum but rather against a backdrop of export prosperity, widespread labor migration, and discriminatory labor practices that would continue until the 1920s.

From the 1850s on, Jamaicans and other *antillanos*, as they were called in Spanish, had settled permanently along the Panama Railroad and in the terminal cities of Colón and Panamá. Old trade linkages through Kingston to Europe revived the South American commerce that had once made Panama prosperous. Historians also trace the beginnings of Panama's Jamaican Jewish community to this era. Many of the United States–Panama–West Indies relationships of the canal period were forged in the days of the railroad.[6] Those West Indians who remained in Panama after mid-century established permanent communities and started schools, businesses, churches, and mutual aid societies. So even though common laborers were transient, several thousand West Indians secured a lasting beachhead.

Jamaicans held education in high regard and early established schools in Panama. Education had been the vehicle of uplift for freed slaves on the island after 1838, as missionaries and government officials tried to spread literacy and culture among the younger blacks. Progress had lagged behind hopes, yet middle-class Jamaicans believed that schools would one day transform the Antilles into modern countries. After emigration, they built schools in their Panamanian townships and brought teachers from Jamaica to staff them. Missionaries from the islands also started schools.[7] This use of education as a source of community cohesion and leadership would last for several generations in Panama.

The English-language press became another source of immigrant solidarity. Begun in the 1850s for North American travelers, it was sustained afterward by West Indian readers. The oldest English paper, the *Star and Herald*, was locally owned. During the next seventy years dozens of West Indian papers sprang up, most of them ephemeral and supported by railroad and canal employees. The last such paper, the *Panama Tribune*, was published until 1972.

Leading West Indian churches dispatched ministers to Panama during the French era, and many of their branches have lasted until the present day. In 1883 Anglicans established regular West Indian services in Colón and maintained mission chapels in construction towns. In 1907 canal officials placed them under the jurisdiction of the U.S. Episcopal church, where they remain today. French Catholic priests from Martinique and Guadeloupe also came with the immigrant laborers to superintend their immigrant flocks. Finally, Methodists, Wesleyan Methodists, Baptists, and National Baptists from Jamaica arrived in the 1880s, and their congregations remained large for two generations.[8]

The West Indians in Panama also formed dozens of mutual aid

[18]

societies. The notices of a few indicate that they offered medical and burial services as well as caring for the indigent. The tradition of voluntary association remained strong among those of the early generations, lasting until the 1960s.

West Indian immigrants also encountered Latin American, or colonial, blacks beginning in the 1850s. Slaves in Colombia, of which Panama was then a part, had obtained their freedom after independence (1819), and they soon blended into the free black population of the towns, which in most cases formed the majority. Most of the blacks already on the mainland were descended from urban slaves or fugitive communities formed in the days of the Peruvian slave trade. Moreover, thousands of blacks from Cartagena migrated to the isthmus in the nineteenth century. By some accounts, native blacks viewed the West Indian newcomers with suspicion, due to cultural differences and economic competition.[9]

Well-to-do white families in Panama managed to control politics and thus protect their property and positions in society. Those in the interior operated cattle haciendas, while those in the terminal cities followed business or professional careers. The rural branch of the elite held more conservative views and guarded their rights more jealously. The urban elite, depending as it did on international trade, had to accommodate outsiders to prosper—smugglers in the seventeenth century, Spaniards in the eighteenth, and Europeans and North Americans in the nineteenth. They tended to be more liberal as a result.

Partisan politics reflected those biases too.[10] Liberals favored gradual integration of newcomers as a means of handling the "lower" racial and social groups, whereas Conservatives preferred keeping them in their place at the bottom of the ladder. In the 1870s several Colombian military caudillos not from the Liberal elite (especially Correoso and Aizpuru) managed to win control of the cities by doing what Liberals preached—giving the vote to the lower classes. This led to the emergence of what one researcher calls the Negro Liberal party, which drew votes from the *arrabal*, or poor section beyond the city walls.[11] The black Liberals monopolized public jobs and exercised considerable influence in city politics, even after the Conservatives returned to power in Bogotá. Attempts to put these upstart blacks in their places could be costly, as was proven in 1885 when one of their leaders, Pedro Prestán, led a rebellion in Colón and caused a fire that leveled the city. For several decades, Liberal oligarchs made peace with the black Liberals, giving them public jobs and other favors in exchange for electoral and military support.[12] This strategy of assimilation made it relatively easy for the Panamanian elite to accept the early West Indian immigrants as another element of the lower classes. These racial-political factors also facilitated the United States' decision to use West Indians as the primary source of unskilled labor after 1904.

Push Factors Influencing Emigration

Because the islands (especially Jamaica) suffered from unemployment, drought, hurricanes, and epidemics in the later nineteenth century, push factors usually greatly added to the pull of Central America in the migration decisions. Island governments welcomed recruiters and facilitated emigration. One Kingston agent bragged of shipping 30,000 men to the French canal works. Barbados officials encouraged and even subsidized emigration to rid the island of its "superabundant" population.[13]

Labor demands on the islands rose and fell with the harvest seasons, and authorities sometimes subsidized importation of identured orientals to replace departing workers. The governor of Jamaica reported that about 1,000 men a month left in 1883, largely artisans from the cities, while about 2,000 East Indians remained to harvest the largest crop in thirty-one years. "I am disposed to anticipate advantage from this ebb and flow in the development of intelligence and habits of industry among our population," wrote the governor; "and whenever the canal works are completed by far the majority of these emigrant labourers will find their way back to their native land." Such was often not the case.[14]

Emigration benefited the West Indies in several ways. The departure of so many workers diminished unemployment, reduced demand for food and shelter, brought cash remittances to families of workers employed abroad, and gave workers training in construction or farming techniques. Few except planters questioned the benefits of the trans-Caribbean labor movements until the collapse of the French project in 1889. In that year some 13,000 Jamaicans, Barbadians, and Saint Lucians were stranded in Panama. British authorities repatriated over 7,000, but the episode badly tarnished Panama's image as El Dorado.[15] Thereafter officials in Jamaica did their best to discourage emigration to Panama.

The general need to redistribute population from the islands to Central America put British colonial authorities in an awkward position. A royal commission sent to study the problem in 1897 recognized the need for emigration yet failed to make specific recommendations. On the one hand they were charged with the well-being of their subjects, which in most cases meant allowing emigration. The governors' reports from the islands during the last quarter of the nineteenth century, filled with accounts of famine, drought, floods, epidemics, depression, and natural disasters, make grim reading. Most islands simply could not sustain their growing populations, due to pressure for land or lack of business opportunities.

On the other hand, those working abroad enjoyed less protection from the British government, and many suffered terrible hardships and death in the Central American jungles. Four thousand men died building Keith's railroad in the 1870s. Perhaps 20,000 died on the French project,

mostly from yellow fever and malaria.[16] Those who survived often returned home in broken health, unable to enjoy their savings from
abroad. And finally, thousands suffered violent deaths. Most men carried
arms, and frontier justice from the barrel of a gun prevailed.

British consuls in Central America did what they could to protect
West Indians, and they cooperated with the Colonial Office by channel-
ing laborers to the most desirable sites and repatriating the destitute and
infirm. Such services from the leading world power undoubtedly gave
West Indian emigrants a sense of security in difficult times. Beginning in
the 1890s, island governments passed new emigrant protection laws to
establish repatriation funds and minimal employment guarantees to be
specified in contracts. West Indian emigrants did not like the contracts,
which smacked of indentured service, but most signed one form or
another between 1895 and 1910. The very survival of the islands required that a portion of the young men work abroad at all times.

Central American prosperity and the canal were both stepchildren of
U.S. expansion at the turn of the century. Leaders like Theodore Roosevelt believed that America had come of age and should exercise the
powers incumbent on a mature nation. Hundreds of scholars in thousands of books and articles have debated the whys and wherefores of
U.S. imperialism. Only a few issues can be discussed here. In the first
three decades of this century, the United States and its citizens invested
heavily in Caribbean basin business, created a system of bases for a
world-power navy, acquired Puerto Rico and the Virgin Islands, and
wielded political and military force in a dozen noncontiguous countries.
The Panama canal served as a unifying element for these Caribbean
enterprises. It captured the national imagination so that the public suspended its lack of interest in Latin America. The canal symbolized the
political, mercantile, and military ambitions underlying this expansionist
tide.[17] West Indian migrant laborers were swept up in it too, in numbers
larger than ever before.

Most authors agree that the Spanish-American War served as the
catalyst of U.S. imperialism. After just three months of fighting, the
country gained the Philippines, Puerto Rico, and Guam as colonies and
Cuba as a protectorate. With possessions in the Pacific and the Caribbean, the United States needed a canal in order to move warships from
sea to sea. The canal was a valuable commercial asset that warranted
strong defenses, and it was a pivotal point from which to "police the
surrounding premises."[18] Revolutions or alien intrusions in the area
might threaten the newly broadened concept of national security and
rising investments. Finally, rising U.S. investments in the region called
for the sort of protection the British had always provided for their
businessmen abroad. European observers, perhaps unimpressed with the
U.S. military victory in Cuba over the inept forces of Spain, nonetheless
took careful note of the new aggressive attitude of America's leaders.

[21]

Many Americans agonized over the responsibilities that had to be faced once the country owned overseas possessions. Were not the business interests abroad the very monopolies that had subverted democracy and exploited workers and farmers at home? Could Filipinos, Puerto Ricans, and Cubans become U.S. citizens? Would foreign bases and territories drag the United States into imperialist struggles like the ones that had plagued Europe for centuries? Was imperialism compatible with the American way of life? (One midwestern senator said that bananas and self-government did not grow on the same section of land.)[19] Would colonial status make some into subjects ineligible for the privileges of the rest? These and other questions—muted by vast pride in expansion and in the construction of the canal—would haunt U.S. relations with Panama and treatment of the West Indian laborers there.

Racism laced much of the debate over imperialism. For one thing, most turn-of-the century scholarship on race claimed that whites were superior to nonwhites, a conclusion seemingly confirmed by the distribution of power and wealth in the world. It was the white man's burden to rule inferior peoples. Racial differences released white nations from the obligation of extending citizenship to the lesser breeds; nonwhites were simply incapable of democracy. Finally, preoccupation with overseas expansion diverted national attention from the resurgent racism at home. The South enacted Jim Crow laws and the North adopted segregationist practices at the very moment U.S. engineers were surveying Central America for the best canal route.[20]

U.S. imperialism was indeed racist. In the name of progress and civilization, U.S. diplomats, military officers, missionaries, business executives, academics, and adventurers controlled and exploited people of other races, believing that it was in the latter's best interests. Neither the American people nor their leaders were consciously malevolent, yet their assumption that nonwhites were inferior led to atrocious behavior on the part of their representatives abroad. Historians have gone to great lengths to explain U.S. racist imperialism as an aberration or an exception, but the fact is Americans treated nonwhites at home almost as badly. Racism helped make U.S. imperialism repugnant to later generations.

The West Indian experience in Panama influenced American and Panamanian treatment of the immigrants after 1904. The blacks had demonstrated their willingness to migrate in large numbers and to work under demanding conditions. They had also been able to adapt to life in the Spanish-American tropics, where Europeans and Americans had failed often. Their towns, neighborhoods, churches, and businesses bespoke permanence. So when U.S. engineers took over the French canal concession in 1904, they relied heavily on black West Indian laborers to start up construction. Eventually they hired as many as 100,000.

Panamanians, meanwhile, had accepted the immigrants as a necessary condition of getting a canal built. Panama was too small to provide a deep enough reservoir of labor for the work, and most native Panamanians expected to live well from commerce rather than to wield picks and shovels. Cultural differences proved stronger than racial ones in the mild reaction of the natives to the growing immigrant community. Most Panamanians had a laissez-faire attitude toward race relations, and thus blacks had risen to high positions in the country. As for cultural differences, nineteenth-century patterns suggested that once the canal was completed, most West Indians would move on. This was not the case. As it turned out, American canal managers used the immigrants to create a third-country labor system that kept tens of thousands in a limbo, prolonged the diaspora, and induced chauvinist reactions from the Panamanians as well.

3

The Construction Era, 1904–1914

OLD-TIMERS WHITE AND BLACK considered the construction years on the canal as the heroic era, one of vast accomplishments, sacrifices, great men, camaraderie, and history-in-the-making. Dozens of books described the canal even before it was finished, and the final success helped rank the United States among the great nations. Yet canal officials made mistakes and poor decisions, and inefficiency dogged the works. From the standpoint of U.S. relations with Panama, the worst errors were the exclusion of Panamanians from managerial positions and the decision to segregate the work force by color and nationality. The Panamanian government, for its part, paid little attention to the massive influx of laborers who, once they decided to stay, would transform sections of the terminal cities into West Indian townships. With regard to labor relations, construction-era leaders avoided some hard decisions and made others that were to become original sins in the eyes of later generations.

Recruitment and Early Living Conditions

No one doubted the need to recruit large numbers of workers for the American canal project—Panama's tiny population simply could not supply them. Moreover, most outsiders regarded Latin Americans as inferior laborers. Consensus ended there, however. Engineers and supervisors argued over which laborers to bring.

A natural choice was more West Indians, since 700 of them formed the bulk of the railroad and canal force inherited from the French. Panama Railroad manager Jackson Smith, on orders from the ICC chief engineer, began the importation of thousands more to start necessary construction. Jamaicans were excellent artisans and could be found in sufficient numbers due to chronic unemployment at home. Yet the railroad's agent met with undisguised obstructionism in Kingston, for the governor simply refused to authorize recruitment. He feared another debacle like the French bankruptcy. In addition, he seemed to be under pressure from planters and the United Fruit Company not to allow emigration. Over the next five years, officials from President Roosevelt down to Smith tried unsuccessfully to change the governor's mind. Perhaps 20,000 Jamaicans emigrated on their own, but without contracts and only after paying their passage and a five-dollar repatriation deposit. On the whole, the Jamaicans came from the skilled artisan class and were said to be more enterprising than recruits from other islands.[1]

Faced with problems in Jamaica, Smith sent his recruiter to Barbados in early 1905, where he found the government cooperative. Officials on the tiny island had long faced the emigration-or-starvation dilemma and welcomed the chance to send off more workers. Canal officials liked the Barbadians, who went to do pick-and-shovel work and harbored none of the pretensions that some Jamaicans had. Most of the 20,000 eventually recruited were under contract and received free passage to Panama. In addition, another recruiter went to Curaçao and Martinique to find workers, and over the years several thousand signed on for canal service. However, French subjects were not held to be as robust or productive as those from the British islands.

The canal's Chief Engineer John Stevens, meanwhile, became pessimistic about the quality of the West Indian laborers. He complained that they quit to take better-paying jobs, would not work unless forced to, and took unauthorized time for holidays and trips home. He wrote the British minister, "I have no hesitancy in saying that the West Indian Negro is about the poorest excuse for a laborer I have ever been up against in thirty-five years of experience." Another engineer told Congress that West Indian blacks were half as productive as U.S. blacks and a quarter as good as northern white labor.[2] Enough complaints arrived to force Washington to consider alternative sources of labor.

Stevens pushed hard to import Chinese workers, because they had performed well for him building railroads in the United States. President Theodore Roosevelt was willing to try anyone who could "make the dirt fly." But Secretary of War William H. Taft, under whose supervision the canal was being built, decided not to use Chinese labor because he thought it smacked of slavery: "Peonage or coolieism, which shortly stated is slavery by debt, is as much in conflict with the thirteenth amendment of the constitution as the usual form of slavery." Panamanian exclusion laws (inspired by those in the United States) presented yet another obstacle, and Stevens abandoned the idea of Chinese laborers in late 1906.[3]

Southern Europe offered a third source of labor. In February 1906 an agent brought 500 Spaniards, and Stevens claimed they did three times the work the West Indians did. Colonel Robert E. Wood, who became the specialist in labor relations, urged Stevens to view "our Gallego and other white labor [as] our dependable nucleus, and the Negro our floating supply." Some also hoped Europeans would be a buffer between the blacks and North Americans, who from the beginning did not get along well. A recruiter stationed in Europe from 1906 to 1908 sent 12,000 men to join the canal force, at double the wages of the West Indians.[4]

Soon after arrival, however, many Spaniards drifted into Panama in search of better opportunities or shipped out for places offering higher wages. Those who stayed demanded quarters and mess halls separate from the West Indians' and often got into fights with them. Spanish anarchist organizers tried to stir up trouble and started a few strikes. In all, the Europeans cost at least twice as much as West Indians in wages and accommodations but accomplished about the same amount of work. By mid-1907, Wood recommended discontinuing European recruitment, which was done the following year.[5]

The canal also recruited white U.S. workers, who signed up at the New York offices of the railroad. White Americans were expected to supervise the unskilled blacks and Europeans and perform the highly skilled crafts and mechanical services needed. They would quickly grasp the complexities of the entire job and fit into the bureaucracy. Although they did these things eventually, the Americans disappointed canal officials in the construction era. The complaints were many. First, this demand for tradesmen coincided with an expansive economic cycle in the United States. The mediocre or adventurous men who applied still demanded high wages and exceptional fringe benefits. And despite these advantages, turnover remained high—the average American stayed in Panama only a year.[6]

Second, U.S. workers quickly formed trade unions that bargained locally, occasionally struck or slowed down work, and used lobbyists in Washington to pressure the administration. Congress extended civil service status to the white-collar staff, but the blue-collar sector remained independent and unruly. Partisanship exacerbated labor trouble because the unions allied with Democratic leaders in the industrial states while management associated with the Republicans.

Finally, the Americans soon adopted a southern-style division of labor where whites supervised and blacks did the heavy, dirty, disagreeable, yet increasingly skilled work. Union procedures prevented blacks from becoming journeymen, even after years as canal apprentices, because they were excluded from union membership. Nevertheless, blacks sometimes became more proficient than their supervisors, and observers noted the inequity of the situation. Officials refused to change it, however.[7]

The recruitment process on the islands foreshadowed the West Indians' second-class treatment as canal laborers. Recruiters paid local agents several dollars for each able-bodied man delivered to the docks. Agents sent runners to the countryside to spread the news, and they published announcements in newspapers. When workers arrived at the docks on appointed days, they received medical exams and vaccination against smallpox. Chief Sanitary Officer William C. Gorgas told recruiters to accept only men between eighteen and forty-five years, of sound mental and physical condition. He recommended a cursory check of eyes, lungs, heart, digestive tract, joints, and skin. They automatically rejected those with venereal disease. Since the doctor in Barbados received only thirty cents a man and twenty cents per vaccination, the exams must have been brief. In 1906 rejections ran between 20 and 25 percent, mostly for VD, poor physical condition, youth, and hernia.[8]

Once passed, the men took their baggage to the docks for the trip to Colón. Because they traveled topside with no protection or comforts except meals, they were known as deckers. Sailing time ranged from five to thirteen days, depending upon weather and port of embarkation. When they arrived in Panama they received yellow fever inoculations. The entire package—recruitment, exam, and passage—cost the canal about ten dollars per person.[9]

Between 1904 and 1909 most recruits signed contracts that were notarized by colonial officials. (See table 2.) The contracts stipulated minimum wages and benefits and included free repatriation. Until 1909 recruiters paid the fare to Colón. Afterward, sufficient numbers migrated voluntarily to discontinue contracts altogether. Men often hoarded their papers for years only to find them unnecessary for repatriation, which the canal provided almost automatically.[10]

At first recruiters had tried to take into account the various emigrant protection laws in the islands, but they soon desisted. Oral contracts sufficed in the various French islands, because authorities could not agree on which language was official for written documents. Besides, places like Bridgetown and Fort-de-France were collection points for people from smaller islands, so colonial officials had little leverage over recruiters. For the most part, they worked together closely.

In order to encourage voluntary migration from Jamaica, canal officials hired men on the docks in Colón, and by 1907 two or three independents showed up for every contract man. Canal officials took advantage of this labor surplus to lower the minimum wage 25 percent, eliminate overtime, and deduct passage over from wages. In 1909 they also stopped recruiting in the West Indies, which produced more savings. In 1912 recruiters returned to Barbados because too few local workers signed up at ten cents an hour. The colonial government at first refused but then allowed about 1,000 men to go. That ended formal labor recruitment in the West Indies until World War II.[11]

[27]

Table 2. Sample Contracts for West Indian Laborers, 1904–1908

	1904	1906	1907	1907	1907	1908
Where issued	Barbados	Barbados	Barbados	Trinidad	Barbados	Barbados
Length of service	500 days	500 days	4,500 hrs.	4,500 hrs.	500 days	500 days
Minimum wage (in U.S. dollars)	$.75/day	$.80/day	$.10/hr.	$.10/hr.	$1.00/day	$.75/day
Work week (days × hours)	6 × 10	6 × 8	6 × 10	6 × 10	6 × 10	6 × 10
Overtime	1.5	1.5	1.5	1.5	1.5	1.5
Medical Care	free	free	free	free	free	free
Unfurnished quarters	free	free	free	free	free	free
Trip over	deducted from wages	free	free	free	free	deducted from wages
Return trip	free	free	free	free	free	free

Sources: For 1904, PCC 2-E-1, ca. December 1904; for 1906, Lancelot S. Lewis, *The West Indian in Panama: Black Labor in Panama, 1850–1914.* Washington, D.C.: University Press of America, 1980, appendix 2; for 1907–08; Mallet to FO, 2 September 1907, 18 January 1908, in FO 371/300/31889 and 493/4644.

Officially, canal authorities brought over 31,000 West Indian men and a few women. But in fact, between 150,000 and 200,000 men and women must have migrated during the construction era, for in most years some 20,000 West Indians were on the canal payroll, and turnover was high. Contemporaries estimated that only about a third of the West Indian community worked for the canal at any moment. The rest were dependents or had jobs and businesses in Panama's terminal cities. These figures are staggering when we recall that in 1896 Panama City had only 24,000 inhabitants and the country as a whole 400,000. The West Indian migrations to Panama constituted a demographic tidal wave, the largest yet in Caribbean history.[12]

Tens of thousands of West Indian women migrated to Panama, and eventually the sex ratio in the immigrant community balanced out. Canal managers early recognized the need for women and brought over 150 Martinican women in late 1905. The incident led to charges of prostitution and the practice was ended.[13] Still, much of the auxiliary work could best be performed by women, and a good market arose for their services. At first, many women simply paid their own passages and went to look for jobs in the construction camps and terminal cities. Others were sent for by husbands or boyfriends. Often the men returned home after completing contracts and, sporting new clothes and savings of "Panama money," married former sweethearts. Then when the money ran out, the new families went back to Panama. Most West Indians chose mates from their own islands.

Immigrant women performed a variety of essential tasks for the canal work force. They cooked for men in camps established along the construction line. They also washed and mended clothes, nursed the sick, and maintained boarding houses. Only a small proportion of the women engaged in these chores were on the canal payroll; most were self-employed or worked for others. As a result, very little information about women is available in canal records, making it difficult to trace their experience in Panama. Two things are certain, though. Canal construction would have taken longer and been more unbearable without women, and women worked as hard as men yet earned less and had less job stability.

Working and living conditions for the West Indians ranged from difficult to appalling. Those employed by the canal had the right to unfurnished quarters in the Zone, but only a small proportion occupied them. Most of the barracks, dating from the French period, were cramped and accommodated only bachelors; the average space in 1906 was twenty square feet per person. Some of the men built shacks near the work sites, which allowed them to keep families and to plant vegetable gardens. Most rented rooms in the tenement districts of Panamá and Colón, where they could catch the labor trains into the Zone. These tenements were death traps, but many men preferred the bustle of life in the city to living in the jungle. Only in 1913 did canal officials begin building permanent quarters for the silver employees who would stay on after the canal was completed.[14]

Canal authorities encouraged men to bring their families, on the grounds that this would make them more stable and productive. Immigration officers objected that such a policy would open the doors to all kinds of undesirables, since it would be difficult to test kinship and means of support. Eventually they and the Panamanians worked out a system by which employed West Indians could request family entry. In addition, independents with fifteen dollars in cash could disembark. As it turned out, consuls approved virtually all requests, since the immigration fees were their principle income. During most of this time, the Panamanian elite permitted free immigration, because newcomers generated more business. Only after the wave receded did leaders seriously consider the consequences of these policies, or their responsibility toward the vast numbers of West Indians who chose to remain in Panama. By that time, the immigrant community had produced its first generation of children born on the isthmus, about 2,000 youngsters.[15]

Feeding the armies of workmen proved a major challenge. At first the men simply bought food from grocers or ate in West Indian diners. In 1905 the canal created silver commissaries for noncitizen employees, after Panamanian merchants had begun charging exorbitant prices. Then, between 1906 and 1912, the canal operated a series of messes serving basic nutritious food. Since the cost of meals was deducted from the men's pay, most felt obliged to eat there, but the fare was hardly appealing to the West Indians. One old-timer described it as "cooked rice which was hard enough to shoot deer; sauce spread all over the rice; and a slab of meat which many men either spent an hour trying to chew or eventually threw away." Authorities reported improvement in the men's stamina due to the meals, but it could also have resulted from daily doses of quinine, an increase in family living, better health service, and a more regular supply of groceries. At any rate, American institutional cuisine was one of the many features of Zone life the West Indians had to adjust to during construction years. Today West Indian cooking is rare enough to be a specialty food in Panama.[16]

Accidents and disease took a heavy toll among the West Indians in Panama. William C. Gorgas became famous for eliminating yellow fever and controlling malaria. But little could be done about industrial accidents, which cast a shadow over the works. Virtually all the old-timers had vivid memories of accidents—train derailments, dynamite explosions, landslides, boat sinkings—that took multiple lives. In 1913 alone, thirty-eight blacks perished in railroad accidents, twenty-three drowned, and fifteen died in explosions. Many suffered falls from scaffolding during construction of the locks and gates.

In addition, diseases dogged the men. Pneumonia and tuberculosis killed the most, amounting to 110 deaths in 1913. Malaria, even though it did not kill, brought down most people at some point in their stay in Panama. Official figures for 1904–1914 show 4,500 deaths among black employees from all causes during the period.[17] Since a larger number of West Indians lived outside the Zone, where sanitation and medical treatment were inferior, the total number of deaths in the West Indian community probably approached 15,000, or one out of every ten immigrants. No wonder so many of the old-timers gave thanks for surviving the dangers of construction days.

Wages for non-U.S. employees remained fairly stable throughout the construction era. Jobs changed rapidly, however, due to shifting demand, rising skill levels, and chance opportunities. Accounts by West Indian old-timers gave the impression of constant turnover. Arriving recruits would be assigned to available jobs according to their preparation. Young unskilled men became water or messenger boys, starting at between five and seven cents an hour. The robust unskilled workers started as pick-and-shovel men at ten cents. Artisans such as carpenters and plumbers earned from thirteen to sixteen cents. Especially able West Indians could become subforemen or machine operators, making twenty-five cents or more an hour. Machinists and boilermakers in the railroad yards could make between thirty-five and fifty cents an hour. Finally, about 10 percent of the West Indians had white-collar jobs as clerks, stenographers, typists, and so forth. Their monthly rates ranged up to seventy-five dollars a month (about twenty-seven cents an hour).

After the labor glut of 1908, officials put a fifty-cent ceiling on West Indian wages and reduced the number of grades of silver classifications. They secretly urged other employers to join them in lowering wages to ten cents for West Indian common labor, thirteen for Spanish-American common labor, sixteen for noncontract Europeans and U.S. blacks, and twenty for contract Europeans. Another round of reductions came in 1913–1914, when the construction neared completion. Many lost their jobs through reductions-in-force, and most suffered wage cuts.

The base of ten cents an hour for West Indian common labor remained quite stable throughout the construction era. Inequities due to race and national origin also persisted. Two other disturbing trends from the West Indian point of view were wage ceilings and compression of grades, both of which prevented West Indians from advancing very far. Occasionally supervisors themselves complained that private firms hired away their best men because the canal wage ceiling was too low. This policy discouraged workers from acquiring additional training and undoubtedly drove off some of the most talented. The main reason for the policy was to preserve a gap between silver and gold wage rates.

The Gold and Silver Rolls

Within months after beginning construction, canal administrators established the system of racial distinctions which was to grow enormously complex over the years. It began in 1904 when they adopted the railroad's policy of different payrolls, gold for American citizens (somewhat higher than pay rates in the United States) and silver for noncitizens (somewhat higher than rates prevailing in the Caribbean basin). Silver rates were always lower than gold, a disparity heightened by the fact that until 1909 silver currency had only half the nominal value of gold. In addition, benefits such as spacious furnished housing, sick leave, and paid home leave were tied to the gold roll. Just as in the French era, the two rolls also connoted skilled and unskilled, and supervisors used gold roll as a reward for especially deserving blacks because of the status it conferred. The dividing line between the rolls had been intentionally ambiguous, and in 1906 over 100 skilled blacks, both West Indian and American, were on the gold roll.

In September 1905, however, canal authorities prohibited transfers from silver to gold, on the grounds that they complicated bookkeeping and violated the color line. Some supervisors objected that this set up pay inequities and eliminated a key incentive for outstanding blacks, but the rule stood. One official wrote, "I believe . . . the original intention [was] that the Gold rolls would indicate the number of white men working and the Silver rolls would indicate the number of colored employees." By the end of 1906 they went a step further, putting gold roll blacks who were not U.S. citizens on the silver roll at the same pay. Some men objected to the lower prestige and benefits, and a few exceptional black machinists and administrators remained on gold. In addition, black teachers, postmasters, and policemen stayed on the gold roll, because they required a higher status to exercise authority in the West Indian community.[18]

By 1908 color became the leading, though not the sole, criterion used to assign men to gold or silver rolls, as revealed in an exchange of memos between two executives:

> I have been endeavoring to transfer all Negroes from the Gold to the Silver roll. Under the former operations of the Panama Railroad this question was not given very much attention. . . . Some of these people resent this transfer. . . . The situation, however, is getting to be somewhat awkward, as we have divided the Gold from the Silver employees in our commissary.

> It is the policy of the Commission to keep employees who are undoubtedly black or belong to mixed races on the Silver rolls.

Gold and silver distinctions applied to public facilities as well, consolidating a system of Jim Crow segregation. It became one of the most objectionable and tenacious features of Canal Zone life.[19]

After 1908 the gold-silver distinction took another twist, when a nationality test was applied. In February Taft issued an executive order that henceforth only American citizens would be appointed to the gold roll. Taft had begun to campaign for the presidency, and his action seemed designed to win the support of the American unions. Union workers in the Zone faced increasing competition from Europeans and West Indians who came with or learned skilled occupations, and a nationality restriction would prevent this. The Panamanian government protested that the order violated Taft's 1905 assurances that natives would enjoy the benefits of the canal and equal employment opportunities. It also had the effect of declaring Panamanians aliens in the Zone, even though Panama retained residual sovereignty there.[20]

Taft modified the order to allow appointment of citizens of the United States *and* Panama to the gold roll. The administration did not apply the rule retroactively, but they did fire aliens first. After 1908 the gold roll increasingly became an exclusive white American club to which a few Panamanian and West Indian trusties might be admitted.

In late 1909 canal managers attempted to define for themselves just what constituted the two rolls. No one had ever laid down coherent rules, and the assumed guidelines were riddled with exceptions. One valiant attempt produced this:

Gold: 1. white Americans receiving over seventy-five dollars a month.
2. white Americans holding Gold jobs at less than seventy-five dollars a month.
3. Panamanians holding Gold jobs at over seventy-five dollars a month.
4. other whites not native to the tropics holding special positions for which Americans are not available and who earn over seventy-five dollars a month.

Silver: all other persons not covered above.

They decided against publishing the results of their exercise, probably because race figured in most of the criteria.[21]

Following the 1908 gold citizenship decision, labor unions began campaigning to remove West Indians and Europeans from managerial or skilled positions. In 1909 they achieved an important victory: President Taft himself agreed with union leaders that no more blacks should be hired as railroad engineers. He wished to protect the older black employees from dismissal, but he nevertheless signaled the start of a decades-long vendetta in which white Americans identified blacks or Europeans in skilled positions and had them demoted or fired.

Colonel George W. Goethals, who became chief engineer and chairman of the Isthmian Canal Commission in 1907, went along with instituting racial segregation under the guise of the gold and silver distinction. He later registered the customary disclaimer about race: "I think the real point at issue is probably the question of citizenship more than color. We cannot very well draw a color line, but we can limit the employment of engineers to American citizens."[22] Unions obtained a series of guild regulations that restricted to journeymen the use of metal-edged and air-powered tools and operation of any major pieces of equipment. Over the objections of many department heads who valued the work and seniority of their black men, the unions succeeded in demoting railroad engineers of all sorts, yardmasters, hostlers, boat pilots, machinists, carpenters, wiremen, and other skilled workmen. It was one of the most vicious episodes in canal history, remembered and resented deeply by the West Indians for years afterward.[23] The effect was to widen the gap between gold and silver workers and to subordinate the latter to the former.

The Americans-only rule and the subsequent purge of West Indians from skilled positions might have resulted from a desire by Taft and Republican leaders to win over a segment of organized labor from the Democrats. During and after the Taft administration, Goethals kept his political ear to the ground and was mentioned for the presidential nomination in 1916.[24] If this was the motive, it failed. After 1913 organized labor found a better sponsor in the Democrats, under President Woodrow Wilson.

Who instituted Jim Crow segregation in the Canal Zone? At the highest level of responsibility were the Republican administrations of Roosevelt and Taft. Both men followed canal affairs closely and concurred in segregation decisions. They could not publicly admit to Jim Crow practices, however, because the Republicans regularly denounced the southern Democrats for the same thing and enjoyed the support of most American blacks. Moreover, the Constitution did not permit segregation by the federal government. But the early twentieth century saw a great rise in racism among all Americans, and Roosevelt and Taft had little power to prevent it from becoming associated with imperialist expansion. The Wilson administration likewise did nothing to disturb the gold-silver system.

Some canal executives favored using southern whites as labor foremen, on the grounds that they knew how to manage blacks. Yet the American work force was mostly northern, from top to bottom. Chief Engineers Stevens and Goethals were from Maine and New York, for example. But more to the point, many of the top executives were officers in the army (segregated until the 1950s), had worked in a variety of regions, and were familiar with racism. Therefore whether or not they were brought up as racists, they had lived in segregated society. Stevens, for example, frequently compared the low productivity of West Indian and southern blacks and saw labor problems in the Zone and the U.S. South as analogous.[25] At any rate, their job, as Stevens and the others saw it, was to dig a canal, not reduce racism in American society.

The rank and file of American employees came mostly from the North and Midwest. Only about a third came from the South in the early days. The oft-repeated view that the Canal Zone was racist due to southern influence is simply a myth. No doubt many arrived without racist ideas or experience with blacks, but when confronted with the need to supervise British colonial subjects, they adopted bigoted behavior. Harry Franck remarks, "Any northerner can say 'nigger' as glibly as a Carolinian, and growl if one of them steps on his shadow."[26]

In 1921, the Zone governor observed, "Our supervisors, of a class above the ordinary bias of race and nationality, are almost unanimous in the opinion that only the most routine mechanical and clerical work can be trusted to the West Indians." In other words, imperialism (the assertion of white superiority over "backward" peoples) reinforced racism (white superiority over nonwhites). The system remained rigid until the 1940s, by which time it compared unfavorably with race relations in Louisiana and Mississippi.[27]

Black West Indians and white Americans formed the poles of the silver-gold system, but three subgroups fit into it at intermediate points: U.S. blacks, Europeans, and white West Indians. The way they fit and interacted with the nodal groups reveals much about the system itself.

Black Americans signing on for canal work in the first few years received appointments to the gold roll. When West Indians were demoted to silver in 1906, U.S. blacks remained on gold. However, officials instructed recruiters in the United States not to give U.S. blacks gold contracts. Instead canal officials devised for them a special silver category which provided sick and home leave privileges but not access to gold housing, commissaries, or clubhouses. American blacks continued to earn more than West Indians, due to skills and nationality, but most on the gold roll were reclassified as silver. In 1912 a White House aide, preparing election materials, inquired about the treatment of blacks in the canal. Goethals's perfunctory answer was that sixty-nine U.S. blacks received average annual wages of $820. He failed to mention that whites earned double that. Because black Americans did not fit well into the gold-silver system, canal authorities hired them only for a few sensitive positions overseeing West Indians. By 1928 only twenty-three U.S. blacks remained, all but a few on the silver roll.[28]

Europeans also posed awkward classificatory problems for canal administrators, especially when gold and silver came to mean white and black. Spaniards, Italians, and Greeks were judged semiwhite, but they ended up on a special rung of the silver roll because they did not deserve home leave nor wages as high as those of white Americans.[29] They had separate quarters and mess halls. Recruitment of Europeans ended in 1908 and their numbers diminished rapidly thereafter.

A final intermediate group was made up of whites and light mulattoes from the islands who could "pass," a group I call the white West Indians. Recruiters avoided sending such people from the islands because they found that this group disliked heavy labor and was sensitive about racial treatment. However, many migrated from Jamaica on their own. They posed as British supervisors who, because of experience in handling Negroes at home, could coax more work out of them. In 1907 about 800 white West Indians worked for the canal. Classic cultural brokers, they used their color and familiarity with two cultures to become intermediaries. Americans and West Indian blacks both trusted them, but neither group could count on their loyalty. White West Indians, hired on both gold and silver rolls at first, suffered status anxiety when demoted to silver and resented their poor treatment at the hands of the Americans. They occasionally played a malevolent role in Canal Zone race and labor relations.[30]

Social Control

Colonel Wood once compared gold and silver workers to officers and soldiers in the army, an analogy that probably revealed more domination of one group by another than he intended. The two rolls, with their racial and national distinctions, served as a powerful brake on laborers' aspirations and were a divisive element. Throwing Panamanians and West Indians together in the same class spurred the desires of each to be different, better than the other. Panamanians resented being classified with blacks, while West Indians disliked being labeled inferior laborers. The competition undermined potential labor solidarity and increased management's power. In effect, being on the silver roll induced Panamanians and West Indians to fight over the scraps that fell from the master's table.

Canal officials established more specific devices for social control in the early days. The police obviously kept order so that the construction could proceed. Three different police units existed, in fact. The hundred or so white American policemen formed the elite. Their duties included coordinating security services, supervising black officers, gathering intelligence through plainclothesmen, maintaining liaison with other agencies, and operating the jails. About an equal number of West Indian police patrolled streets and labor camps, their job being to control their own people, potentially the most volatile element. Finally, Americans sporadically tried to supervise the Panamanian police. From all accounts, the Canal Zone police system was intimidating and effectively kept the Zone peaceful. Virtually all contemporaries remarked on the peaceful behavior of the West Indians, and white Americans left no record of fearing violence from the blacks.[31]

The vast majority of persons arrested received fines or short jail sentences. Peak activity came in 1912, when 7,000 arrests occurred: Barbadians made up 24 percent of the total, Jamaicans 19 percent, Panamanians and Americans 9 percent each, and Martinicans 4 percent. The most frequent crimes were disorderly conduct, loitering, petty larceny, and vagrancy.[32] The canal deducted fines from employees' wages. Those convicted of serious crimes went to the army-administered penitentiary for longer sentences. The highest number of convicts there was 133 in 1913, a number never again matched. West Indians, Americans, and

Panamanians composed the bulk of the inmates and lived in separate cell blocks. Prison population steadily declined after the end of construction.

The effectiveness of the police forces in the Zone and low levels of serious crime have several explanations. First, the British claimed to have taught their subjects respect for law and order. Second, the work regime of sixty hours a week kept the men under close watch during their waking hours and left little time or energy for getting into trouble afterward. Third, the summary justice meted out by U.S. and Panamanian courts was so harsh as to be a positive restraint. British Minister Claude Mallet wrote, "Much of my time is taken up in receiving complaints," a fact borne out in his reports. Even though the West Indian was said to "dearly love lawsuits" and to have "the habit of writing directly to his king about his many grievances," in fact he must have done all he could to avoid contact with the police and courts.[33]

The Canal Zone police spent much of their time averting or solving labor troubles. A 1904 planning document foresaw that "the enforcement of contracts for services made with these ignorant people will be a very difficult matter, unless the power exists somewhere of arbitrarily controlling imported contract labor." The police served that function. They used spies, deportation, strike-breaking, intimidation, and diplomatic intervention. The latter consisted of bringing in representatives of the country whose nationals were involved in a dispute. A final technique was to have the Panamanian police arrest unemployed men and threaten them with jail or deportation if they did not sign up for work on the canal.[34]

Panama's police worked closely with their canal counterparts. In 1904 the Panamanian government disbanded its army altogether to prevent its meddling in politics, and the police force remained weak, especially in view of the explosion of population during construction days. Police relied to a great extent on the good behavior of the West Indians and, failing that, on the intervention rights of the United States.[35] This police relationship had resulted partly from a 1905 incident in which Panamanian police attacked protesting Jamaican laborers in Panama City. The episode embarrassed U.S. officials and further reduced hopes of recruiting Jamaicans.[36]

Panama's police adopted a rather predatory attitude toward West Indians living under their jurisdiction. At best, they tolerated the foreigners as a temporary inconvenience caused by canal construction and employed normal tricks of the trade to extort money from them. At worst, they harassed and intimidated the outsiders to demonstrate their own intermediate position in the pecking order. The British minister finally prevailed upon Panama to hire West Indians to police their own neighborhoods, which apparently proved successful.[37]

Physical and verbal abuse of blacks by whites constituted another form of social control in the Canal Zone. In 1906 the police chief listed

nine cases ("a small percentage") in which white Americans were fined
for accosting blacks. The U.S. government had decided not to use juries
in Zone courts because of their ineffectiveness in handling racial violence
in the South. Whites still managed to intimidate witnesses. An observer
noted in a letter written in 1907, "Race feeling . . . is at a fever heat and
is liable to develop seriously at any moment. Every man who resorts to
the courts, or is a witness in any case, is immediately discharged."[38] In
1908 jury trials were introduced, and in several scandalous cases whites
were acquitted after murdering blacks. But the everyday verbal abuse by
whites never made headlines and was only recorded by scattered observers. Most of the black old-timers, however, recalled the intimidating
treatment they received as "niggers." One remembered, "Life was some
sort of semislavery."[39]

Not all forms of social control required force. Zone officials encouraged other institutions designed to preserve harmony. Male immigrants
could bring their families, and eventually they got better quarters in the
Zone. Taft and Roosevelt recommended offering small salaries to priests
and ministers, in order to prevent "dissipation and dissolute habits"
among the workmen. However, Stevens did "not regard it as prac-
ticable . . . to use the same church for both blacks and whites . . . the
color line should be drawn." Nondenominational churches for whites
were built at several construction sites. Blacks at first used school buildings for worship, but soon they erected chapels with the help of the
canal. By 1908 authorities had expended $100,000 to build churches or
remodel other structures. They paid about a dozen priests and ministers
as chaplains under the hospital budget, and they granted them housing
and other privileges as well.[40]

The Anglican-turned-Episcopalian church proved the most popular
West Indian sect, with some 15,000 members, followed by the Baptist
and the Catholic. Religion served to reassure the West Indians, and
perhaps the very dangers of construction made them more religious. One
chaplain wrote at the time: "Religion means very much to the West
Indian. He prefers his Church to everything else." It certainly became a
stabilizing force in the community.[41]

A final method of social control, at least in the long term, was the
educational system for West Indian children. With the frenetic work of
construction going on, children playing near work sites could cause accidents. Moreover, schooling and child rearing at home could distract the
West Indians from the primary job. So from the very beginning, municipalities in the Zone operated schools for the workers' dependents. At
first, five schools accommodated 140 white children and over 1,000
blacks in racially mixed schools with segregated classrooms. Most children rode the train to school. As part of an administrative centralization
in 1906, the municipalities were extinguished and the schools put under
a superintendent from Nebraska, David O'Connor. Chief Engineer Ste-

vens's main goal in appointing O'Connor was to reduce discontent among U.S. workers by providing as many support facilities for families as possible. By mid-1906 four schools had entirely white student bodies, while the other twenty-three were mixed but predominantly black.

The Zone schools followed an American curriculum. In the words of Superintendent O'Connor, "The present public school system . . . is essentially American, conducted by Americans, supplied with American textbooks, and in large and increasing measure with American teachers using American methods, with American songs and literature, which should in a short time affect the pupils with American ideals and American patriotism." From the very beginning, the black schools were a nether appendage of the white system, and the color line was rigid.[42]

In order to improve morale among American parents, O'Connor expanded the number of white schools to twenty-eight by 1908, so that few white children had to ride the trains. Black schools dropped to only nineteen, even though they had five times the white enrollment. Jamaicans predominated among teachers in the black schools, because of Jamaica's reputation for educational excellence. Those with three years or more of high or normal school earned sixty dollars a month on the gold roll, compared to ninety to a hundred dollars a month earned by U.S. teachers. No matter how good the Jamaicans were, though, they could hardly have taught much with an average class size of 115 students in 1909. In 1910 and 1911 the schools recruited teachers in Kingston, and by 1915 they lowered the average class size for blacks to 65. Even at that, they did not make attendance compulsory because they could only take in about half the black children of school age.[43]

White children attended schools designed to provide education at least as good as they would receive in the United States, and teachers aimed for college preparation. Black children marked time in overcrowded rooms using cast-off supplies from the white schools. West Indian teachers emphasized rote memory, discipline, oration, and manners—a curriculum tailored for social control. Administrators assumed that black children were intellectually deficient, so they put black schools on a twelve-month schedule. This also kept the children under year-round adult supervision.

Toward the end of the construction period, officials set up vocational studies for the blacks, so they could move onto the lowest rungs of the employment ladder. Alda Harper has concluded that "the educational policy for colored schools . . . became one of preserving the status quo . . . of keeping the West Indian and his progeny in positions of common labor.[44]

Few people at the time realized that West Indians and Panamanians, but not Americans, paid the taxes that sustained all of the Zone schools. In other words, the nonwhites paid for the whites' quality education while their own children got inferior schooling. One could never point to

[39]

the early Canal Zone schools as an example of the civilizing influence of American imperialism. They were merely an instrument of social control paid for by the controlled.[45]

Early Relations Between the United States and Panama

The United States exercised a protectorate over Panama during the construction era. Although the canal was built for the benefit of both countries, Panamanians had little to say about how it was done. They viewed the worker army of West Indians as a necessary element but also as an opportunity to make some profits. Property owners and entrepreneurs immediately threw up stores and rooming houses to cater to the immigrants. They fought unsuccessfully against the 1905 decision by canal officials to operate commissaries for silver roll employees. Thereafter Panama's chief benefit from construction was rents, so even more tenements went up in Colón and Pananá. An early study on immigration urged continued exclusion of Chinese (who controlled a major share of retail commerce) but did not mention West Indians. Well-to-do Panamanians hoped to live comfortably from commerce and real estate investments.[46]

Many Panamanians also sought access to better-paying jobs, and in the early days canal authorities appointed about a hundred members of the local elite to the gold roll for public relations purposes. That had also been the policy of the railroad. Roosevelt assured Panama of "full and complete and generous equality between the two republics," confirming Taft's agreement of two years before.[47]

When Taft issued the executive order in early 1908 to appoint only Americans to the gold roll, Panamanians objected and Taft amended it in December. This appeared to be a victory for the State Department, which forwarded the Panamanian protest with a favorable recommendation. Goethals and other executives, however, gave the order the most narrow construction possible. They *could* hire Panamanians for gold roll positions when they had the best qualifications, but they were not obligated to appoint equal numbers. Moreover, U.S. employees still enjoyed preference over Panamanians in promotion and retention.[48]

Internal rules since 1905 provided paid home leave for U.S. citizens but only one or two months' unpaid leave (schedules permitting) and two weeks' paid vacation for noncitizens on the gold roll. The reasons for this policy derived from the third-country national system. Panamanians competed with West Indians, not Americans, and needed an edge over the aliens to maintain parity. Zonians never dreamed of giving Panamanians opportunities or treatment equal to those they themselves enjoyed.[49]

In 1914, as part of the transition from construction to permanent operation of the canal, Zone officials got an executive order renewing that of 1908 and extending access to gold roll employment to Panamanians.[50] Again, Panamanians saw it as giving them an edge over aliens, but aliens could become Panamanian citizens quickly by bribing a few bureaucrats. A number of Europeans and immigrants from elsewhere in Latin America did so after 1908, but Goethals discouraged the practice by refusing to recognize Panamanian naturalization certificates issued after 1 January 1914. He assumed that anyone receiving papers afterward did so for the purpose of qualifying for the gold roll and was not a genuine citizen of Panama. Nobody seemed to realize that in several years West Indian children born in the Canal Zone would also qualify for the gold roll if Panama extended them citizenship.[51]

A final aspect of early U.S.-Panamanian relations requires mention, because it elucidates how North American racial attitudes affected diplomacy. From 1903 on, the Roosevelt administration had preferred the Conservative party, which had close ties to the railroad and had led Panama's independence movement against Colombia. As a rule, the U.S. government favored Conservatives in Latin America throughout the imperialist era.

In Panama, racial preferences reinforced the tilt toward Conservatives, because the Liberal party drew upon the black lower class in the cities and was led by a mixture of whites, mulattoes, and mestizos. U.S. Minister Squiers, for example, made no secret of his partisanship. In 1906 he backed a measure to disfranchise many of the blacks: "There is no question that a limited suffrage will guarantee a better and more conservative government. The voting population is said to be seventy-five percent blacks, of whom only ten percent can read or write."[52] Most observers reported that the Liberals enjoyed majorities in the cities and rural areas.

Several times in the early years the United States became embroiled in Panamanian politics without wishing to, and in 1908 Taft decided to back a moderate Liberal for the presidency, apparently hoping he could govern more successfully than the Conservatives. Taft forced the Conservative candidate to desist and the Liberal won unopposed.[53]

In 1910, another complication arose and nearly brought U.S. military occupation. The president and vice-president of Panama both died, and a Liberal, Carlos Mendoza, succeeded to the highest office. Mendoza, a mulatto, enjoyed great popularity and now commanded the Liberal party. He had participated in the 1903 revolution against Colombia and had written Panama's declaration of independence. The constitution stipulated that if (as in this case) more than two years of the presidential term remained, the National Assembly would select an interim president. Since the Liberals controlled the Assembly and Mendoza controlled the Liberals, his selection appeared to be guaranteed.

Conservatives approached the U.S. chargé d'affaires, R. O. Marsh, and requested American pressure to prevent Mendoza from remaining in office. Goethals and Marsh disliked the prospect of dealing with a black president for two years, and they cited a no-reelection clause in the constitution as a reason for opposing Mendoza. This rule did not seem to apply to Mendoza, and the Assembly had the power to interpret such questions. The opposition, therefore, stood on soft ground. In June the British minister judged Mendoza's chances a toss-up.[54]

Marsh, with Goethals's approval, tried to convince Washington of the need to bar Mendoza's succession. His argument rested principally on race: "I believe him to an able, clever and comparatively high-minded politician, but I consider the unfortunate circumstance of his race will produce more harm . . . than his able qualities will produce good." Non-whites in Panama and Central America would become unmanageable, while the United States would lose the respect of the white elements. He also objected to a timber contract with an American firm, rumored to be favored by Mendoza. Summing up, Marsh wrote, "Mendoza's election will strengthen the hold of the Liberal party, which includes the Negro and ignorant elements and is most apt to be anti-American."[55]

Over the coming weeks Marsh and Goethals met several times to coordinate activities, taking care to avoid scandal due to the congressional election under way at home. Mendoza soon agreed to desist if he could be finance minister, so all that remained for the Assembly was to choose another Liberal as interim president. By this time, Goethals had grown fearful that Marsh's high-handed dealings with the Panamanians would strain relations to the point of jeopardizing work on the canal. He warned him not to meddle in the presidential selection. Marsh, however, continued to do so without authorization from Washington—or worse, from Goethals. As his frustration rose, so did his audacity. The climax came when Marsh threatened occupation or annexation should the Assembly not follow his suggestions regarding the presidency. Goethals counteracted Marsh, who eventually went home in disgrace.[56]

The 1910 crisis would not have occurred had U.S. officials not objected to Mendoza's color, because he was among the abler politicians available. Marsh, of course, committed gross errors and deserved censure. But behind his action was Goethals's desire not to deal with a black president. And Goethals made U.S. policy for Panama. Sir Claude Mallet, Britain's ranking diplomat in Panama, a thirty-year resident married to a Panamanian, wrote, "I am in a position to state positively that the attitude in Washington was taken entirely on the initiative and recommendation of Colonel Goethals, who is prejudiced against señor Mendoza on account of his colour."[57]

Important results flowed from this episode. White Panamanians, who had been aware of American racism from the start, learned how to manipulate it for their own benefit. In doing so, however, they surrendered a measure of sovereignty. An informal alliance of sorts emerged between Panama's white elite of *both* parties and the canal executives, whereby racially mixed persons were kept in subordinate positions. Since Panamanian prejudices were milder than American ones, the net effect was less disadvantageous to the native mestizos and blacks than to the West Indians, who had to contend with racism in the Canal Zone and chauvinism in Panama. Panamanians rarely admitted to race prejudice, and when they did, they could blame the Americans for having introduced it.

In this way American racial practices during the construction era left a deep imprint on formal and informal relations between the United States and Panama. The West Indians who came to build the canal and then settled as immigrants found themselves in double jeopardy, caught between two hostile forces.

By 1912 Goethals could make plans for the permanent organization of the canal. He foresaw a small civilian force composed of about 1,500 Americans and 2,500 West Indians. In addition, the army would station about 8,000 troops there for defense. Such a small population compared to the 60,000 at peak construction must have appealed to Goethals, and he asked foreign consuls to discourage laborers from coming and to prepare for repatriation of tens of thousands to the islands. At one point his architect, designing a permanent commissary, asked if he could dispense with divided gold and silver areas and assume that the two rolls would use the same premises at different hours. Goethals responded, "This arrangement has worked very well so far and I do not know of any good reason why the present plan should be discontinued." He already envisioned a permanent canal force of whites and blacks (and a few intermediaries), separated by the color line.[58]

A few years later Goethals was asked about the gold-silver system. He explained that it was "customary in these tropical countries for white men to direct the work and for Negroes to do the harder parts of the manual and semiskilled labor. The relative proportion of the white and black races in these countries fixes to a large extent the division of labor. . . . It is not compatible with the white man's pride of race to do the work which it is traditional for the Negroes to do."[59] This statement reveals how officials sought to hide the imperialist and racist character of their actions. The canal caused some 150,000 West Indians to migrate to Panama, greatly disrupting the "relative proportion of the white and black races." In order to keep costs down and to control vast numbers of laborers, authorities devised a sui generis system of segregation based upon race and nationality. It began as a simple color line, but soon took on more complexity, with gradations for American blacks, Europeans, whites, West Indians, and Panamanians. The gold and silver system distributed rewards—wealth, power, and status—in a unique and caste-like fashion. In addition, U.S. officials interfered openly in Panamanian affairs, controlling presidential successions and imparting a racist hue to subsequent relations between the two countries.

To say that segregated payrolls were the custom in tropical countries would be false. The British and French governments did not treat their

Caribbean subjects in this manner, nor did major employers like the banana and petroleum companies. The Panama Canal Zone was a unique American creation for a unique enterprise. Had it occurred in another country, gold and silver might have faded away after the decline of imperialism in the 1940s. As it happened, the system became even more complicated and entrenched in the decades after construction.

4

Consolidation of Zone Life and Panama's Reaction, 1914–1929

AS AMERICANS ABSORBED the shocking news of World War I, another dramatic but unheralded event occurred in Panama: the first oceangoing ship traversed the canal in August 1914. Americans in that year felt an upsurge of isolationism, a desire to stay out of Europe's troubles and to get on with the constructive task of making the Americas prosper. The canal would aid that effort immeasurably, allowing trade, capital, technology, and people to flow more freely around the hemisphere. European imperialism meant restrictions, while American expansion brought freedom, people believed.

Goethals had managed to get his way in most decisions regarding permanent organization of the canal, despite his being a Republican in a Democratic administration. He thwarted Secretary of State Bryan's plan to put the canal under civilian control. Fending off attempts by the navy to take jurisdiction, he kept the canal firmly under the secretary of war. The army moved in troops and in 1917 set up the Panama Canal Department. Goethals (still only a colonel) retained his right during peacetime to report directly to the war secretary instead of going through the commanding general.[1]

Goethals kept the railroad as a separate quasi-private corporation to operate commercial enterprises that could not properly be run by the government. The railroad collected revenues from these businesses, while the canal got appropriations for operations and administration in the Zone. Goethals even handled the tricky labor question with finesse, using the West Indies as a threat against the white unions, but taking from the former's wages to buy peace with the latter. Finally, he won appointment as the first governor of the canal, a job he held until the end of 1916.[2]

British officials on the islands braced themselves for a backwash of laborers from the canal after construction ended, and many feared the impact they might have on the islands. The war and a worldwide recession clouded the picture even more after 1914. For a time men moved to other parts of Central America to work on banana plantations, but the war disrupted that industry, too. Most West Indians who had worked in Panama either stayed or returned to the isthmus after failing to find work at home. Those who remained on the canal force found their wages and benefits reduced just when they had begun to establish families.

Panamanians, realizing that 40,000–50,000 West Indians had decided to stay in their country, developed a love-hate attitude toward them. They needed the West Indians' business but resented their presence. They allowed them to vote and publish newspapers, but they passed legislation restricting immigration and naturalization of West Indians. In fact, Panamanians hated the Americans for the inequities of canal administrators but could not touch the colossus. Thereafter they vented some of their anger and frustration on those brought to build the canal and compete with native laborers. The 1910s and 1920s were dark years for the West Indians throughout the Caribbean basin.

Repatriation and Depopulation

In November 1911 the governor of Jamaica, Sir Sydney Olivier, visited Panama and Puerto Limón to view firsthand the problem of excess laborers after the canal was finished. He went beyond that question, however, to ponder British interests in the Caribbean and the part labor would play in advancing them. He predicted that the West Indians, having learned business methods from the American and British companies there, would exploit the potential for tropical agriculture. Their communities along the north coast would prosper and bring attempts at control by Spanish American elites in the highlands. Governor Olivier wrote: "This . . . is . . . destined to be . . . a chapter in the development of the transplanted African race and its relations with white races in the new World."[3]

The United States, meanwhile, had become the dominant power in the Caribbean since the Hay-Pauncefote Treaty of 1901. Britain faced a choice, then, between graceful withdrawal (including what was regarded as the probable cession of Jamaica to the United States) and a pro forma presence in collaboration with the United States. Favoring the latter, the governor suggested that London appoint a special agent for Central American labor and emigration affairs. He implied that the blacks would establish an Anglo-American beachhead for the development of tropical agriculture. One conclusion underlay all his speculation: the islands could not reabsorb the scores of thousands of workers still abroad. They must remain in Central America or go elsewhere.

Canal officials knew by 1912 that they would lay off large numbers of West Indians once the canal was finished, yet they could not say exactly how many. An early guess was 10,000 workers with their 15,000 dependents. Authorities hoped that the United Fruit Company would hire 5,000 for new plantations in Bocas, Nicaragua, and Colombia. The governments of British Honduras and British Guiana offered inducements for agricultural settlers as well. Island governors stressed that at best they could take back their own people and legitimate offspring, not persons from other islands. The legislative council of Jamaica eventually turned down the governor's suggestion for a special labor agent. The moment was awkward, with well over 100,000 West Indians residing in Central America while at home unemployment and suffering had become endemic.[4]

Another problem arose in the Canal Zone as construction ended. The waters of Gatun Lake inundated former towns and work camps along the canal route, forcing many to abandon their homes and farms. Panamanians dubbed these the *pueblos perdidos* and submitted claims for property losses. The Joint Land Commission that considered the indemnities to be paid favored native over West Indian claimants, although some of the latter had lived there since the French project. Representing his constituents, Minister Mallet managed to get some payments from the canal. Many West Indians remembered bitterly that American officials had assured them of generous compensation if the lands were taken away but later forgot those promises.[5]

Goethals decided to depopulate the entire Canal Zone, limiting residence to employees and having everyone live in canal quarters. Only those aliens for whom housing already existed would live in the Zone. Goethals believed depopulation would facilitate government, defense, and sanitation: "I did not care to see a population of Panamanians or West Indian Negroes occupying the land, for these are non-productive, thriftless, and indolent."[6]

Depopulation created more work for the Joint Commission and forced West Indians to choose between the Zone and Panama. Goethals began charging noncitizens rent for newly constructed or remodeled quarters and forced the rest to go into Panamá or Colón. Zone rentals ran from $7.50 to $10.00 per month, somewhat less than the rates in Panama. Finally, depopulation tended to reduce canal outlays for services such as schools and hospitals.[7]

After 1914 Zone authorities put more pressure on West Indians to leave Panama altogether. Some feared that large numbers of unemployed in the terminal cities would create social unrest. Wood reported: "West Indians, who have been accustomed to the high wages and higher standard of living prevalent on the Canal Zone, have not chosen to return to their homes in the islands." Between 1914 and 1917 the canal provided

Figure 1. The Canal Zone, 1920

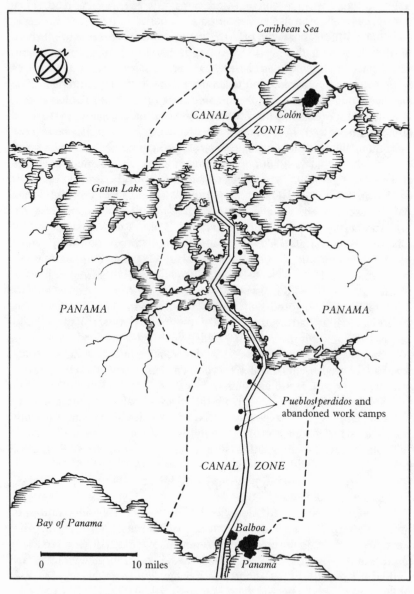

free passage home to virtually all unemployed who desired it and to their dependents. Some 13,000 left in those years. Yet with unemployment everywhere, most West Indians preferred to stay. "They [are] too proud to return as poor as when they left [the islands]," wrote personnel officer John Collins. "The lack of ability to accumulate a fund, and being too proud to return practically paupers, may be at the bottom of . . . the disinclination of the West Indians to return."[8]

Immigrants kept arriving in Panama even after the canal was finished, despite attempts to discourage them. The net outflow between 1914 and 1921 was only 4,000 people because so many returned. Immigration officers doubled the deposit that arriving passengers had to leave as proof of self-support, yet most had already obtained less expensive papers from greedy consuls on the islands. By 1917 the canal discontinued wholesale repatriation on the grounds that it simply furnished a free vacation to men who would return when their money ran low. Repeated efforts to get Panama to restrict immigration apparently failed. Yet the failure to stop the flow was not all bad. In 1921, an official wrote: "We have to be careful in trying to check immigration, so that we may not later find ourselves embarrassed for want of labor."[9]

Canal administrators made it as unpleasant as possible for West Indians to stay in Panama after 1914. Layoffs cut the number of silver employees from 38,000 in 1913 to 8,000 in 1921. Three out of four lost their jobs. Wages fell precipitously, especially in 1914, when virtually all silver workers were demoted. The earlier floor of ten cents an hour became the standard wage for most employees, no matter what skills they had. In January 1915 the silver employee received an average of $1.17 for a ten-hour shift, and eighteen months later pay fell to $1.12. At the same time, the cost of living rose sharply because of shortages of supplies and shipping during World War I. Officials evidently tried to discover the lowest wages the West Indians would take.[10] (See figure 2.)

The Silver Rates Board debated just what standard of living should prevail, and they hit upon a formula in 1916. No reference would be made to the relatively high wages of the construction era, but rather pay should "enable the laborers to live in reasonable comfort and decency." When increases were in order because of a rise in the cost of living, they should help those at the bottom rather than those at the top. Thus the compressions of grades that had occurred in 1913–1914 became even more pronounced.

Only much later did the Silver Rates Board consider three other factors that aggravated the cost-and-wages squeeze that trapped the West Indians during the war. Some supported relatives who had been laid off; many had families whose costs rose as the children grew; and more were living in Panamá and Colón, paying higher rents than in the Zone and without access to land for cultivating gardens. The board did not consider such factors, so few laborers could live in reasonable comfort and decency.[11]

Figure 2. Silver Employees' Cost of Living and Average Monthly Wages, 1914–1922 (in U.S. dollars)

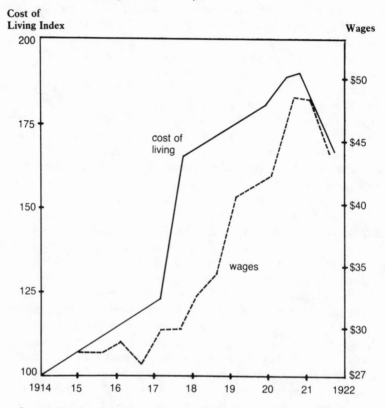

Sources: Minutes of the SRB, 15 January 1920, in PCC 2-D-40/B; Collins report, 7 October 1921, in PCC 2-D-40.

The spirit of the silver wage and benefit cuts became clear when President Wilson ordered free rent for all resident employees of the Zone in 1916. Two years earlier Goethals had instituted rents, but gold employees appealed to Washington and had theirs suspended. In 1915 Colonel Wood recommended that Silver rentals be reduced, because "the colored employee is in worse shape than ever before." No change was made. Then when Wilson's executive order of July 1916 provided free rent for both gold and silver workers, the acting governor cabled Washington and had Wilson exclude silver employees from the order. For the next thirty-five years silver residents paid rent, while gold did not.[12]

More hardships resulted from the continuing campaign by white unions to remove West Indians from all skilled jobs. These unions, now numbering about thirty, had coalesced into two peak organizations, the craft-based Metal Trades Council (MTC) and the white-collar Central Labor Union (CLU). These groups urged Goethals to replace blacks in skilled positions with whites whenever possible. But Goethals refused to conduct a wholesale purge because he would lose his best leverage with white labor: the threat of replacing them with West Indian blacks. However, he did widen the gap between the gold and silver rolls—an inhumane strategy but one seemingly necessary, given economic and political pressures.[13]

Everyone suffered in the cutbacks after 1914, even the gold employees, whose numbers declined from 5,300 in 1911 to 3,300 in 1918. Given falling demand for gold employees, and the instability of the U.S. rates on which their pay was based, Goethals could not (nor did he wish to) raise the wages of gold workers. However, he did protect their perquisites: the construction pay bonuses (after 1912 called the 25 percent differential), free housing, paid home leave, excellent medical care, schooling, commissaries, and recreation facilities.

In addition, by lowering silver wages and benefits, Goethals increased the *relative* standard of living of gold compared to silver employees. And in what had become a close-knit, defensive, inbred, status-conscious, white supremacist society, that symbolic gain became extremely important. Gold employees and their families constituted a local oligarchy, supervising a mass of destitute blacks. Blacks should not even compete with whites, and their status should indicate that clearly. As one union leader testified before Congress in 1913: "We do not feel inclined to work on a level basis with a Negro. . . . We are willing to use the Negro as a helper, but [not] as far as 'Mr. Negro' being on a job with me, as my equal."[14] If it took race segregation, nationality rules, closed-shop unions, politics, violence, or any other means, that distinction had to be observed. Goethals gave supremacy to the Zone whites.

Intermediate groups found themselves in an anomalous situation during the consolidation of white supremacy. Well-to-do Panamanians resented being lumped together with West Indian blacks and sought to get on the gold roll. Some, because of family, politics, training, or language skills, made it. But the Panamanians' anger inspired a letter of 1918 complaining that race discriminaton undid all the democratic influences the United States had brought. It cited the case of a young woman of good family who was unceremoniously escorted from a washroom because of her color.[15] Panamanian laborers and artisans worked side by side with the blacks, but off the job in Colón or Panamá, they associated little with West Indians.

U.S. blacks tried but failed to get back onto the gold roll. White Jamaicans on the silver roll suffered status deprivation, but they and the remaining Europeans were favored for gold jobs when no Americans were available.[16]

Canal management began to consider maintenance of a West Indian reservoir or pool from which to draw laborers when the need arose. They did not discuss the idea openly because it violated the spirit of agreements with Panama to the effect that unemployed workers would be repatriated. Therefore they were not too distressed when, despite the squeeze during the war, thousands of West Indians stayed in the terminal cities.

Protests and Strikes

West Indians formed organizations to defend their wages and benefits after the 1914 cuts began, and strikes and walkoffs erupted. For example, Samuel Whyte, who played a leading part in his generation, formed the Isthmian League of British West Indians in 1916 to lobby for rent-free quarters. But not all efforts were limited to lobbying, as was demonstrated by the October 1916 strike.

The strike began in the dredging division when a supervisor announced a cut in pay. The men walked off the job and returned to Panamá, where they conferred with Latin Panamanian labor representatives. After calling a joint strike, they managed to close down several businesses in Panamá. On the second day some 5,000–6,000 men failed to report for work on the canal. In Colón the mayor prevented the men from meeting, and the strike failed to catch on. The British Club, representing white West Indian businessmen and professionals, met with acting Canal Governor Harding to mediate the dispute. Harding promised to reinstate the strikers and to look into any grievances they cared to present. They went back to work forty-eight hours after calling the strike. Harding appointed the Silver Rates Board to develop policy and statistics, and two months later he announced wage increases averaging 11 percent.[17]

Observers in the West Indian community concluded that confrontation was an effective means for redressing grievances, since the strike had produced results despite inexperienced leadership and lack of organization. They believed they had conducted the first strike against the U.S. government and had won improvements. The fact that a Panamanian absconded with their $8,000 strike fund only convinced them of the enormous need for West Indian organization. Press comments stressed that mistreatment by Zone whites spurred them too.

The Colón Federal Labor Union (CFLU) had begun on the Atlantic side, where the black community had deeper roots. Organized just before the strike, it obtained recognition under Panamanian law and began a successful membership drive. CFLU president Víctor de Suze, an Antiguan, played a double game, assuring canal authorities they had not participated in the recent walkout but advocating strikes to prospective members. Asked for canal recognition, Harding wrote that no such formality existed and that the CFLU could engage in peaceful organizing in the Zone. In fact, he put them under police surveillance.[18]

Throughout 1917 the CFLU did remarkably well, drawing as it did on the wounded sentiments and pocketbooks of the West Indian canal employees. Within a few months it had 8,000 members, and revenues came in at close to $2,000 per month. Membership soon dropped, but by that time a sizeable capital had accrued. The CFLU obtained a land grant of 2,500 acres from the Panamanian government, where directors started a housing and farming community. They purchased a hall where they conducted union business as well as operating a lunch counter and movie theater.[19]

The CFLU took on a life of its own in Colón, and most meetings concerned the union's business activities more than labor questions. For one thing, the leaders got nowhere with Zone officials. They also tried to affiliate with the AFL, but were rejected because the MTC opposed admitting blacks to union membership. For another thing, the union gravitated toward politics because its members, although foreigners, could vote in municipal elections. In Panamá and Colón, West Indian leaders could usually count on support from local officials. Finally, union leaders could get away with more graft in Panama than they could in the Zone, where spies reported constantly on their activities. Evidence suggests that tens of thousands of dollars melted away during the CFLU's three years of existence in Colón. Nonetheless, this first experiment proved that West Indians would support a more aggressive union with money and loyalty.

Samuel Whyte formed a second group in 1917, the Silver Employees Association located on the Pacific side of the isthmus. Whyte, a Canal Zone police officer who knew full well how tough the Zone authorities could be, developed a deferential style for petitioning his bosses on behalf of the community. Strongly imbued with British Caribbean manners of formality and protocol, Whyte would never challenge canal officials. Rather, he tried to persuade them, using quasi-legal briefs and moral arguments. At the same time, he was haughty and overbearing with his followers. He had little sociological understanding of the gold-silver system beyond its obvious injustice, and his efforts over the years produced scant results. A newspaper announcement of a meeting reflected Whyte's leadership style: "The subjects to be covered are the necessity of more love, unity, oneness, and consolidation of the Negro race, which will establish more fully their strength, might, and ability." His advocacy of restraint and reason kept the Silver Employees Association membership small, because the mood of the times demanded militancy.[20]

The stakes rose considerably in early 1919, when two white Americans from the United Brotherhood of Maintenance of Way Employees and Railroad Shop Laborers arrived to organize silver canal workers. Nicholas Carter, a black American laborer in the railroad car shop, had begun to interest coworkers in the union five months earlier, and he soon became a leader himself. Representing an essentially black U.S. federation, the United Brotherhood sought to mobilize the canal workers in a period of heightened union activity and leftist influence at home. Governor Harding vehemently opposed their efforts, on the grounds that they bred racial hatred, and he had the police and mail censors impose round-the-clock surveillance on the men. The secretary of war tried unsuccessfully to get Samuel Gompers, head of the AFL, to call off the two organizers. Given a populist upsurge in his own ranks, Gompers decided to lead a movement to bring blacks fully into the AFL. Meanwhile, the MTC joined Harding in urging the AFL to stop organizing silver employees.[21]

Another strike broke out in May 1919, when supervisors told 1,200–1,500 longshoremen that they would be cut back to an eight-hour day without any increase in hourly rates. After eleven days off, they went back to work with a few concessions but far less than they demanded. Just as in 1916, the men walked off the job spontaneously and without backing from local unions. The United Brotherhood organizers avoided involvement, and the SEA urged the men to go back to work.[22]

The British minister regarded the 1919 strike as evidence that the West Indians were too easily misled: "Avid of grievance, the West Indian will give ear to any agitator or allow himself to be carried away by any movement that seems to afford him an opportunity to indulge his ruling passion." By going on strike, the men made it difficult for legitimate representatives to negotiate any improvements.[23] Still, the strike signaled a rising wave of discontent and aggressiveness among the West Indians.

The United Brotherhood made great advances in 1919. They claimed to have enlisted 13,000 silver workers, or nearly 80 percent, by July. Police reported fewer members. Meanwhile some 1,100 dock workers in Colón won a charter from the International Longshoremen's Association in New York, and the carpenters union was admitted to the AFL. The *Workman,* a weekly newspaper founded in 1912 by Barbadian H. N. Walrond, became the quasi-official organ of the United Brotherhood, with a circulation of about 6,000. Prominent figures in the West Indian community contributed editorials attacking the mean treatment and wages given silver employees of the canal.[24] The United Brotherhood sent about $30,000 to the international headquarters in Detroit in 1919. The West Indians believed that affiliation with a U.S. international carried substantial force and warranted the hefty dues required.

In September 1919, union spirit crested in a mass Labor Day parade designed to embarrass canal management and in particular the Silver Rates Board. Some of their placards and banners read: "Shame on the Wage Board for causing our children to be underfed"—"Help us get rid of the Wage Board"—"Are we slaves or free men?"—"Let your might protect the right and your justice know no color"—"Now is the time for action: Be prepared"—"Must our children die and mothers plead in vain? No!"—"Here we are—Negro advancement"—"Half-bound, half-starved"—"Must our girls be sacrificed on the altar of vice? No!" These protests, though not threatening in a physical sense, embarrassed the U.S. government at a time when it was trying to assume moral leadership of the world in the Paris peace talks.[25]

Governor Harding had even more trouble on his hands in 1919. Roosevelt's death in January provided an opportunity for congressional critics to probe canal operations. A delegation visiting in March found gross inequities and waste in the gold-silver system and recommended a thorough reorganization. The strike in May and reports of mismanagement prompted the secretary of war to send a special investigator, Colonel Williams, to look into the charges. Williams reported that silver employees were organizing, but he did not expect them to achieve much success due to the surplus of laborers. The real problem was excessive power in the hands of the MTC, which virtually dominated the governor in a "socialistic utopia." His extremely critical report jarred the canal administration and set in motion a two-year shakeup. News of Harding's troubles, leaked through clerks and messengers in canal headquarters, elated leaders of the silver unions.[26]

Harding decided to get tough with silver employees. In mid-1919, a white Jamaican spy in the CFLU leadership began actively to confuse and disrupt the movement. Muscett (code-named Marshall) had been sending voluminous secret reports to the police and to Harding, in exchange for thirty dollars a month and expenses. In June 1919, he thwarted a plan to merge the ailing CFLU and a local chapter of black nationalist Marcus Garvey's United Negro Improvement Association (UNIA). He also managed to discredit some of the abler union men.[27]

In September, police issued orders to prevent the expected arrival of Garvey himself, who apparently was attracted by the success of the silver mobilization. (Garvey had worked for a Colón newspaper years before.) Canal officials also fired William Stoute and Sam Innis, Barbadian teachers who had been elected officers of the United Brotherhood. In November, police refused entry to two United Brotherhood organizers returning from the United States. This left Carter and Stoute in charge (the original white organizers had returned home in May) and virtually cut off from the international headquarters in Detroit.[28] As a military officer and government administrator, Harding felt he could not lose control over his rank and file.

The Silver Rates Board, meanwhile, proposed settling thousands of West Indians in a colony known as Las Cascadas, on the west bank of the canal. Depopulation had cleared the entire area except for a small Seventh-Day Adventist encampment. The settlement idea had arisen after the 1919 strike, as a way to keep a reservoir of workers in the Zone. They would be a dependable force in times of labor strife, and when not needed they could raise crops and animals to feed the local population. The colony would reduce unemployment in the terminal cities and separate the men from labor agitators.

[55]

The governor began to implement the Las Cascadas plan in November 1919, but the West Indian community did not find it appealing. The *Workman* denounced it as a means to make the canal strike-proof. Landlords in Panamá started rumors that the residents would be abandoned in the jungles because train service would end. And many remembered the miserly indemnities paid to former residents of the *pueblos perdidos*. Nevertheless, the colony slowly grew from 60 in 1921 to 5,000 in 1929, enlarged mostly by retiring employees and Chinese immigrants excluded from Panama. It never provided sufficient reserve labor to make it worth the cost, and officials eventually discontinued settlement.[29]

Secretary of War Baker visited the Canal Zone in December 1919, and in an interview with United Brotherhood leaders he stated that their circumstances were pathetic and that "the United States is too great a nation to oppress any people." This seemed to signal a willingness to make concessions, and indeed in January the Silver Rates Board came under considerable pressure to make adjustments commensurate with cost of living increases. Leaders of the United Brotherhood met with the board to offer statistics supporting their claims.

By January 1920, the United Brotherhood had operated for eight months without professional leadership, largely because Harding would not allow Detroit to send anyone. Carter and Stoute had emerged as leaders from within the ranks of canal employees, and although they were effective, they had little experience or familiarity with the labor scene in the United States. They were unaware of the fact that the government and the AFL had turned against black unions like the United Brotherhood, once the rival Industrial Workers of the World began to crumble. Neither did they know that graft corroded the management of many unions, especially those representing blacks and immigrants. Stoute held an idealized view of unionism and faith in its eventual triumph.

None of the other local leaders had much experience in union affairs, although many were active in lodges and benevolent societies. The list of seventeen compiled by Zone police included five Barbadians, three Panamanians, and nine others from various Caribbean basin locations. Their occupations ranked them among the top silver employees of the canal. Most were foremen and clerks; Stoute and Innis were teachers; and several were skilled tradesmen. They were from the group that had suffered demotions in the reductions-in-force and been reclassified from the gold to the silver roll. The majority lived in Colón, but men also represented twenty towns spread along the canal route.[30]

Some West Indian leaders in Panamá and Colón collaborated too: Walrond of the *Workman;* Dr. Milliard, an ardent black nationalist; and lawyers Nightengale and Flowers. Luis Baptista led the Panamanian lodge of the United Brotherhood, called Aurora del Istmo, and Julio Arjona established a liaison with Presidents Porras and Lefevre of Panama. The only outsider was Henrietta Davis, an aide of Marcus Garvey sent to promote the UNIA movement and to lend moral support to the laborers. In short, strike leaders came from the elite of the West Indian canal workers, and they sought bread-and-butter gains.[31]

Two things forced the hand of the United Brotherhood and triggered the strike of 23 February: Harding's decision to be tough and not give in to labor demands; and stop-and-go communications from Detroit indicating that the international sanctioned a strike against the canal.

Harding kept the Silver Rates Board in session through most of January and February, and workers waited anxiously for the outcome. Labor inspector Gilkey conducted a survey of 133 West Indian families living in the tenement districts of Panamá to determine their living conditions. He learned that the average family had three children and ran out of food and money before the end of each month. Fifteen children and ten adults were sick or underfed, but nobody was found to be starving. Gilkey reported: "Many of the families have darned and ragged clothes and the children no shoes or poor ones. The children of only one or two of these families were going to school on account of claimed inability to pay school fees of a dollar per month."[32]

January rumors suggested a minimal raise of two cents an hour. In early February Harding confirmed it. Carter protested that such a small raise would not assure them a life of "ordinary decency and comfort." In fact, the laborers were fighting mad and demanded raises of seven cents an hour.[33]

Minutes of the Silver Rates Board show that they adjusted cost of living figures to justify the rates they wished to grant, and the employees undoubtedly knew this. When the union refused to accept the two-cent raise and threatened to strike, Harding asked an aide to look into possible concessions. The latter tinkered with the cost of living figures and concluded that they could justify another penny per hour. Even that, he said, would not achieve the goal of "reasonable comfort and decency" adopted in 1916. Harding met one last time with the silver board and then decided to make no further concessions. Minutes were not kept. But by then a one-cent additional raise would probably not have changed events nor dissuaded the men from striking.[34]

Talk of an organized strike had begun in September 1919, when Detroit headquarters planned a nationwide rail shutdown in conjunction with thirteen other unions. If the Panama Canal also ceased to operate, they could paralyze East-West transportation. Talks continued and the crisis was averted, but again in February they threatened a coast-to-coast rail strike. Detroit cabled Stoute and Carter in Panama to be prepared to strike on the seventeenth. Over the next few days, Detroit officials admitted that raises for canal workers did not figure in their demands. Then they called off the strike in order to hold discussions with President Wilson. That was on 15 February.[35]

During these tense days in mid-February, Stoute, Innis, Carter, and the others debated what course to follow. Carter apparently urged moderation, and on the fifteenth he was obliged to resign because the others thought he was a spy. Stoute continued to trust Detroit officials, despite the fact that they had not sent any more representatives. He was sure that if they went out, Detroit would approve and return the $30,000 strike fund the union had set up the previous year. He could not explain, of course, why they had not returned a draft contract he had submitted weeks before. Stoute thought they should show it to Harding before deciding on a strike. After the fifteenth, Stoute led the union virtually alone and without advice from Detroit, because Harding had ordered all their cables impounded. Now it was Stoute against Harding.

Harding had known of Detroit's orders to strike and issued a warning on the fourteenth. He would terminate any employees who did not work and would cancel their commissary and housing rights. Two days later, he rejected Stoute's fourteen-point draft contract. Included in the list were a seven-cent-an-hour pay raise for common laborers; reclassification of skilled jobs now rated common labor; eight-hour days; equal pay for women; grievance procedures; five-day layoff notices and preference in rehiring; recognition of the union; and automatic step increases such as gold employees received. Stoute got the *Star and Herald/Estrella de Panama* to publish this proposal and cost-of-living figures showing the need for a raise. Union officials were angered by Harding's rejection and many favored a strike, yet Stoute held back in hope of getting sanction and funds from Detroit. He was unaware that his cables were not getting through.[36]

Stoute had about $28,000 on hand, in addition to the funds in Detroit. He estimated that his men could subsist on twenty cents a day. That meant that he could finance 15,000 silver strikers for nine days with local funds and for another ten days with reserve funds, if they arrived. Harding's spy Muscett, who passed along these figures, favored a strike then and there, before money could come from Detroit. He did not have long to wait: on the twenty-second, Stoute decided to go out the following day.

The international did not send their money. Harding kept the situation under control and finally defeated the workers. Those nine days burned into the silver employees' memories as deeply as any brand. Twenty-six years would elapse before another union arose, to organize not this group of West Indians but rather their children.

About 80 percent of the silver employees joined the strike, and the canal virtually stopped operations except for moving a few ships through. Workers who lived in Panamá and Colón due to the depopulation policy simply stayed at home to join the strike. They held frequent meetings in parks and fields, and by all accounts the strike was extremely popular. Harding's intransigence had unified people of three races and about ten nationalities. Marcus Garvey cabled his support and contributed $500. The Panamanian lodges joined wholeheartedly, as did several smaller unions. For a moment the labor policies of the canal had been in jeopardy.

Harding succeeded because he could afford to wait until the strikers exhausted their funds. The strikers did not use violence or sabotage, so the gold workers and the canal were never threatened. No military forces were deployed. Stoute even ordered hospital, postal, and military personnel to stay on the job. As one canal official summed up later, "It was splendid; . . . there was absolutely not one case of disorder—the niggers behaved splendidly."[37]

Harding was vindictive, however, and earned the lasting hatred of the West Indians and Panamanians. He ordered police to evict the families of strikers, not only from their prepaid quarters but also from the Zone itself. They removed 391 families, including women, children, and sick people, stacking their furniture in the streets. These families moved into Panama after the union posted a bond to cover import duties. Harding also issued orders that men returning to work be hired at lower grades, which probably prolonged the strike several days. Silver foremen, clerks, timekeepers, and craftsmen were replaced with Americans, often servicemen or teenaged children of older employees.[38] Orders went out to arrest and deport strike leaders. Harding became the worst villain in the West Indians' memory.

Panamanians despised Harding for other reasons. President Lefevre had assumed a neutral position after taking over from Porras on the eve of the strike. Among other things, a good many of his citizens were participants, and since the men were peaceful they violated no laws. Harding obtained permission to occupy the terminal cities with troops if Lefevre did not ban all meetings and arrest and turn over the leaders. Faced with an ultimatum to this effect, Lefevre did end meetings, and occupation was averted, but at great cost to U.S.-Panamanian relations. Moreover, by breaking the strike Harding was able to keep wages and benefits low, forcing the West Indians back into a subservient position. This of course depressed wages for Panamanians and made it even more difficult for them to qualify for positions on the gold roll. Breaking the strike strengthened the third-country labor system.

For eight more months, Harding and strike leaders engaged in a desultory dialogue, the latter from the refuge of Panamanian territory. Police watched for the men in the Zone and managed to arrest most of them for deportation. Stoute, however, evaded capture and continued the struggle. Thousands flocked to parks to hear him speak, and a network of supporters raised money for his subsistence. He tried to get his final naturalization papers from Panama, but Zone officials managed to block them. Finally, police caught him on the Colón-Panamá train (which went through Zone jurisdiction) and eventually deported him. He died years later in Cuba. The strike had been an utter failure from the West Indian point of view.

In the largest sense, worldwide events trapped the West Indians in Panama, though they had little awareness of them. The U.S. government, threatened with a general rail strike, took a forceful stand against unions at home and in Panama. Gompers backed away from unionizing blacks, and the AFL actually suspended the Detroit international for its dubious role in the silver strike. Moreover, the red scare of 1919–1920 embraced the West Indian organizers, who were denounced as Bolshevists, Wobblies (of the IWW), white-haters, and anti-Americans. Officials in Detroit, meanwhile, gave little leadership. Twice they called on canal workers to strike but did not include their objectives in the demands. They did not attempt to send any more representatives, nor did they return the money sent from Panama. Indeed, a year later the same officials were indicted for embezzling $200,000. Finally, 1919–1920 was a period of antilabor action throughout the Western world, in reaction to the Russian Revolution. The West Indians who worked for the canal suffered the same fate as strikers in a dozen other places.

The British government played a part in the denouement of the strike. Two days after it began, the new foreign minister, A. Percy Bennett, offered to mediate. But the governor set impossible conditions, and the effort was aborted. Neither Bennett nor the British consul in Colón believed the men had the slightest chance of winning, but they were bound to do what they could to protect the British subjects among the strikers. Should violence or an exodus to the islands occur, they would have major problems on their hands. A Foreign Office bureaucrat in London remarked that the timing was unfortunate, since the Prince of Wales was scheduled to land at Colón on 23 March and might become embroiled in labor troubles.[39]

After the strike ended, Bennett proposed forming a commission to investigate the grievances, to be composed of the Colón consul, a French diplomat, an official from Jamaica, and three labor representatives. In the early months they had trouble because Zone officials did not wish to provide them with information. In addition, the Jamaican representative, following a line by now traditional in the Colonial Office, accused the diplomats of neglecting the West Indians. He tried to steal the show and made statements highly critical of the canal administration to the Jamaican press.

After he left, however, the British commissioners got on with their task. More than a year after the strike, they issued a report that found Zone wages seriously inadequate for married men. Most disturbing was that "the rising generation appear to be the chief sufferers, as children cannot be expected to grow into vigorous manhood unless properly nourished." Analyses of household and dietary expenditures showed that minimum needs for a family of four rose from forty to seventy-three dollars between 1914 and 1920, while the average earnings increased from forty-three to fifty-two dollars. Single persons could support themselves well enough, but not those with families. By this time 60 percent of the canal employees had families or dependents and were permanent residents. The children the commission believed to be in greatest jeopardy were first-generation Panamanians of West Indian descent.[40]

By mid-1921, the West Indians in Panama realized they would not get strong backing from the British government, so the predictable findings of the commission report drew little attention. Nor did Zone officials pay any heed: in July and October the governor actually reduced the wages of the lowest paid by 9 percent. Several thousand West Indians left Panama after the strike, though even that alternative was narrowed when some countries erected immigration barriers against blacks.[41] But one hope still burned: that the U.S. government in Washington would recognize the inequities of the canal system and bring justice to the silver workers.

The Connor Board: 1921

The canal became something of an embarrassment to the U.S. government by 1920, due to the inequities of the gold-silver system and to the growing anger of Panamanians kept at the fringes of what had become a Garden of Eden for white Americans. The Republicans had just regained the presidency with a campaign promise to make "America efficient," and their proclaimed traditions were violated by many of the canal's practices: mistreatment of blacks, waste in government, public enterprise competing with private, alienation of Latin American elites, and strong trade unions overpowering management. The silver strikes also indicated something wrong in this important American outpost. So after Theodore Roosevelt and Woodrow Wilson left the stage, the canal underwent a thorough probe by the new Harding administration.

Colonel Williams's investigation of 1919, it turned out, signaled the start of an intensive study of the Canal Zone, as well as one of the strongest attempts yet to reform it. In May 1921, Senator William B. McKinley attacked the canal waste and mismanagement. The secretary of war appointed Brigadier General William Connor to head a special commission that spent about a month scrutinizing canal operations. The commission interviewed a variety of people in the Zone, including delegations of silver workers.[42]

The Connor Board report, buttressed with many appendices, could be reduced to one word: silverization. They recommended replacing most gold employees with West Indians. Some silver employees already did highly skilled work, while gold men presumably supervised them. In fact, as one department head admitted, many West Indians had taken over their supervisors' trades. The commission recommended a system of apprenticeships to allow replacement of virtually all Americans except those in security positions. Silver wages should rise to match the quality of work performed. Silver workers also needed schools, training, and incentives. They should be allowed to live and farm in the Zone and to police their own communities.

The core problem, as Connor saw it, was the de facto closed shop policy of the canal. All of the Americans belonged to unions, and many executives had moved up from unions to which they still belonged. In effect, unions controlled management. An open-shop policy would release that stranglehold and permit talented natives to move up in the ranks. The Connor Board also recommended charging Americans rent and utilities and cutting their leave privileges, which would save some $5,000,000 a year. Underlying these recommendations was the conviction that whites could never be very productive in the tropics, due to the degenerative effects of climate and isolation.[43]

The Connor Board report attacked the gold-silver system frontally, and the MTC and executives of the canal lost no time building their defenses. The new governor, Jay Morrow, testified that very few gold employees could be replaced by silver ones. To do so would effect a false economy, he said, because "a poor workman is a great luxury." Besides, the whites would become demoralized and perhaps quit if blacks replaced many of them. One supervisor argued that blacks capable of doing first-class mechanical work were "as rare as a red ear of corn in a field." His argument rested on racial theories of the day, according to which the mixed-blooded people of Central America were inferior to whites. They also claimed that security demanded that U.S. citizens occupy key positions to prevent sabotage.[44]

In mid-October, the MTC lobbyist in Washington met with President Harding and extracted a promise not to implement the silverization proposal and to postpone decisions regarding gold workers' rent and other benefits. A day later, the secretary of war sent Morrow a directive to pursue silverization but to leave Americans in "responsible positions which involved any element of the national defense, or where [alien] employees might imperil the proper operation of the canal." He should substitute blacks for whites slowly in order to avoid problems for Americans. As for silver workers, he wished to give them training for better jobs and to expand education for their children, including vocational studies. Finally, he favored opening the Zone to colonization by West Indians and other settlers.[45]

In the months following this decision, department heads queried supervisors regarding gold jobs that could be reclassified silver. Not surprisingly, they only found a few. In late November, Morrow advised the MTC that at most several dozen gold employees would be affected, usually upon retirement: railroad hostlers, wood caulkers, drivers, planing mill operators, and a few clerks, foremen, and craftsmen. Morrow had decided on token compliance with the silverization order. A few department heads and supervisors seemed to favor silverization, but the governor and the MTC overruled them. Should the one-to-three ratio of Americans to aliens decline, the entire system of separate gold and silver installations would become too costly to justify. By early 1922, the Connor Board reforms lay moribund, and the few layoffs that occurred did not alter the existing ratio of gold to silver.[46]

The West Indian community retrenched after the twin defeats of the strike and Connor Board. Layoffs reduced the silver roll to an all-time low of 7,600, producing devastating unemployment in Panamá and Colón. A canal labor official estimated that 30,000 people, including dependents, were destitute. Nonetheless, they did not leave the country because prospects elsewhere seemed worse. Instead, they doubled up in rooms, and those with jobs fed the unemployed. A few thousand took up the offer of cheap land in Las Cascadas, to become farmers and casual laborers. British officials, alarmed at the prospect of mass repatriation, requested that any official change be gradual in order to cushion the impact on the islands. British Minister Mallet opposed repatriation, believing that "a West Indian who has become accustomed to living in the Central American states is an undesirable person for return to a properly governed and law abiding country."[47] Yet little movement took place in the region, because to be unemployed in Panama was still better than to be poor in the islands.

Silver wages remained low for the rest of the decade. Canal officials recognized that they paid less than most employers in the surrounding region and that the purchasing power of wages had fallen by about half since 1914. Gold wages, meanwhile, rose rapidly, paced by those paid in the United States. In 1928 the governor suggested a gradual increase in silver pay, because "it is difficult indeed to see how a number of these employees manage to exist and to provide for their families."[48] Before any change could be made, however, the Depression cut the overall budget and eliminated plans for silver raises.

The cutbacks in the canal employment afffected gold as well as silver employees, because the overall budget fell sharply in the early 1920s. The MTC, realizing that silverization might be resurrected, tried a number of tactics to protect members' jobs. Their lobbyist sponsored legislation in Congress to reserve some positions for U.S. citizens, especially those of clerk, timekeeper, mechanic, and foreman. Morrow opposed this bill, which would have restricted his staffing freedom and forced reconversion of hundreds of jobs from silver to gold. The effort failed, but for the next quarter-century the MTC introduced some version of this bill in every session of Congress.[49]

The MTC also used the AFL to strengthen its hold on higher-paying jobs. Just before the Connor Board visit, the AFL executive council urged the secretary of war to reclassify several hundred positions for U.S. citizens. The MTC then arranged for Samuel Gompers and a special AFL delegation to visit the Zone in early 1924 to forestall cuts in jobs and benefits. After a week of meetings, Gompers urged the governor to protect the rights of MTC members. His sole reference to the West Indians came when he chided the governor for using cheap aliens to depress the wages of Americans. Gompers also attended the Second National Labor Convention held in Panamá, where he gave a prolabor speech. He did not understand Spanish, so he missed the criticism of canal authorities for low wages and retention of cheap West Indian laborers. The British minister observed, "The West Indian labourer is becoming the object of attack both from the canal American employees and the Panamanian labourers."[50]

Panamanian Responses to the West Indians

In the five years following completion of the canal, Latin Panamanians had come to view the West Indians as a necessary inconvenience, a by-product of the canal and related commercial activities. They adjusted immigration procedures to accommodate canal labor requirements, raising and lowering the cash deposits needed to disembark. They did not object to large numbers of West Indians moving into the cities during depopulation, because they brought money and business. The commercial and real estate sectors got a boost from the West Indian community. Besides this, on paper Panamanians were preferred for employment over West Indians, so they did not have to compete for the lowest-paying jobs, which went to the blacks.

After the labor troubles of 1919, however, many Panamanians developed a positive dislike for West Indians, based on several factors. Layoffs and wage cuts reduced the amount of money in circulation, and some resented the fact that the canal's reserve labor force should be lodged in their cities. A delegate to the first International Labor Organization conference in 1919 objected to the burden of "tens of thousands of Antillians who are intellectually and racially inferior to the Panamanians, whose religion and customs differ from ours, speaking a language different to ours." The 1921–22 recession had increased competition for jobs in and out of the Zone. British Minister Wallis defended the blacks: "Unfortunately friction has been difficult to avoid between British West Indians and native born Panamanians, and . . . the unpopularity of the British West Indians extends to the economic sphere. Undoubtedly a considerable amount of ill feeling is attributable to a realization of the superior efficiency of Negro labour compared with that of natives."[51]

The West Indians had become more visible in the tenement districts and now looked like permanent residents. Panamanians doubted whether the West Indians and their offspring could be assimilated into Latin American society. The growing spirit of rejection toward the blacks manifested itself in a 1924 newspaper: "Are we going to stand aside and permit an inferior unassimilable foreign element that is objectionable from a sociological point of view, to take advantage of the few jobs that our native element could fulfill?" Cultural differences seemed insurmountable and bothered Panamanians.[52]

By 1925 the lack of jobs and continued rise in the cost of living sparked a rent strike in Panamá and Colón. The strike mobilized mostly the poor Latin American population and did not involve the West Indians directly. However, the 25–50 percent rise in rents since 1920 clearly stemmed from the movement of West Indians into Panama. Speakers at mass meetings attacked the government and landlords for raising rents, and Panama's police got into a fracas with strikers in which four persons died. From 12 to 23 October the U.S. Army actually took over the cities.[53]

The 1925 rent strike served notice to Panama's elite as well as to Zone authorities that the squeeze in wages produced by the third-country labor system could engender social disorder and jeopardize United States–Panamanian relations. Due to these fears and growing awareness of West Indian unemployment, local politicians proposed a limit on West Indian immigration.[54]

The year 1926 marked an important turning point in Panamanian–West Indian relations. The National Assembly passed Law 13 to block immigration of non–Spanish-speaking blacks, and Law 6 to require that 75 percent of the employees of any business establishment be Panamanians. These acts began a series of anti–West Indian laws that would culminate in the exclusionist 1941 constitution. The legislation both drew upon and stimulated chauvinist opinion and probably contributed to racist acts by the public.

Shortly after it convened in September 1926, the Assembly received draft legislation to require all industries to employ at least 50 percent Panamanian citizens. By the time it reached the president, the figure had risen to 75 percent. The bill could not be enforced without grave disruption of the economy, and little evidence exists that it ever was. It did not apply to the canal, of course. However, it served notice to many West Indians that their jobs might be in jeopardy.

The bombshell of 1926, however, was a bill to end immigration of Negroes, who would henceforth be known as "undesirables." It called for a census of all aliens and a heavy alien registration tax. The chambers of commerce of Panamá and Colón recognized that if passed the law would spark an exodus of West Indians and prove devastating for business, so they urged a veto or amendment. The president favored amendment of the law for several reasons. First, he viewed racial exclusion as deplorable and insulting to friendly countries whose blacks would be denied entry. Arguing that the real objections were to job competition and cultural incompatibility, he amended the law to bar non–Spanish-speaking blacks. As for economic competition, he noted that they could keep out casual immigrants by raising the cash bond required before they could land. Finally, he changed the census to a simple five-dollar registration procedure. The Assembly accepted these changes on the grounds that "immigration of Negroes should not be forbidden merely because they are Negroes. . . . [The] intention of the National Assembly . . . is to free the Panamanian workman from the ruinous competition of the Antillean Negro."[55]

Racism was one of three different and confused motives behind Law 13. The assemblymen, dominated by the so-called chauvinist party, knew what they wanted when they originally banned Negroes: to avoid racial "degeneration" of the population. But they also hoped to protect their constituents by offering them some degree of job protection. Finally, they wished to preserve the Hispanic culture of the country. This was evident from an exemption made for those blacks who had exercised an honorable profession for ten years or more, married a Panamanian, or owned real estate, these being signs of stability and assimilation.

Panamanian labor groups emphasized the economic motive in urging adoption of Law 13, and afterward they pressed the government to include immigration restrictions in renegotiation of the U.S.-Panama treaty which the National Assembly had shelved in January 1927. The Panamanian government did not bring the matter up, however, because it lay in the jurisdiction of the canal administration.[56]

In 1927 and 1928 the British ministers urged the foreign secretary to make changes in Law 13. The latter proved amenable and soon most of the objectionable terms were removed or softened. However, another setback occurred when the Assembly passed a constitutional amendment withholding until the twenty-first birthday citizenship of children of prohibited foreigners. Previously the constitution granted Panamanian citizenship to anyone born in national territory, but now they would have to appear before authorities within a year after coming of age to demonstrate knowledge of Spanish and Panamanian history and customs.

Since the amendment did not apply retroactively, it affected only those born after 1928, who were cast into a nationality limbo. Canal officials made certain that birth in the Zone would not confer U.S. citizenship; Britain admitted to citizenship only legitimate children of at least one British subject when registered at a consulate; and now Panama recognized only children of prohibited foreigners at the age of twenty-one. The generation born after 1928 had no secure nationality.[57]

Birth of a West Indian Subculture

By the late 1920s the West Indian community had suffered a decade of wage cuts and labor defeats at the hand of canal administrators and the MTC. Panamanian chauvinism had led to several laws inimical to their interests. Scant opportunities existed elsewhere, so most elected to remain in Panama, where they now numbered 50,000–60,000. In these unfavorable circumstances, the community raised its defenses and formed a subculture with which to fend off American and Panamanian hostility. The cohesion and defensiveness of the subculture afforded protection but by the same token slowed the processes of integration.

In physiological terms, the West Indian community was robust, healthy, and had a full complement of age cohorts. The migration and selection process during construction days assured that most adult male West Indians in Panama were physically strong. They had received above-average wages and free medical care, which tended to keep them healthy. By the 1920s the principal causes of death were tuberculosis, pneumonia, diarrhea, and enteritis. The highest mortality rates occurred among infants. Those residing in the crowded tenement districts of Panamá and Colón faced the greatest risks from disease, even though all canal employees and their dependents could use Zone hospitals.[58]

Most of the oldest West Indians, who had arrived in the French period, were infirm in the 1920s. Some of them had been repatriated after construction, but the island governments took them back reluctantly, and many had established families in Panama and preferred to stay there. This generation was quite small.[59]

The second generation of immigrants had arrived during the U.S. construction era and made up the bulk of the community by the 1920s. Men outnumbered women, but the ratio declined steadily as movement back and forth became common. Many domestic and menial jobs in the Zone and in Panama became the province of West Indian women. Most members of this generation knew how to read and write and had some skilled or semiskilled occupation, either brought from the islands or acquired in Panama. By the 1920s they were middle-aged, and some had begun to retire.[60] Two things kept them on the job longer, though. Service during construction days gave them seniority when there were layoffs, and the canal had no system of retirement pensions. Only in 1928 did a few railroad employees begin receiving monthly stipends when they could no longer work. This generation was the "heroic" one that had paid a high price in labor, family disruption, and physical danger and impairment to build the canal.

The West Indians had formed families and borne children; these were first-generation black Panamanians. Birth rates remained high throughout construction but fell sharply afterward, due to instability, depopulation, and the advancing age of childbearing couples. By 1930 the West Indian birth rate in the Zone stood at 18 per thousand, substantially lower than that of the Panamanians.[61] All West Indian children born before 1928 enjoyed Panamanian citizenship, and a small number British as well. Their education was haphazard, entrusted to inferior Zone schools, local West Indian schools, or occasionally Jamaican ones. Virtually none enrolled in the crowded Panamanian public schools. Most boys upon reaching fourteen obtained jobs on the canal; girls could look forward to domestic work or marriage.

This first generation of Panamanians of West Indian descent provoked the strongest reaction from the natives, because its members rarely spoke Spanish or knew anything of local customs. Yet one could eventually become president. In addition, as this generation passed through childhood, it seemed to promise that there would be a high rate of fecundity in the community. The Panamanians' fear of this first generation led to the 1928 constitutional amendment postponing conferral of citizenship.[62]

The development of a unique subculture eroded the community's ties with Britain and with the West Indies in the 1920s. To be sure, many turned out to receive the Prince of Wales in 1921 and the Duke of York in 1926, but few ceremonial visits followed. Well-to-do West Indians returned to the islands on occasion and praised the neat orderliness of the "old country."[63] Over 2,000 volunteers from Panama served in a special West Indian regiment in World War I. When it came time to muster out, however, the Jamaican government refused to receive them. The volunteers returned to Panama, where the British eventually gave each of the men $150. Much bitterness resulted from the episode.[64]

Symbolic of the declining loyalty to Britain was the eclipse of the *Workman*, whose motto read, "Learn all the important happenings in your West Indian home," and the rise of the *Panama Tribune*, "dedicated to the West Indians and the Panama Canal." The latter began publication in 1928, and the former ended in 1930. British diplomats maintained ties with the community through the 1940s, but by 1929 they realized that the West Indians would probably never return to the islands.

The new subculture blended elements of the West Indies, the United States, and Panama. Labor organizer Stoute had noted that unionism and other U.S. influences came from the work place and Canal Zone schools: "The instinct of imitation asserted itself and a gradual, almost imperceptible change has taken place." Old-timers' recollections confirmed the influence of American customs in West Indian life. In particular, a few young men who took jobs or attended school in the United States returned to become leaders in the community. Among them were Lloyd Carrington, Arthur Nightengale, Alfred Osborne, James Edwards, and R. H. Thorbourne. Finally, a unique work ethic arose in the Canal Zone, characterized by pride, ritual deference to gold supervisors, and cynicism regarding rewards for initiative, individualism, and responsibility.[65]

Schools played a major part in shaping the emerging West Indian subculture. Teachers were natural leaders and taught young people skills and attitudes that would prepare them for adult life in Panama. The Zone educated less than half of the first-generation Panamanian children, because officials did not wish to pay for their schooling. Depopulation pushed most families into Panama between 1913 and 1921 and forced parents to pay tuition for Zone schools. The new housing policy of the 1920s caused enrollments to rise, but the depopulation program of the preceding decade coincided with the greatest demand for education.

Even with expanded capacity in the 1920s, overcrowding in the colored schools alarmed administrators. The Connor Board ordered more schools and teachers, a recommendation upheld by the secretary of war. Only in 1928–1929, when they hired twenty-four new teachers, did enrollments rise to 89 percent of eligible school-age population.[66]

Curriculum for the Canal Zone blacks had originally been the three Rs acquired through rote memory, a course dictated by large classes (an average of forty-three students in 1927). West Indian teachers still used texts discarded from the white schools, but they did not follow them very closely. In the 1920s they added gardening, homemaking, and carpentry to the eighth grade curriculum, to fit the students' most likely adult jobs. Parents did not approve of vocational studies, which seemed to lock the children into manual work, but they probably had little to fear: the schools spent nothing on equipment and supplies. Annual expenditures per student stood $29 for blacks and $100 for whites. Teachers seemed dedicated and enjoyed great prestige in the West Indian community. Their pay, however, fell farther behind gold salaries and even cost-of-living increases. In 1919 West Indian teachers earned half what gold teachers did; by 1929 they earned less than a third. A Columbia University survey in 1930 found the black schools inadequate.[67]

A large number of children attended private schools operated by West Indians. Jamaican schools enjoyed good reputations, and in fact some Latin Panamanian children studied in Kingston. West Indian schoolmasters stressed discipline and social decorum in addition to the academic pursuits. Claude Mallet once boasted that the fifty Panamanians taking their studies in British schools were acquiring some refinement of manners and moral character "totally void in the ordinary U.S. collegian." A Jamaican inspector in 1923 found the private British schools better than the Zone ones.[68]

Yet British schools had drawbacks too. The culture they conveyed had little relevance to the islands, much less to Panama, unless the student went to Britain for university education. None did. Rote learning failed to produce problem-solving techniques young people could apply in a rapidly changing world. Overcrowding affected the private schools too, when they reduced tuition to accommodate parents squeezed by wage cuts. And finally, they did even less than the Zone to teach the Spanish language and Panamanian social studies.[69] So the private British schools met some of the demand in the 1920s but did not provide a permanent solution. In the end the Zone schools, managed increasingly by West Indians and first-generation black Panamanians, would fill the need.

After the schools, churches were the most important institutions shaping the new subculture. Following construction, little change occurred in the distribution of parishioners—Episcopalians, Baptists, and Methodists easily had 80 percent. Canal authorities, however, did reduce privileges once afforded to the West Indian clergy, while their American counterparts continued to enjoy gold services. The black churches offered refuge in adverse times, and many performed welfare services. They operated in the Zone as well as in Panama, changing with community residential patterns. Only a few churches had substantial buildings, so they could move easily. Protestant ministers often acted as community leaders, especially after the unions were discredited in 1920.[70] Religion operated defensively, protecting the West Indians in a hostile environment but doing little to promote constructive change or integration.

The only labor group to function effectively in this period was the PCWIEA, organized by Samuel Whyte after the 1920 strike. Whyte, a member of the police since 1906, had not competed well against the CFLU and United Brotherhood, but now that the field was clear he emerged as practically the only community leader. In 1924 he announced the formation of the PCWIEA and petitioned Zone authorities for recognition and access to silver clubhouses for meeting purposes. These were denied. Yet soon Whyte submitted a long letter to the governor complaining about a variety of things, from community toilets to sick leave. The Silver Rates Board, impressed with the careful reasoning and documentation, examined each point. Although they rejected all of Whyte's requests, they assured him they stood ready to consider future petitions. That initiated what became a twenty-year dialogue between canal officials and the only acceptable West Indian labor group.[71]

Whyte believed that confrontation must fail, so he perfected a style of deferential petitioning that never challenged but had a touch of controlled anger. He tried unsuccessfully to affiliate with the AFL, though he never thought he had sufficient backing. A bachelor with little else to do, he dedicated his free time to the organization and expected everyone else to recognize him as supreme leader. He acted with stiffness and arrogance toward any other leaders. He had no time for Hispanics and restricted membership to West Indians and their children. His annual report carried his messages to the membership and reprinted his correspondence with Zone officialdom. He took full credit for the occasional improvements granted.

Whyte saw his first task as educating the workers to act in their own best interest—by following him loyally. Due to his overbearing manner, the PCWIEA never had many members: several hundred in the 1920s; a peak of 2,800 in 1931 because of unemployment and threats of deportation; and a smaller peak of 1,400 in 1942.[72]

A wide variety of other black associations sprang up in the 1910s and 1920s. Lodges and friendly societies proved especially popular because they offered group insurance and community activities. In 1919 the *Workman* listed 32 friendly societies, and in the early 1930s estimates ranged from 140 to 500 associations, with combined assets of $1.8 million. The West Indian Committee had early been formed to coordinate these groups and to maintain liaison with the British legation and consulates. In 1929 the Central Board of Colonial Societies played a similar role.[73]

One of the largest societies was the Jamaica Provident and Benevolent Society, established in Panama City in 1927. An initiation fee of two dollars and monthly dues of fifty cents entitled a member to death and sick benefits. The society soon built its own hall and held regular meetings, at which speakers and performers appeared. Membership on the board of directors conferred status, and elections drew heated competition. By the early 1930s the society had 400 members in Panamá, a prosperous branch in Colón, and a new one in the Zone. The Canal Zone governor and the British minister both spoke at meetings, an indication of the society's importance.[74]

Garveyism proved popular in the 1920s. A branch of Marcus Garvey's United Negro Improvement Association (UNIA) started up in 1918, and an aide had recruited in the days preceding the 1920 strike. In 1921 Garvey himself visited Panama and made a great hit among the West Indians. He sailed in on the flagship of his Black Star Line and gave six public speeches. He concentrated on Colón, where several branches of the UNIA existed. He charged a dollar admission to his meetings, and in addition he sold five-dollar shares in the Black Star Line and the Liberia International Loan, both of which would supposedly promote blacks' resettlement in Africa. Having already had trouble with authorities in the United States, Garvey avoided radical statements and focused on the ideal of an African commonwealth to end the diaspora. With regard to race relations he said, "The whites have no right to rule the Negroes and if necessary the Negro should and must fight to rule himself. . . . The Negro is not to dig any more canals or cut any more cane or bananas for the white man." Police reported no unrest among the blacks and estimated that Garvey collected $35,000. He received similar amounts in Puerto Limón a few days later.[75]

Garvey returned once more, following his acquittal in the U.S. fraud trial of 1927, but canal officials refused to let him land. He met local leaders aboard his ship and gave them encouragement. Several prominent West Indians carried the torch for Garvey long after his death in 1940, but even by the late 1920s some leaders doubted the efficacy of his organization. Walrond of the *Workman* approved of Garvey's aims and ideals but not his methods. In 1930 a *Panama Tribune* editorial stated, "After 12 years of [the UNIA's] existence, many people are beginning to expect more from the organization than perpetual oratory. The serious economic condition of our people cannot be improved by beautiful phrases."[76] In a few years, Garveyism ceased to exist as an organized movement.

The West Indian press itself helped to define the emerging subculture. Weeklies by and for West Indians had existed since the French period, but most had operated close to bankruptcy and played little role in community leadership. In the 1920s, however, their readership stabilized and was anxious to gain canal and Panama news affecting them. West Indians had much to worry about, and forewarned was forearmed. The pro-British *Workman* (1912–1930) clearly dominated the West Indian press in the 1920s, but as already noted it ceded leadership to the *Panama Tribune* late in the decade. In addition, the English editions of major Panamanian dailies—the *Star and Herald* and the *Panama American*—also began West Indian sections in the mid-1920s, relying heavily on West Indian staffs.[77]

The dailies, however, were largely interested in circulation, so serious community journalism fell to the weeklies. Indeed, a racist incident in the *Panama American* had led to the formation of the *Panama Tribune*. In 1926 Sidney Young, wire service editor of the former, quit when the publisher told him, "No matter how much work you do, I could never think of paying you the same salary as I pay a white man." Two years later, Young started his own paper with borrowed capital and volunteer writers. The *Panama Tribune* sought to provide service to the West Indian community and to hold together its many members. It featured columns by local writers and picked up material from the Negro wire services in the United States. It was to enjoy the longest run of all the West Indian papers, forty-four years.[78]

Only a few West Indians found lasting success in business, and some observers believed that the subculture discouraged private enterprise. Many had started little shops and stores after construction ended. In 1918 Mallet remarked that while few large companies existed, British subjects possessed interests valued at not less than $5 million. They operated bookstores, dress and tailor shops, barbershops, photo studios, shoe stores, pharmacies, furniture stores, and the like. Colón had an even more active West Indian business sector than Panamá.[79]

The three most prominent West Indian businessmen, Stirling, Deveaux, and Omphroy, had started in Colón. All three made their fortunes in automobile distributorships and garages, but they worked in other fields as well. Deveaux, for example, sold shoes, bananas, and real estate before investing in property himself. Omphroy imported bicycles, tires, and scouting supplies in his early years.[80] Yet the fortunes of these men, while impressive by West Indian standards, were soon dwarfed by those of Panamanian entrepreneurs.

The lack of a large, prosperous West Indian business sector impressed observers. Some attributed it to a service mentality and a lack of aggressiveness. Others noted the unwillingness of the black community to patronize fellow West Indians. Yet another factor was a lack of saving habits. For whatever reason, though, the West Indian community failed to gain a foothold despite the lucrative business opportunities that existed in the 1920s.[81]

In sum, a unique West Indian subculture emerged in Panama and the Canal Zone in the 1920s, one centered in the schools, churches, voluntary associations, and the press. It still resembled the parent West Indian culture of the islands, with increasing influences from the Canal Zone and Panama. The actions of the latter were usually antagonistic and so prompted defensiveness and isolation. Since the West Indians could not survive without the canal for employment and Panama for residence, they were forced to live in a hostile environment. Perhaps this, too, discouraged West Indians from pursuing business opportunities. The more dependent they were upon the Zone and Panama, the more they fitted into the third-country labor system; they were a vulnerable work force with scant political and legal rights living among people who did not want them.

As life and work in the Canal Zone settled down following construction, many of the temporary and improvised solutions to immediate problems became enduring. The third-country labor system, with its gold and silver rolls, would plague the West Indians and irritate Panamanians for decades. Whether intentionally or not, Zone officials failed to repatriate the bulk of the West Indians, and indeed they pushed most into the cities of Panamá and Colón. The West Indians had some skills but few job opportunities, and their presence in large numbers created fears of demographic inundation among the Panamanians. Canal authorities barely responded to Panamanian protests, since to them the West Indian presence was an insoluble issue, and overnight Panama became a more complex place, racially, culturally, and economically.

West Indians themselves protested low wages and mean treatment through union organization and strikes between 1916 and 1920. The protest climaxed in the nine-day strike of 1920, which broke their organizations completely and eliminated unions for the next twenty-five years. Canal authorities soon had to respond to another threat: the Connor Board proposal for silverization, that would have robbed white American unions of their existence by replacing gold employees with silver. Gold unions resisted successfully and retained their relative advantage over the West Indian labor force.

Finally, Panamanians, seeing that a large, destitute population of West Indians would remain permanently in their cities, passed legislation declaring them undesirable immigrants in the future. Moreover, the children of West Indians would not automatically enjoy Panamanian citizenship. West Indians, repressed by Zone authorities and increasingly rejected by the Panamanians, turned inward and built up a defensive subculture with which to sustain themselves. By this time, however, only a few submissive leaders remained. Many of the enterprising ones had moved on to other countries—Cuba, Costa Rica, even the United States.

The strike leaders had been deported. Those who had sought alliances with Panamanians found the ties severed. In the end, the community was left in the hands of teachers, priests, journalists, and obsequious labor leaders like Samuel Whyte.

5

Depression, War, and Chauvinism, 1930–1945

WHEN CANAL AND PANAMA authorities realized the severity of the Depression that began in 1929, they made policy decisions of lasting importance to the West Indian community. Zone officials again offered to repatriate unemployed persons from Panamá and Colón, and they devised a minimal retirement system for those unable to continue working. Yet large numbers of destitute West Indians remained in the cities, and by now their children nearly equaled them in number. Native Panamanians began to agitate for their removal, feeling that the West Indians were subsisting on their piece of a shrinking pie. Anti–West Indian sentiment grew and peaked in the early 1940s. It coincided with and was partly caused by a levy of 5,000 West Indian workers brought in to build a third set of locks wide enough to take a new generation of capital ships. The West Indians had become pariahs in their adopted homeland, but they had no place to go. As they retrenched, their leaders became more assertive and finally managed to find sympathetic ears in Washington during the Second World War. The Depression and war years proved to be the worst for the West Indian community in Panama.

Repatriation and Disability Relief

Unemployment headed the list of crises brought on by the Depression. Between 1929 and 1933 the canal laid off 3,400 silver employees, roughly a third. Because losing a job meant losing one's quarters, most moved to Panama and tried to scratch out an existence. The West Indians called this "scuffling." Timing could not have been worse. The

[75]

governor had just decided to raise silver rates in the late 1920s, but the Depression prevented him from doing so. In 1931 the secretary of war even vetoed an appropriations request for public works to absorb unemployed men.[1]

The decline in payrolls and reduced shipping had an adverse effect on Panama's economy, so there was less income to go around. The West Indian weeklies outdid each other in depicting a gloomy future. The *Workman* editorial, "Between two Fires," portrayed the West Indian community as living at the suffrance of the Americans, while Panamanians rejected them as racially undesirable, exploited them in slums, and yet drew them into political disputes. They were caught between "hell and the powder house." The *Panama Tribune* noted that despite the threatening times, West Indians did not band together in self-defense. A Central Organization died stillborn, and the Confederation of Colored Societies was moribund too. The PCWIEA picked up few new members. This organizational paralysis fed on a growing mood of fatalism among the West Indians.[2]

Governor Burgess urged Congress to appropriate more money for silver workers. He wanted new housing (because only 4,000 of the 11,000 silver workers lived in the Zone), cash relief or superannuation pay for those too old to work, better colored schools, and slight increases in pay. He invited the House Committee on Interstate Commerce to visit Panama so its members could see for themselves the deplorable conditions in which the West Indians lived. The committee did not accept, but the following year two budget specialists did. One, after seeing the tenements of Panamá, said, "I would not live in them."[3]

Evidence of poor silver conditions accumulated. In 1930, a team from Columbia University Teachers' College examined the schools, largely for the purpose of accrediting the white schools so that they could send graduates to U.S. colleges. Their findings, called the Englehardt survey, also addressed the backward state of the colored schools. Starting from the premise that the black children would be U.S. citizens in the future, they urged that minimal standards be met. Classes were excessively large, they reported, especially since the schools operated two shifts and even then turned away many children. Enrollments of 90 percent of the school-age children (and attendance of only two-thirds) were too low. An illiteracy rate of 15 percent in the colored population was too high. Colored achievement scores fell far below those of blacks in the United States, especially in math, reading, and composition. They noted that if the graduates could not find employment they should be given secondary training, with the emphasis on vocational education: "The colored schools offer nothing more than a bare academic training, with no opportunities for self-expression, appreciation, or training for the task of earning a livelihood. Inefficiency and discontent . . . are inevitable under such universal maladjustments," the survey concluded.

The Englehardt team recommended expansion of the colored schools to ten grades, from kindergarten to ninth, with additional schooling for potential leaders in the community. The future welfare of the Zone, they concluded, depended on provision of adequate education to the black children of this generation.[4]

Despite the governor's repeated pleas to Congress for more money, he did not consider redistributing wages from the gold roll to the silver roll nor narrowing the gap between them. Partly this resulted from the MTC's influence on the Silver Rates Board. Two decisions in the early 1930s provide a glimpse of how the board operated. Laundresses petitioned for a raise from their average fifteen cents an hour, but their supervisor opposed it on the grounds that a West Indian laundry in Colón paid that rate. The executive secretary reminded him that supply and demand was not the principle upon which they set wages but rather what was required to live in reasonable comfort and decency. He doubted that anyone, especially with children, could live on those wages. But rather than increase all levels, the Silver Rates Board simply raised the minimum from ten to thirteen cents an hour and made fifteen cents the average pay after six months. Most laundresses remained in the same predicament as before their protest. Another example of tight-fistedness concerned paid vacations for silver employees. Samuel Whyte built a solid case for such leaves, on the grounds that they would enhance overall productivity and employee welfare. Major employers in the region, including the army and the United Fruit Company, gave vacations. The board turned him down. Silver leaders could scarcely believe in the good will of canal officials after such decisions.[5]

Growing Panamanian discontent with unemployed West Indians gave urgency to canal plans for older employees being laid off. Since 1928 the railroad had provided monthly stipends for employees too old to work. However, they would need congressional approval for adding in noncitizen canal employees, something doubtful in the economic crisis of 1930. In May 1931 the Panamanian government formally requested repatriation for unemployed or retired workers and a month later threatened to refuse reentry permits to persons of prohibited immigration who left the country. Already they had begun denying entry to thousands of West Indians, so canal authorities had to give serious consideration to the possibility of repatriating many unemployed workers and their dependents.[6]

C. A. McIlvaine, executive secretary of the Panama Canal, a career administrator and the most powerful civilian in the Zone, informed the governor that while in theory they ought to send home any unemployed West Indians likely to become public charges in Panama, any wholesale deportation would be cruel and inhumane. Some old-timers had been there for forty years and could hardly be expected to readapt to life in the islands. Others had married Panamanians—of Spanish or West Indian descent—and should not be forced to take their families away. Nor would the island governments be pleased to receive elderly persons or their non-British dependents. Given these complications, McIlvaine suggested requesting congressional funds with which to offer cash inducements for unemployed West Indians and their families to return to the islands. He spoke of free transportation and a lump-sum payment of between ten and fifteen dollars for each year of work. He believed the U.S. government had a moral obligation to repatriate all those who could not show strong family or employment reasons for staying.[7]

Governor Burgess did request funds for large-scale repatriation, and his successor Julian Schley followed suit. Speaking before the Jamaica Provident and Benevolent Society in late 1932, Schley urged unemployed West Indians to take advantage of the canal's offer of free transportation home. A local paper responded that without a cash payment, repatriation would be a humiliating end to long canal service, no more than a pauper's deportation.[8]

Meanwhile, the newly elected president of Panama, Harmodio Arias, urged the United States to repatriate West Indians and to give Panamanians preference for silver jobs. In 1933 he visited Washington to urge changes in canal operations, including the institution of a definite policy of repatriation. The upshot was full-scale negotiations leading to the 1936 treaty. In addition, President Roosevelt offered to request a congressional appropriation for repatriation. Congress demurred until Roosevelt made a personal plea in March 1934, and then it approved $150,000.[9]

Yet even before Congress appropriated funds for sending West Indians back to the islands, doubts arose as to the adequacy of the measure. Canal officials admitted privately that $150,000 would only take care of 700–800 ex-employees and their families, a drop in the bucket when compared to the numbers of unemployed workers. Moreover, the few signing up for repatriation were older men. Young ones could afford to wait for jobs to become available again. Some Panamanians also realized that wholesale repatriation of the West Indians would be harmful to Panama. Property owners and businessmen urged restraint to prevent a mass exodus, which would cause grave economic damage. Harmodio Arias, whose family owned rental property, moderated some of the more radical appeals for deportation. The U.S. ambassador extracted a promise from Panama to bolster immigration controls and contribute $15,000 in cash toward the repatriation fund, but Panama never complied.[10]

Repatriation had been a charade all along, Schley later admitted to the British minister. They were happy to have a large labor reserve in Panama, but they had to go through the motions of sending the unemployed home. The effort failed because so few accepted the offer, and he had to ask British authorities to encourage people to apply. Limited as they were, the repatriation funds lasted until the 1950s.[11]

Several factors besides official indifference contributed to the failure of repatriation. The black community itself experienced mixed feelings, as revealed by vacillating editorials in the *Panama Tribune*. Many of the old-timers had little to look forward to in the islands except loneliness and death, if they left their friends and families behind in Panama. Timing also undermined the effort. Those willing to accept repatriation waited for the appropriation that would provide a lump-sum payment. Yet by the time it arrived, in late 1934, employment was rising and prospects were good for an even more attractive alternative: the disability or cash relief program.[12]

The first attempt to provide some retirement pay for silver employees came in 1928, when the railroad, because of its greater financial freedom, began paying fifteen to twenty-five dollars a month to those too old for service. The retired men moved into Panama or back to the islands and continued receiving checks until their death. Governor Burgess set up a disability relief board in 1929 to consider procedures for covering all canal employees, but Depression budget cuts curtailed his efforts. Most of the employees received medical exams and reassignment to light work so they could go on receiving pay. A few returned to the islands with cash payments. Based on this experience, the board drafted legislation to authorize a regular system of relief, which they avoided calling pensions or retirement because of budget constraints.[13]

For seven years Congress failed to pass the disability relief legislation, adding to the unemployment problems in Panama. For charitable reasons, supervisors tended to keep older men on the payroll and to let younger men go in reductions-in-force, even though the latter were least likely to leave Panama. And after the government made a big pitch for congressional approval in 1935, the older men had even more incentive to stay on the job until Congress acted, rather than accept repatriation. By the time legislation was passed on 8 July 1937, many men hired in the construction era were in their sixties.[14]

Canal officials set up a small bureaucracy to handle claims under the disability relief program. Benefits were set at a dollar per month for every year of service, plus allowances for dependents, the total not to exceed twenty-five dollars per month. They faced a major problem of documentation, because after 1908 records had no longer been kept on silver employees. Therefore each case took months to process, requiring medical exams, reconstruction of applicants' service records, house visits to verify the number of dependents and actual need, and possible transfers to lighter duties. Because they were not retirees, the annuitants (as recipients were called) lost housing and commissary benefits and had to move out of the Zone.[15]

Processing became sufficiently complex to require some monitoring, and Samuel Whyte—who never seemed to tire of bureaucracy—became a broker for the workers. Many objected to demeaning house searches to prove their poverty. Others claimed more service than clerks could verify in payroll records. And finally, the twenty-five-dollar ceiling, meager at first, became unrealistic after some years of inflation. The *Panama Tribune* criticized the low amount approved in an editorial entitled "Pension or Charity?" During the active life of the program (1937–1959), the ceiling was raised only once, in 1954, by about 50 percent. Officials privately claimed that the canal actually saved money by getting inefficient elderly workers off the rolls.[16]

Anticipation of the cash relief program, then, undermined repatriation efforts in the mid-1930s. Few West Indians went back to the islands. Whether or not canal authorities intended this outcome, Panamanians became increasingly vehement in their attacks on unemployed West Indians.

Anti–West Indian Sentiment

In 1930 Panama's National Assembly passed legislation barring naturalization of persons of prohibited immigration, the main target of which was the West Indians. The government from time to time pressured aliens to comply with registration procedures, although the repeated orders suggest lack of enforcement. In 1931 a new passport law required the foreign ministry to stop issuing return permits to those of prohibited immigration, largely the West Indians. Panamanians had the impression that West Indians and their children took all their savings to the islands for vacations and then returned broke. Authorities explained that they did not intend to discriminate against any particular group but merely to prevent people from selling their passports while abroad.[17]

The British minister, however, perceived an element of racism in these measures:

> The native Panamanians—and more especially the small upper class, which still shows evident traces of Spanish blood in its veins—have come to resent intensely the presence of the Negro in their midst, and they realize only too well that there is a danger of his imparting an African taint to the whole population. . . . To the student of racial interactions and antagonisms, Panama offers an interesting spectacle just now.[18]

Unfortunately for the West Indians, the aversion permeated all layers of society.

An informative exchange of views occurred at this time, one which helped to clarify positions and soften racial antagonism. In 1930 Abel Villegas Arango, the editor of *El Diario*, denounced the West Indian community in especially derogatory terms, using such epithets as *meco* (black) and *chombo* (nigger). Called to task by the *Panama Tribune*, he explained in a letter to that paper:

> Antipathy exists since your race came down to the Isthmus because of the divergence in manner and habits; animosity since it deprived the native of his natural field of endeavor. . . . Neither is there racial prejudice. . . . There can be no prejudice when there is such a wide chasm of religious,

social, and racial features between the white Panamanian and the colored West Indians. Prejudice is envy, and this can only exist between two communities of similar racial, cultural, and financial standing.

Panamanians, he continued, were disgusted by the "law-breaking tendency" of the West Indians. "There can be no affection between two races so far apart." Mutual esteem and respect could only come through "submission by [the blacks] to the standards and habits of the country, which bespeak legal protection, social toleration, and equality of possibilities. . . . There is no denying that the West Indian element is hard working, intelligent, and energetic, and that they make fine laborers in all fields of human activity." To get along with Panamanians and realize their constructive potential, West Indians should act politely, dress modestly, stop importing British wares and exporting their earnings, and end vagrancy.[19]

Panama Tribune editor Sidney Young knew he had a good thing and encouraged the exchange of letters. He himself denied the contention that West Indians committed the most crime. Only one murder had occurred in the preceding year in the community of 50,000. Crime statistics reflected the fact that police patrolled West Indian districts almost exclusively and arrested people indiscriminately. And if the slums were appalling, should the hapless residents or the landlords be blamed? After several more exchanges in this vein, the editor of *El Diario* offered to serve as liaison between his and the West Indian communities.[20] No matter how bad things got in later years, West Indians could count on some Panamanians, like the editor of *El Diario*, to defend them.

West Indians had another defense against bigotry: the ballot. Throughout the 1920s they had voted in municipal elections and had found political allies among the Panamanians. West Indians were especially active in Colón politics, and several sat on the municipal council. When the government threatened to enforce an onerous registration tax in 1929, community leaders hired Harmodio Arias, a lawyer and respected politician, to fight it. Arias had received his degree from Cambridge and served as legal advisor to the British minister to Panama. The latter described Arias as the closest thing Panama had to a statesman. As a member of the advisory board to the foreign ministry, he could suggest changes in laws and procedures which would help the West Indians. Lloyd Carrington, a U.S.-trained Jamaican lawyer, handled Canal Zone cases for Harmodio Arias's law firm and served as liaison with the community. The firm's West Indian stenographer, Claudio Harrison, also kept up ties with leaders.[21]

By early 1932 some 10,000 first-generation Panamanian West Indians, who called themselves criollos, were eligible to vote in national elections scheduled for later that year. As long as they voted in block, the criollos could have an impact. Harmodio Arias decided to run for president, and the criollos supported him since he had defended the community in the registration tax and reentry permit disputes. Claudio Harrison became front man to line up voters and arrange public appearances.[22]

Arias's opponents, however, sought to prevent criollos from voting by having the electoral jury refuse to register them. They alleged that the 1928 constitutional amendment had made citizenship contingent upon meeting certain requirements that few children of immigrants could satisfy. This retroactive application of the law, patently illegal and partisan, failed to disfranchise the criollos and heightened their resolve to vote for Harmodio. They did several months later, and Harmodio won.[23]

The criollo vote of 1932 proved to be a turning point, because it established the political rights of the first-generation West Indians and gave them an influential friend in high office. In a period of rising nationalism and exclusionism, exercise of the franchise served to confirm the criollos' patriotism.

In the 1936 election, candidates went to great lengths to court criollo votes. Juan D. Arosemena reportedly spent $7,000 and made a campaign trip to Jamaica. Partly as a reward for services in the 1936 election, Arosemena appointed Claudio Harrison district court judge, the highest post yet held in the republic by a member of the West Indian community.[24] In the late 1930s another West Indian, Desmond Byam, won appointment as Colón's inspector of schools. Over the next twenty-five years the size and effectiveness of the criollo vote increased substantially and prompted greater acceptance of the group by Panamanians.

Harmodio's views on race and unemployment probably represented those of most responsible Panamanians of his day. His September 1932 inaugural speech defended the restricted immigration of certain racial and national groups in order to reduce labor competition, prevent further miscegenation, and discourage unemployed foreigners from coming to Panama. He, like many of his contemporaries, hoped to prevent mixing of the predominantly mestizo population with black immigrants. Yet he believed that the West Indian community already there should be treated with respect, since it was necessary for the canal and the economy.[25]

The West Indian community soon called in Harmodio's electoral debt to them, in the rent strike of July–November 1932. The Labor Federation called the strike to protest rent levels made intolerable by high unemployment. Soon another group, the Tenants' League, claiming that landlords profited by as much as 16 percent a year on their slum property, demanded a 50 percent cut in rents. Outgoing President Alfaro decreed a $1.50 monthly reduction in rents, but neither side accepted it. Harmodio took office promising to reduce rents and protect private property, but he soon lost control of the situation. Angry crowds milled in the streets, violence broke out on several occasions, and police arrested scores of strikers.

The West Indians found themselves caught in the middle. Panamanian labor groups had for some time blamed them for taking the few available jobs in the canal and for bidding up rentals and prices in general. Yet leaders needed the cooperation of West Indians to make the strike succeed, so they printed broadsides in English and Spanish.[26] Most West Indians did stop paying rent and many participated in marches, but they carefully avoided illegal acts and violence. In October leftist assemblyman Demetrio Porras sponsored a bill to cut rents by 30 percent, but it failed to win passage because of strong opposition from landlords. (Porras later commented that Harmodio, elected as "candidate of the poor," himself owned tenements and hence could never resolve the strike and merely frustrated mass expectations.) Thousands of people gathered outside the National Assembly and the presidential palace to hear the debates, and when the bill failed, a fracas ensued in which another assemblyman ran down Porras in a car.

Harmodio eventually defused the crisis in November with a new bill to freeze rents at $1.50 less per month, subsidize the destitute, create a Tenant Board, and encourage new construction. He prevented the strike from becoming an anti–West Indian movement, but the entire episode alerted him to the dangers of race conflict. Over the next dozen years Harmodio would be a key figure in mediating conflicts and controlling potential Panamanian–West Indian antagonism.[27]

The National Assembly, composed of what the British minister called wild, inexperienced, ignorant, and self-seeking men, continued to introduce highly nationalistic bills disadvantageous to the West Indians and other foreigners. One proposed a seventy-five dollar fee for reentry permits. Another sought to limit fishing, journalism, and retail trade to native Panamanians. Yet another would prevent foreigners from starting businesses without at least $15,000 capital. In 1934 the Assembly passed Law 70, for the nationalization of commerce, which took effect in January 1935. It limited foreign-owned stores to an employee ratio proportional to the number of foreigners in the market region. Although Panamá and Colón were excluded, they would be affected by a 1941 version of the law. In these cases Harmodio tried to mitigate the impact on the foreign community without appearing unpatriotic himself, a difficult role under any circumstances. Quietly he urged the British and Americans to repatriate as many unemployed West Indians as possible, at least 15,000.[28]

The year 1933 brought some employment gains but also the worst agitation against West Indians yet experienced. The canal began relief projects to be paid for by Panama out of its annuity, especially a new water system linked to Madden dam. Later in the year the U.S. government appropriated $1 million for public works and jobs. This temporary respite from reductions-in-force encouraged competition for employment between West Indians and Panamanians, showing that the third-country labor system still operated.[29]

Harmodio had begun arguing that more Panamanians should be

hired by the canal, whereas supervisors preferred West Indians because they spoke English and were more experienced. One executive thought they should ignore Panamanian applicants who "demand employment . . . in many cases with arrogance. . . . Their demands for more jobs increase with the number employed." Besides, every Panamanian hired meant an unemployed West Indian, and canal officials believed they owed something to their loyal employees.[30]

In June the *Panama American* began a sensationalist series on the need to rid the country of unemployed West Indians. The highly inflammatory articles suggested that the West Indians were on the verge of armed revolt to resist deportation. The reports were not true, but they turned public opinion more against the West Indians. Soon the campaign spread to the Spanish papers, and a group called Panama for the Panamanians (PPP) was formed to arouse further antipathy toward West Indians. Led by former police chief Nicolás Ardito Barletta, the group claimed to have several hundred members. Barletta cited Hitler's campaign against the Jews as a model for what they should do with the "hated West Indians."[31]

Shortly afterward another group, the Advance Guards, organized by Demetrio Porras (of the rent strike), defended the West Indians. It represented labor and intellectual leaders on the left who opposed fascist tendencies and racism.[32]

On July 9 the PPP and a sister organization, the Society for National Defense, staged a march of 3,000 persons to the presidential palace to protest the presence of unemployed West Indians and job competition in the canal. Before receiving the crowd, Harmodio called in his associates Carrington and Nightengale and requested them to urge destitute West Indians to return to the islands. He was especially concerned about unruly youths of the first generation born in Panama. Then he spoke to the crowd in conciliatory tones, telling them that he had assurances from West Indian leaders that everything was being done to repatriate the unemployed. He cautioned against singling out a particular group or race during hard times, saying that "prejudices of that kind have never existed in Panama." The crowds dispersed peacefully after the president's assurances.[33]

The peak of the anti–West Indian campaign in 1933 demonstrated that some Panamanian leaders and intellectuals would speak up for fair play and that economic competition added urgency to the situation. Although agitation died down for several years, it would flare up again in 1935 and 1941.

Living and Working Conditions

During the 1930s and 1940s little change occurred in the housing stock available to the West Indians. Most still lived in Panamá and Colón, and those who had quarters in the Zone regarded themselves as fortunate. The entire outlay for new silver workers' quarters between 1928 and 1939 was only $620,000. Because rents were so low in the early 1930s, the canal lost $95,000 a year operating them. In 1934 the subsidy ended and rentals rose in two steps to make quarters self-supporting. About two-thirds of the silver housing was occupied by families, each with an average of 3.5 children.[34]

Virtually no improvements were made in the tenement districts of Panamá and Colón, which still consisted of highly crowded two-story wooden buildings dating from the construction era. The typical tenement was built in a square around an interior courtyard, with rooms facing inward and outward. Communal washing and toilet facilities were located in the courtyard. Second-story rooms had access by wooden walkways stretching around the building. A 1942 survey of four larger tenements in Colón revealed an average of thirty-eight rooms and 123 residents in each building, and an average of a little more than three persons per room. Rooms rented for between $6.50 and $20 a month.[35]

Conditions in Colón had become especially bad following a major fire in 1940, which left an estimated 10,000 homeless. Some movement into suburban areas occurred in Panamá, as developers platted and opened new eastern districts in Rio Abajo, Sabanas, Parque Lafevre, and Juan Díaz. Some retired West Indians moved there, and other silver employees purchased land for future residence. Those districts took on the look of Canal Zone silver townsites and relieved crowding in the tenements. They constituted the nucleus of a West Indian middle class that would arise in Panamá.[36]

Silver wages remained depressed in the 1930s, and the MTC continued to oppose any improvements. The 1932 U.S. presidential election campaign revealed partisan factions at work. Many "old Republicans" wrote the secretary of war to protest the gradual takeover of the canal's clerical jobs by blacks. Meanwhile, labor representatives exacted a platform promise from Franklin Roosevelt to employ more U.S. citizens on the canal. The principal reason for removing West Indians from clerical positions was to make room for the gold employees' children, who were now reaching working age. Governor Burgess authorized the conversion of clerical jobs to gold status, although he opposed the perennial bill in Congress making such conversions mandatory.[37] Burgess and his successor, Schley, overruled many of their department heads and prepared estimates to show that a substantial increase in gold employees would cost a vast amount. They also testified that the West Indians possessed a perfect loyalty record—none had been interned during World War I for security reasons, although dozens of Americans had.[38] Unstated among the reasons for not appointing more Americans to clerical jobs was the fact that silver wages could be held down more easily than gold, which were pegged to wages in the United States.

Governor Schley tried to curb the MTC lobbying in Washington, because it endangered the gold-silver balance the canal had established. All he accomplished was to cause the secretary of war to send down a public relations specialist in 1935 to look into labor troubles in the Zone. In a briefing paper, the head of canal personnel admitted that the silver employees were underdogs, denied benefits given to Americans, and kept down by the ceiling on silver wages of eighty dollars a month. Still, he believed they had a "relatively high degree of contentment in their work, which may be attributed to the relatively beneficent conditions of employment under the Canal."[39] The specialist, who was quite familiar with the Zone and who spent nearly six months investigating, concluded that paranoia was rampant among the Americans, whom he described as an "isolated employee community conditioned to the paternalism of benevolent autocracy." Gold employees were exceedingly conservative and defensive and would "not mingle with the [Spanish-speaking] Panamanians, whom they regarded as 'niggers.' " He recommended that canal administrators commission a history of Panama that stressed positive accomplishments, urge executives to learn Spanish, and prevail on the Zone police to treat Panamanians courteously. The report did nothing to mollify the MTC activists, and its suggestions for better relations with Panamanians fell on deaf ears.[40]

MTC lobbying to exclude non-U.S. citizens from skilled, clerical, and supervisory positions rankled Panamanians and prompted Ricardo Alfaro, a diplomat in Washington in 1935 to negotiate a new treaty, to press for a clause guaranteeing Panamanians parity with Americans on access to gold roll jobs and privileges. President Arias backed these efforts wholeheartedly, as a way to ease unemployment. Those rights, he claimed, had been stated in the executive orders of 1908 and 1914 regarding administration of the Canal but were never made effective.

Alfaro presented a draft article for the treaty specifying that "Panamanian citizens shall be eligible to positions on the Panama Canal . . . on a footing of equality with American citizens, in regard to pay, promotions, vacations, retirement, protection against accidents in the line of duty, and other facilities and guarantees; . . . preference shall be given to Panamanian citizens over foreigners." On the face of it, this simply reiterated existing policy.[41]

Alfaro's proposal hit a stone wall of opposition, however, because officials feared that it would make personnel policies subject to diplomatic haggling. The legal adviser from the State Department raised another objection: preference for Panamanians might violate most-favored-nation treaties with Britain and France. The latter could claim for their West Indian subjects treatment equal to that afforded the Panamanians, which would ruin the gold-silver system.[42]

Governor Schley sent a long note opposing a treaty article or even an informal commitment to equal treatment. Existing policy guaranteed about a hundred gold roll positions for Hispanic Panamanians, which was all they could reasonably qualify for, Schley argued. They did not speak good English and lacked commitment to the canal enterprise; moreover, hiring Panamanians would undermine the color distinction between gold and silver. He noted that the canal was gradually hiring more Panamanian West Indians on the silver roll, now that a generation of local-born children was reaching maturity.[43]

The under secretary of state, Sumner Welles, in charge of negotiations for the United States, tried to bury Alfaro's proposal, but it cropped up several more times in the talks. Welles said that Roosevelt himself found the matter inappropriate for an international treaty. Late in 1935 he offered a compromise that would give Panamanians equality with Americans but would not mention particulars nor give them preference over other nationalities. Alfaro objected, saying, "To be frank, Mr. Welles, I think the Government of Panama would prefer not to have any assurance of this kind rather than having any hint of an equality of a Panamanian with a Jamaican and a Negro and that is the actual problem."

After sparring around a little longer, treaty negotiators finally agreed to Welles's compromise language, not in the treaty itself but in a separate note ancillary to the treaty: "The Panama Canal . . . will maintain as its public policy the principle of equality of opportunity and treatment . . . and will favor the maintenance, enforcement or enactment of such provisions, consistent with the efficient operation and maintenance of the canal . . . and its auxiliary works and their effective protection and sanitation."[44]

The note, signed by Secretary of State Cordell Hull, confirmed existing policy but provided no means of enforcement. On paper it gave Hispanic and first-generation black Panamanian employees preference over other nationalities to the extent that they had special privileges not afforded other aliens. Had it been carried out, this concession would have worked to the relative disadvantage of the immigrant West Indians, but in fact neither the State Department nor canal officials intended any change in personnel policies. As more children of West Indians attained Panamanian citizenship and joined the canal force, they would gradually raise the proportion of Panamanians, black and Hispanic, in the work force from the existing 20 percent to 100 percent. It was simply a matter of time. In fact, McIlvaine urged the governor to recognize Panamanian naturalization of West Indian descendants to speed up the process, but the latter refused.[45] The competition between natives and third-country nationals gave management too effective a tool to be relinquished so easily.

Treaty negotiators touched on immigration procedures, which were almost entirely in the hands of U.S. authorities. Panama wanted more compliance with restrictions passed since 1926 and hoped to put their officials on board arriving ships. Welles refused to accept this point, but agreed that the Zone would have to advise disembarking persons that they might not be free to move into Panamanian territory. Since the new treaty established freedom of transit between the Zone and Panama, the latter could not in practice keep restricted aliens from crossing. Eventually, though, an agreement in 1942 obliged the U.S. government to help enforce Panamanian immigration policies.[46]

In sum, the 1936 treaty did not appreciably change the status of West Indians in the Canal Zone, although the Hull note, if enforced, could have moved them to the bottom of the pecking order. The episode showed Roosevelt willing to make minor concessions to promote good will but not to alter United States–Panamanian relations substantially nor inconvenience canal administrators.

By the time the Senate ratified the treaty in 1939, conditions had changed considerably and the issue of equality in employment was overshadowed by other concerns. War planners had projected a third set of locks parallel to the existing ones to accommodate larger battleships and carriers. The necessary legislation passed in 1939 and immediately raised new labor problems. On the one hand, the Third Locks Act contained an MTC-sponsored clause reserving skilled and supervisory positions for U.S. citizens. Roosevelt objected to it on the grounds that it violated the 1936 note on equality, and Congress changed the wording to read "U.S. and Panamanian citizens."

In subsequent years, the same restriction, at the request of the MTC, was attached to the army and navy appropriations bills in the form of the McCarran amendment. The administration used an escape clause to suspend application, but it continued to hang over the heads of West Indians like a sword. If applied, it would have removed hundreds of West Indian immigrants from skilled and supervisory jobs at a time of severe labor shortage.[47] The McCarran amendments persisted throughout the 1940s, a continuing threat to the West Indian employees.

From mid-1939 canal administrators planned to bring in more West Indian laborers for the third locks project. Panama did not have sufficient laborers available, even counting the West Indian communities in the terminal cities. Yet because of anti–West Indian sentiment, officials considered some alternatives: Puerto Ricans, Spaniards, even black Americans. In each case, two main objections arose. Non–West Indians would not fit into the gold and silver system, and they would require higher pay and benefits that would arouse envy among the existing workers. Therefore, canal officials proceeded on the assumption that from 6,000–10,000 West Indians, principally Jamaicans, would make up the bulk of the new force. The British Colonial Office heartily approved these plans, which would relieve island unemployment.[48]

The Panamanian government, however, objected to new levies of West Indians, on the grounds that they would violate immigration restrictions and further unbalance the ethnic and racial composition of the country. When canal officials said they would keep the laborers in Zone camps and out of Panama, businessmen protested that they would lose sales to which they were entitled. The answer given was a proposal to bring in laborers ethnically and racially similar to Latin Panamanians. General George Stone of the Panama Canal Department (army), made supreme commander of the Zone due to the war in Europe, assured Panamanians that they would not recruit West Indians.[49]

Yet in January 1940, a team of canal personnel officers toured Jamaica to make arrangements for recruiting laborers. They brought back detailed information for a labor contract, and by February they reached provisional agreement on terms and set up an office in Kingston. The canal offered free transportation to and from Panama and wages and benefits similar to those of silver roll employees. Workers would serve a minimum of one year or 1,000 hours. Unlike earlier contracts, the new agreement did not permit the workers to take or send for their dependents, to leave the Zone to live in Panama, or to stay once the contract was fulfilled. The men were to be kept isolated in the Zone and repatriated when work was finished. These terms applied to employees of the canal or the armed forces or any firms under contract to them. Some 600 men came in early 1940 to do preliminary construction work.[50]

The Panamanian government, meanwhile, convinced Roosevelt to have the canal bring a contingent of Spanish or Spanish-American workers who could blend in more easily with the Panamanians. The president wanted to accede to the Panamanians' wishes if possible, yet their desires ran directly counter to the Canal Zone plans. For the next six months a desultory argument went on between the State Department, the Panamanian government, and the War Department, the latter trying to convince the former two that West Indian labor was essential for the third locks project. After construction began in July 1940, they stressed that the project might even fail due to insufficient labor.[51]

In October the ambassador and governor met with newly inaugurated President Arnulfo Arias to discuss further labor needs. Arnulfo, Harmodio's younger brother, had already won a reputation as a nationalist, and he believed that the war gave him an opportunity to demand more respect and benefits from the United States. He admired the Nazis and Fascists and expected Panama to become more disciplined in imitation. Although he referred to the United States and Panama as Siamese twins and pledged full support in the event war spread to the Western Hemisphere, still he planned to extract advantages from the growing emergency. An important part of his program concerned limiting West Indian immigration and strengthening the Hispanic culture of the country.[52]

Arnulfo's inaugural address focused on the ideas of "Panama for the Panamanians" and "assimilation and incorporation of *desirable* foreigners who sincerely wish to contribute to the development and progress of the country." The West Indians, he said, constituted a "grave ethnical problem." While some of them had assimilated and become constructive elements of society, "the majority continued . . . to constitute a foreign body, encrusted in our two great terminal cities with their descendants born on Isthmian soil, protected by [British] citizenship or by ours, as may suit their personal convenience." New contingents of West Indians were an added threat to his plan to preserve the racial integrity of the nation.[53]

In the two weeks following Arnulfo's inauguration, the canal and State Department got his reluctant approval to import 4,000 more West Indians. Arnulfo knew that in the long run he could not continue to veto labor importation, but he could make it as difficult as possible and use it to gain other concessions. He insisted that any new recruits be confined to the Zone and repatriated upon termination of service.[54]

The outcome of these deliberations was a moratorium on recruitment until early 1941, after which Roosevelt could not devote as much attention to the canal. The canal brought in 1,000 more West Indians as well as some Spanish Americans, especially Salvadorans. Their impact on the existing West Indian community was therefore small.[55] Then the Joint Chiefs abandoned the third locks project in May 1942 and cut back the silver labor force. Virtually all West Indian recruits stayed in the Zone and were later repatriated.

The third locks project and Zone officials' insistence on importing West Indian laborers raise important questions about the labor and racial policies of the canal. Why did two canal governors defy Roosevelt on the matter of recruiting non–West Indian laborers? To what extent did the State Department influence key decisions affecting United States relations with Panama? How did the third locks recruitment affect implementation of the Hull note regarding equality of treatment of Panamanians? And what impact did wartime policies regarding racial discrimination have on the Zone?

A major reason for insisting on West Indian labor despite Roosevelt's preference to the contrary lies in the racial policies of the Zone. During the late 1930s nonwhite American employees put considerable pressure on the personnel department to be transferred to the gold roll, and in 1939 the director approved their request. This bookkeeping measure applied to some eighty-three American citizens and simplified administration of fringe benefits. By the middle of 1940, however, officials encountered problems because new nonwhite employees and military personnel coming to the Zone did not understand or accept the color line in gold and silver facilities. Officials also claimed that importing large numbers of Puerto Ricans "would threaten the alien-U.S.-citizen pay standard that was working so satisfactorily in the Zone in keeping pay costs down." Recruiters were instructed not to send white West Indians, who might object to silver segregation, and the personnel department in Colón turned away Latin Panamanians for the same reason.[56]

Worse yet, black American and Puerto Rican soldiers who held gold commissary cards insisted on using gold clubs and postal services as well. The head of personnel recommended that the canal should discourage defense contractors from bringing Puerto Ricans or blacks from the United States, while those already in the Zone should not be allowed in gold commissaries: "It appears to be necessary to adopt frankly the principle of segregation by races and to allow the use of the white club-houses and commissaries on the basis of color." The canal stopped hiring U.S. blacks altogether in 1940 and even discouraged black clergymen from coming to the Zone. Thus canal officials hardened the color line in 1940 and 1941 to prevent an influx of nonwhite U.S. citizens who could undermine the gold and silver system.[57]

Yet at the same time, the federal government took the first steps in fifty years to reduce racial discrimination. Roosevelt had managed to win the black vote away from its traditional Republican allegiance in 1932, and he felt a commitment to bring gradual improvements in U.S. race relations. In June 1941 he signed an executive order setting up a fair employment practices committee for defense industries, to see that no criteria of race, religion, or national origin be applied in hiring.[58]

Though soon promulgated in the Canal Zone, the order was not enforced there.[59] Several months later Arthur Springarm, president of the NAACP, complained to Roosevelt of open segregation in the canal, and the letter made its way to Panama for a response. The acting governor, Mehaffey, drafted a long reply in which he stated that access to gold and silver facilities was "not wholly a question of race or even of nationality but instead is essentially a matter of the wide differences in education, training, skills, customs, and personal habits." He affirmed that no objectionable segregation of races existed. Springarm did not accept the explanation, but Roosevelt did not pursue the matter further.[60] It is clear that canal governors defied Roosevelt's wishes to employ nonblack workers on the third locks because compliance would have undermined the gold-silver system.

The State Department's role in canal policies between 1935 and 1942 revealed that it had little power to affect the canal and hence U.S.-Panamanian relations. Roosevelt authorized the State Department to negotiate a new treaty to improve relations, yet because he would not force the armed services to make necessary changes, the treaty left the canal labor policies largely untouched. The Hull note on employment equality was never enforced. In the third locks recruitment controversy, State sided with the president and Panama in trying to get a preponderance of Spanish-American laborers. Canal officials insisted on West Indian recruits and for a year made only token efforts to comply with these wishes. Therefore, State took a back seat to the War Department at a time when diplomacy counted for less than the exigencies of war.

In some respects, the war, by creating an emergency, undermined the

1936 treaty and the improvements it might have brought in U.S.-Panamanian relations. Labor, defense sites, and other issues brought new pressures to bear and exacerbated tensions. Details such as greater opportunities for Panamanians in canal employment were submerged in the drive for military preparedness. Relations became so bad that U.S. officials welcomed a coup against President Arnulfo Arias in October 1941. The West Indians played virtually no part in these events, and their living and working conditions remained depressed from 1935 to 1945.

The West Indian Community on the Defensive

Like most immigrants faced with adversity, West Indians banded together in self-defense in the early 1930s, strengthening key institutions and reinforcing their cultural identity. The earliest years of the Depression had a disorganizing effect on the community due to distress, unemployment, and insecurity, but by 1933 strong leaders began to unify it again. Not surprisingly, the resurgence appeared first among the teachers in the Zone colored schools.

As in Jamaica, school principals and teachers enjoyed high status among the West Indians in Panama and often ended up leading community organizations. The poor quality of Zone education for nonwhites and the inaccessibility of Panamanian schools reinforced this tendency, since the black community demanded decent training for its children. (See figure 3.) By the early 1930s, however, the generation of teachers from the islands was nearing retirement, and Zone authorities decided to train new ones from among the graduates of the colored schools. This group, the first La Boca Normal School class, contained the next generation of leaders of the West Indian community and also marked the rise to prominence of its instructor, Alfred Osborne.[61]

Osborne's father had left Antigua to work on the canal in 1911, and two years later he sent for his family, including his five-year-old son Alfred. The elder Osborne rose in the colored schools to the rank of principal, and he made sure Alfred received a good education. In 1924 he sent Alfred to live with an uncle in Chicago so that he could attend high school. Alfred graduated second in his class at Hyde Park in 1928 and entered the University of Chicago, where he tried a number of majors before settling on Spanish literature. He worked straight through summers and graduated in a little more than three years.[62]

Osborne's studies in Chicago changed and inspired him. Because of his long residence there, he took out U.S. citizenship, became accustomed to American manners and attitudes, and gradually lost his boyhood Episcopalian faith. A number of studies excited him, but a freshman honors course, "Nature of the World and of Man," made him appreciate the Renaissance ideal of broad education. Teaching became his way to synthesize the extraordinary learning experience he had received in Chicago.

[92]

Figure 3. Average Daily Attendance in Canal Zone Schools, 1905–1975

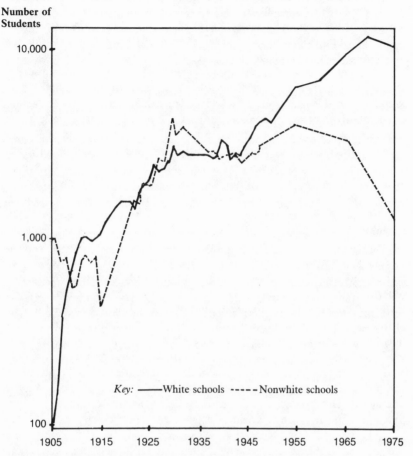

Sources: Canal Record, 3 March 1920, p. 240; Webster papers, tables 7, 9, 12, and Speir memo of 18 February 1975; Governor, *Annual Reports*, various years.

Note: Scale is semilogarithmic.

The New School movement dominated educational philosophy in the United States during Osborne's residence, and he became its apostle in Panama. Beginning in 1935, he returned to the United States every summer to attend Columbia University Teachers College, where he eventually earned his master's degree. The New School philosophy stressed that learning should begin with the child, who should be encouraged to seek out knowledge and personal growth. Students should be awakened to the world around them and be given the tools to understand it on their own terms. Their personalities, skills, and ambitions all interacted with the environment to guide them into adulthood. Schools should inspire students and bring to the classroom as broad a spectrum as possible of

[93]

life's experiences. Everyone should experiment with music, art, carpentry, literature, science, and social studies, in order to form preferences. Avocations shaped personality as much as vocations and played a positive role in learning. These and other elements of the New School educational philosophy opened Osborne's eyes to the inadequacies of his generation's training in the Canal Zone.

Osborne returned to Panama in early 1932 and applied for a teaching position with the canal. His father had been promised that Alfred would go on the gold roll because he was a U.S. citizen, but the acting superintendent proposed starting him at the lowest silver wage instead. Osborne won appointment at the top of the silver scale and five years later, by threatening to quit, he got himself transferred to the gold roll. Given racial and gold-silver prejudices of the time, Osborne's advancement paid high tribute to his qualities. In early 1935 he became principal and sole instructor of the La Boca Normal School.[63]

American educator Lawrence Johnson, hired a year after the 1930 Englehardt survey conducted by Columbia University Teachers' College, was charged with carrying out its recommendations for colored schools, especially for more and better vocational study. Johnson had fought for money and supplies to push the schools beyond the eighth grade. School superintendent Ben Williams, a crusty white supremacist from Georgia, gave him no backing, however; Williams believed that taxpayers' money should not be spent training aliens who would then compete with Americans for jobs. So in 1936 the average class size in the black schools stood at forty-five, a slight increase over 1930. In addition, Johnson had to deal with West Indian objections to teaching farming and manual skills in the schools, which they felt foredoomed the children to menial occupations. Therefore, Osborne's designation as director of the normal school was Johnson's first breakthrough in improving the colored schools.[64]

The first La Boca Normal class ran from January 1935 to June 1938 and graduated thirty-seven teachers. Original plans called for twenty new students each year, but instead it operated sporadically, reopening whenever administrators foresaw a shortage of teachers. The second class ran from 1941 to 1944, and thereafter the school took in new teachers each year. Selection for the first class was stiff: only 40 out of the 358 who applied were accepted. All were under twenty-five years of age. This competitiveness and Osborne's dedication gave the participants a sense of importance and esprit de corps. Osborne himself described the normal school experience as seminal and extremely significant for his generation. He of course recognized that as a one-man faculty he had to rely on student contributions and self-education, so in some ways the normal school merely gave the brightest youths of that decade a chance to expand their own knowledge.[65]

Osborne provided philosophical direction and style to the students of La Boca Normal. The New School became a methodological beacon and the Engelhardt survey their chart. Apart from providing new theory, Osborne insisted on eliminating authoritarian West Indian educational techniques. In fact, he attacked the methods of the older teachers ruthlessly, giving the impression of arrogance and intolerance toward the preceding generation. He ridiculed West Indian mannerisms, which he said were a mockery of British colonial society.

Because his training had been in the United States, Osborne tended to Americanize instruction, but he also had an acute sense of his community's insecurity in Panama and the Zone. He had studied Spanish literature at Chicago and emphasized language skills above virtually all other areas. His message proclaimed: "Weed out West Indianisms and learn Spanish!" By speaking correct Spanish, his generation would get along better with the Latin Panamanians. Participants in the first normal school remember Osborne as imperious, haughty, intellectual, and very impressive. He turned thirty while teaching at La Boca Normal.

In early 1938, Osborne and two of his associates wrote a curriculum guide entitled *General Objectives of the Canal Zone Colored Schools,* which served for the next generation of teachers.[66] Their guide summarized the techniques and materials they had worked with in the preceding three years. The unit on social adjustment stressed the cosmopolitan character of Panama and teachers' responsibility to help children get along but also to preserve group identity. The economic unit suggested contrasting the pseudo-socialistic organization of the canal with capitalistic Panama. It noted that in an economy dominated by trade, their role should be to provide services. Teachers should bear in mind that their graduates would mostly find semiskilled and unskilled jobs and that polite manners were essential. "Young people must be told that keeping one's head, keeping one's mouth shut, and being courteous to superiors and subordinates will pay large dividends in the end."

The section on citizenship noted that the children in the colored schools enjoyed Panamanian nationality and needed to know more about their native country. Geography, history, social studies, culture, and language needed emphasis. Yet "owing to the peculiar situation of this group within the larger group which represents the nation, political discussions should not be attempted." The guide went on to develop the concept of world citizenship, an inspired attempt to understand the place of the West Indians in a larger scene. Osborne and his associates could not rule out the possibility of moving on again with the diaspora, so the idea of world citizenship proved especially relevant. They ended the guide with a catalogue of leisure activities and sports in which the first generation excelled. New School philosophy held that constructive pastimes promoted growth and development long after formal schooling ended.

Taken together, the La Boca Normal class and the publication of *General Objectives* signaled the rise of first-generation black Panamanians

[95]

to responsible positions and a subtle subversion of canal administrators' plans for the colored schools. Osborne served as an outside agent and catalyst, because he did not belong fully to any group. But his students represented the brightest and ablest of the West Indian children born in Panama, and many became the leaders of their generation. Canal officials, of course, had no intention of training leaders nor even good teachers. La Boca Normal was a stopgap solution to a teacher shortage, as Osborne himself admitted. With the exception of Lawrence Johnson, canal officials preferred *not* to give the colored children a good education but rather the minimum necessary to make them efficient employees. The New School stress on adjustment unwittingly complemented efforts to train compliant future employees, but Osborne and his students certainly did not accept that goal, nor did the West Indian community as a whole. They turned their classrooms into laboratories for studying democracy, science, literature, and the world at large. La Boca Normal inspired this new generation of teachers and leaders.[67]

Canal authorities refused to budget funds for improvements in the colored schools, despite the enthusiasm of the younger teachers and repeated requests from Johnson and the PCWIEA. A Columbia University follow-up report in 1941 listed the only improvements made since the Engelhardt survey: Johnson had been hired to improve vocational education; the colored schools now administered health exams; they added minimal Spanish instruction in the seventh and eighth grades; and teachers' qualifications had risen. Meanwhile, colored teachers' salaries declined in absolute terms and so had scholarship.

In 1940 Superintendent Williams agreed with a proposal to add a ninth grade, but only if the colored schools suspended the first grade for a year and raised the matriculation age from six to seven. This plan was implemented in 1942 because the canal experienced shortages in several specific employee categories. They used the ninth grade to train new workers: waitresses, carpenters, helpers, sign painters, clerks, seamstresses, and elementary teachers. An Osborne protégé, Leonor Jump, taught in the reopened La Boca Normal, which took in a combination of new and mid-career teachers.[68]

The pressure to improve the colored schools intensified in 1942, and officials realized that some concessions would be necessary by the end of the war. The Association of Colored Teachers submitted a long petition calling for secondary education, both academic and vocational. Simultaneously, they sponsored a series of lectures and meetings in the silver townsites to build support for high schools. Leonor Jump and an enterprising thirty-two-year-old newspaperman, George Westerman, collected funds to buy 1,000 books emphasizing black studies and got the canal to open a public library in La Boca for colored students. Westerman also obtained autographed photos of fifty prominent black Americans, which he hung on the walls of the library. Finally, Westerman and several

[96]

teachers helped found the Isthmian Negro Youth Congress (INYC) to serve as a bridge from their generation to the teenagers just finishing school.[69]

Unemployed teenagers had been a problem in the black community since the early 1930s, when they formed gangs and seemed omnipresent in the streets of Panamá. By 1940 Westerman saw their unruliness as a serious threat to the community. In July 1942, he, Sidney Young, Osborne, and several others sponsored the INYC as a Canal Zone youth club. Their slogan, "Progress Through Education," revealed that cultural and literary activities would dominate their agendas. They hoped to create a healthy outlet for the energies of bright young people and a spirit of pride in Negro history and in their own community. Secretly they hoped to obtain U.S. citizenship for those born in the Zone. Harold Williams, who would become prominent in labor circles, formed a branch of INYC in Colón. From 1942 to 1946 the INYC published a quarterly *Bulletin*, to which members contributed articles, essays, poetry, and information of public interest. Canal authorities approved of the INYC and provided some facilities in the silver workers' clubhouse. The INYC helped pave the way for the first generation of Panamanians of West Indian descent to assume leadership of the community after the war, and it also convinced authorities that the young people could be serious and warranted better educational facilities.[70]

In 1943 Samuel Whyte and other community leaders addressed a memorial to President Roosevelt requesting an appropriation for two high schools, one at each end of the canal. Governor Edgerton had promised to forward the request through the secretary of war, and Whyte believed it had his support. But Edgerton sent it up with a negative recommendation. His reasoning began with the premise that very few of the black children could aspire to skilled, technical, administrative, clerical, or supervisory positions because of the McCarran amendment, an unfortunate policy but one they had to live with. He took refuge in what had become a perennial excuse: the canal could not improve silver standards of living without specific appropriations from Congress.[71]

Edgerton's reasoning erred on two counts: first, Roosevelt had suspended the McCarran amendment and would continue to do so; second, the canal generated millions of dollars in revenues that could be expended without congressional approval. Edgerton, coached by his MTC-dominated staff, simply refused to take action that might threaten the gold-silver system.

Sidney Young revealed the indignation felt by many when he asked the MTC

whether a population of uneducated aliens residing in the Canal Zone would not be a greater expense to the United States, a graver problem and a more serious menace to public order and safety, than a population of well-educated and intelligent people able to solve for themselves the problems of life, to control in a measure their own destiny and engage in such pursuits as would make them prosperous and independent?[72]

Had canal authorities been candid, they would have admitted preferring uneducated people whom they could control.

Canal intransigence on the school issue lasted until 1945, after which Williams and Johnson instituted many improvements. By then, however, the inferior schools had turned out nearly two generations of young people with only minimal education and a subservient attitude toward authority. The graduates of La Boca Normal felt such anger and frustration at these policies that they formed the first post-1920 union, the Canal Zone Colored Teachers Association, which would become the nucleus of Local 713 in 1946.

The 1941 Constitution

Of the myriad problems faced by the West Indian community in the early 1940s, none posed a more serious threat than the constitution promulgated during Arnulfo Arias's short term in 1940–1941. Intellectuals and politicians had long discussed the need for a new charter, and the nationalistic experiments in Europe enhanced the appeal of a stronger state. Arias appointed a constitutional commission shortly after taking office.[73]

To the horror of West Indian leaders, the commission proposed denying citizenship to children of prohibited immigrants born in Panama after 1928 and declaring that those born before would be considered naturalized. Some Panamanian lawyers and politicians decried the measure. Ricardo Alfaro, former president and negotiator of the 1936 treaty, argued that a cosmopolitan country like Panama should honor birthplace (*jus solis*) over parental criteria (*jus sanguinis*) in awarding citizenship. Juan de Arco Galindo, a contractor in Colón, denounced the constitution in the Assembly. Juan D. Moscote and Felipe J. Escobar spoke up as well. Most Panamanians, however, remained silent.[74]

Panamanians of West Indian descent, whose nationality stood in jeopardy, formed the National Civic League, modeled on the NAACP, to urge Arias to strike down objectionable features of the proposed constitution. They again engaged Harmodio Arias (Arnulfo's older brother) to defend their interests, legally and politically. In fact, the U.S. State Department had also asked Harmodio to keep watch over his impulsive brother, for American officials doubted his stability. Rumors circulated that Harmodio would overthrow Arnulfo if the latter endangered U.S. interests.

The British minister, who had all but washed his hands of the West Indian problem in Panama, took up the matter with Arnulfo too. He noted that tens of thousands of illegitimate children of West Indians could not claim British citizenship and would also be denied that of

Panama under the draft constitution. Arias admitted that they would become stateless persons. He did not, however, regard the West Indians and their children as "a bad colony, on the contrary they were hard-working people, who did not trouble the police courts too frequently." Arias said he would deal with the matter "from a large point of view." He added jokingly, "At any rate, I will not do as the Nazis do: I will not shoot them." The minister of foreign relations elaborated that they could not allow a black, English-speaking person to be elected president: "The Panamanians are anxious to guard against the danger that Panama, situated at the crossroads of the world, should degenerate from a Spanish-speaking, white nation into a cosmopolitan congeries, a babel of tongues, an utterly bastardized race."[75] The National Civic League and the minister persuaded Arnulfo to include a transitory clause giving the president the power to issue naturalization papers to prohibited immigrants for six months.

The 1941 constitution became law on the second of January. The Arias administration applied the so-called denationalization clauses retroactively, taking away the citizenship of children of prohibited immigrants. This interpretation survived a supreme court challenge in June 1942. West Indian leaders protested that denationalization left 50,000 people without a state, and it caused hardship and anxiety for tens of thousands more. It most affected those who wished to travel abroad, because they could not obtain passports or received ones stamped "nationality unknown." Many others fell victim to shysters who promised to obtain naturalization papers for fifty or a hundred dollars.[76]

Most West Indians, however, simply ignored the constitution and tried to keep out of trouble, as they had been doing for a long time. The authorities did not deport any West Indians, who by now constituted a relatively safe minority. Yet the constitution renewed feelings of hostility and rejection on the part of West Indians and prompted racist demonstrations by some Panamanians. Its greatest evil, then, was to bring about worsened relations between the immigrants and the host society. The 1941 constitution culminated a decade and a half of rising intolerance and chauvinism among Panamanians.

The constitution had another deleterious effect on the West Indian community: it gave the canal administration an excuse to harden the color line while posing as benevolent protectors. On a number of occasions, they cited the Panama constitution in order to discourage U.S. blacks from canal service, when they really intended to keep out people who would not fit the gold-silver criteria. The West Indians had not been so vulnerable since the early 1920s. Real wages fell during the war because of the abundance of Jamaican labor, and no additional benefits were given.[77]

The Nationalization of Commerce and Commercial Carnet Laws (number 24 of 24 March 1941 and Decree-Law of 28 July 1941) worried the British legation more than the constitution itself, because they threatened the business community. These laws prevented prohibited immigrants from running retail businesses or from holding any but the most menial jobs. The laws primarily targeted Chinese retail merchants, yet they potentially affected some eighty British subjects: forty East Indian merchants, nineteen Englishmen, eleven Palestinians, two British Chinese, and twelve prosperous West Indians.[78]

Minister Dodd fought for British rights and received assurances that genuine British subjects had nothing to fear. Some West Indians could be affected, however, should the government wish to persecute them: 300 small shopowners and some doctors, lawyers, dentists, and newspapermen. Because Britain found itself severely taxed by the war, the Board of Trade decided not to fight the laws but to hold out for sufficient time for affected persons to sell their properties.[79]

An Anglo-Panamanian trade agreement of 1928 had established most-favored-nation treatment for businessmen, and Panama could not move against them until March 1942. The Panamanian government hoped to convince the British to sacrifice nonwhite subjects in exchange for immunity for whites, but to their credit the British held out. The foreign minister declared, "The benefits conferred upon British subjects generally by commercial treaties shall be enjoyed by all British subjects . . . without any distinctions whatsoever."[80] By stalling, the minister bought enough time to prevent wholesale attacks on the business community. When Arnulfo fell in October 1941, some of the worst zealots fell too, and the new government gradually reduced the pressure and mended relations with London.

By the end of 1943, the British minister reported that some East and West Indians suffered losses of property and employment through the applications of the 1941 laws, but he found "no case of extreme hardship." By that time, most enforcement came about due to pressure from the Merchants and Industrialists Association, whose members profited from buying up victims' businesses at low prices. Apparently the artificial prosperity of 1942 and 1943 from wartime spending provided sufficient easy money to make pillaging nonwhite foreigners unnecessary.[81] In the long run, these laws drove a deeper wedge between the West Indian immigrants and the Panamanians and made their integration more difficult.

Ricardo Adolfo de la Guardia overthrew Arnulfo Arias in October 1941 and assumed the presidency. He did not enforce the citizenship provisions of the constitution or the 1941 laws very vigorously, yet he displayed more racism. Arnulfo had always admitted that West Indians who acculturated could become good Panamanians, and the strongest drive behind his actions had been a nationalist desire to forge a unified people. De la Guardia, on the other hand, seemed motivated by racism alone. In a meeting with West Indian leaders, he said that their people had to be prevented from overrunning the country. They were subhumans who bore children twice a year. He refused to authorize any more Jamaican recruitment and insisted that those already there be confined to the Zone and repatriated upon termination of service. Finally, he objected to a construction team of black U.S. soldiers operating in western Panama and told Roosevelt he "did not want any more niggers brought in."[82]

The ostracism West Indians experienced in Panama during the war and their inability to break down the gold-silver system of the Zone led them to bolder action. In part, this new initiative reflected the coming of age of a younger generation of black leaders, Panamanian by birth, fluent in Spanish, and convinced that their only hope lay in political action. Their efforts in 1943–1945, coinciding with Allied successes in the war, began to find sympathetic ears. These initiatives, stimulated by the peak of chauvinism in Panama and the recrudescence of segregation in the Zone, would bear fruit after the war.

During a March 1943 visit to the Canal Zone, Vice-President Henry Wallace received Noel Austin, a West Indian labor leader. Austin presented him with suggestions for improving silver working conditions on the canal. They concerned opening up Zone lands for retired or laid-off employees, providing more quarters, and allowing freer movement to and from the United States. The governor soon quashed these suggestions, since they either violated the 1936 treaty or fell outside his jurisdiction.[83]

Another group, the Society of Panamanians Employed by the U.S. Government, also requested an interview with Wallace, apparently unsuccessfully. Formed in 1941, the society represented intellectuals and leaders in Panama's labor movement and did not reach very far into the rank and file. Zone intelligence analysts believed that the president, Víctor Urrutia, had political aspirations because of his close ties to Liberal party boss Francisco (Pancho) Arias Paredes. The group focused on securing more gold roll jobs for better-trained Latin Panamanians, as intimated in the Hull note of 1936.[84]

Urrutia, with a U.S. college degree, proved an effective leader. In July 1943 he urged Nicaraguan diplomat Nicanor Chamorro to write to Roosevelt about noncompliance with the equal employment note. In September he hosted a labor federation meeting featuring Vicente Lombardo Toledano, the Mexican labor boss. The Panamanians gave Lombardo a power of attorney to present their case to Roosevelt in Washington. His letter, drafted in October, called attention to the 1936 Hull note, to the Fair Employment Practices order, and to blatant racial discrimination. He characterized the MTC as a cabal of old-timers and a labor aristocracy bent on preserving white supremacy. The letter would touch off a serious debate when it reached the White House in February 1944.[85]

In December 1943, Samuel Whyte, learning that Eleanor Roosevelt planned to visit the canal the following March, wrote to request a meeting to discuss White House support for silver workers' high schools. The governor put on a show for Mrs. Roosevelt and assured her they were doing everything possible to improve the lot of the West Indians. The main problems outstanding were housing, schools, and recreational facilities. Mrs. Roosevelt did not pursue the problem.[86]

Meanwhile, President Roosevelt had asked an assistant, Jonathan Daniels, to deal with the Lombardo letter and other complaints that had surfaced. Among these was a potentially embarrassing protest by the Panamanian government at the May 1944 International Labor Organization conference in Philadelphia. Panama's delegate, Diógenes de la Rosa, presented a memorial to Secretary of Labor Frances Perkins regarding unequal treatment of non-U.S. citizens employed on the canal. Simultaneously, West Indian leaders in Panama held a mass meeting, at which they collected 5,000 signatures on a petition requesting answers to the questions presented to Vice-President Wallace the previous year.[87]

By this time Daniels had become convinced that canal labor policies had already jeopardized U.S. relations with Panama and could potentially undermine those with the rest of Latin America as well. He drafted a strong letter from the president to the governor concerning the Panamanian and Lombardo protests. He asked the governor to give close attention to the charges and to present a full report on actions planned to remedy the situation. "It is my desire that there be nothing in our employment or other policies in the Canal Zone which might serve as justifiable basis for any charge that the United States of America deals with its neighbors of any race or nation in anything less than the fairest and most neighborly spirit." Governor Mehaffey flew to Washington to discuss these accusations with the president and the secretary of war. To his relief, he found Roosevelt less concerned about the situation than Daniels, but he took advantage of the opportunity to get the president's support for funding better silver employees' schools and housing.[88]

Daniels also convinced the president to send down an expert to study the need for more silver housing. In August the National Housing Agency detailed Jacob Crane to Panama. Crane's report, the first of many in the 1940s, recommended designing better housing for the tropics and building enough to accommodate all silver employees and their dependents. This program should proceed in conjunction with similar Panamanian efforts, to eradicate what he termed the worst tenements he had ever seen. Two million dollars would be required at the outset. He also urged immediate improvements in schooling, job training, and promotion of Panamanians. He viewed segregation as the most painful problem and urged that housing and other policies be gradually changed to facilitate "a greater community of interest and activity" between whites and blacks. Mehaffey used this and other recommendations to show good-faith efforts to improve silver workers' conditions and to deflect attention from the racist gold and silver rolls.[89]

Mehaffey realized that a campaign was under way to dismantle the gold-silver system, but he stuck to his guns in hopes that the end of the war would bring respite. Daniels and the State Department had in fact used up most of their ammunition and had not modified canal policies. Roosevelt did not wish to deal with the problem, only to keep it from diverting his attention from Europe and the Pacific. In January 1945 Mehaffey refused a request for a statement to the International Labor Organization on social policy in dependent territories and gave scant attention to Diógenes de la Rosa's protest to Perkins.[90] The most disturbing development from his point of view proved to be changes in Panamanian attitudes toward the West Indian community.

By mid-1944, the de la Guardia government faced a formidable challenge when Pancho Arias (no relation to Harmodio and Arnulfo) managed to build a majority coalition in preparation for elections two years hence. Don Pancho, as the masses referred to him, put his people in the cabinet and began planning for a new constitution to replace that of 1941. He looked favorably upon the West Indians and their descendants and promised to eradicate all racist legislation from the books. The National Civic League responded with a 900-signature petition asking for changes in the constitution and laws that affected them. Foreign Minister Samuel Lewis (son of a white Jamaican immigrant) eased passport and immigration regulations and sped up naturalization cases for 5,000 West Indians. He explained to the British minister that they were using Panamanians of West Indian descent employed on the canal silver roll as evidence that the United States did not comply with the Hull note of 1936. Therefore their nationality could no longer be considered in doubt.[91]

Writer-politician Gil Blas Tejeira and his daughter Otilia advocated integrating Panamanians of West Indian descent into society, rather than treating them as outcasts. By August 1944, President de la Guardia disavowed responsibility for the racist policies of previous years. Bowing to pressure, he abrogated the 1941 constitution and restored citizenship to those who had lost it. Yet he fooled no one, and his career ended ignominiously the following June.[92]

Whether Mehaffey realized it or not, this new Panamanian attitude toward the West Indian community, plus fresh attacks from other branches of the U.S. government, would force a retreat from the gold-silver system and from racist policies. So although little outward change had occurred during the Depression and war years, the changing generations and the evolution of Panamanian attitudes left the canal ripe for an overhaul in the postwar years.

In the period 1930–1945, the West Indian community in Panama experienced severe hardship and forged strong defenses with which to assure its survival. Mass unemployment in the early 1930s and the inability to keep old-timers on the job forced the canal administration to set up repatriation and retirement systems. Panamanians, meanwhile, campaigned to get rid of the West Indians, treating them as scapegoats for all of the problems that beset the country. Agitation rose to alarming proportions, and Harmodio Arias (who enjoyed the support of Panamanian West Indians in their first presidential election) seemed the only politician capable of ameliorating racial tensions. Despite his efforts, Panamanian chauvinists passed legislation to limit immigration and employment of undesirable aliens, especially West Indians. This trend peaked in 1941 with the promulgation of a new constitution and several nationalistic laws.

Canal officials did virtually nothing to improve silver living and working conditions, and gold employees lobbied for more jobs for their children. The McCarran amendment of the 1940s, which aimed to limit skilled and supervisory positions to U.S. and Latin Panamanian citizens, symbolized the height of this gold-silver competition. Canal officials also hardened the color line in the war years, despite opposite trends in the United States.

West Indian leaders reinforced their defenses in the face of such adversity, using their associations, diplomacy, and the Zone schools. Alfred Osborne led what amounted to a philosophical reform of the colored schools, and while his actual accomplishments remained small, the effort galvanized community leaders. A new generation had emerged. In Panama, too, new leaders arose in 1944 to build bridges to the West Indian community. They turned back the tide of chauvinism and forged what became a politico-diplomatic alliance that would prove powerful in the years following the war.

6

The First Generation
Comes of Age, 1945–1964

WORLD WAR II and the Panama canal's role as a maritime link between the Pacific and European theaters of war prevented Panamanians
and West Indians from achieving changes in personnel policies before
1945. Roosevelt seemed attentive to their complaints but did not take
action. After the war, however, long overdue reforms became urgent,
and canal administrators yielded to pressures from many quarters. First-
generation Panamanians of West Indian descent assumed leadership of
the community and mounted a vigorous union movement among silver
workers. Latin Panamanians accepted them as citizens, and the government used them to attack the old gold and silver rolls. Segregation went
into retreat also, though in one area—schools—it continued. U.S. government agencies in Washington also participated in the debate over
canal reforms. Three events in this period set a rapid pace of change: the
reorganization of the canal in 1950, the Eisenhower-Remón Treaty of
1955, and the flag riots of 1959. By the early 1960s, the canal Zone was a
different place, and the descendants of the West Indians were far removed from their parents and grandparents who had dug the "big
ditch."

Reform from the Top

The passing of the original immigrants created poignant scenes. The
Panama Tribune bade farewell to fifty-six West Indians repatriated in
1945. For the next several years the canal gradually settled its obligations
by sending old-timers back to the islands. Their children, now accepted

as Panamanians, experienced both nostalgia and rebelliousness as they came of age. In Panama to stay, they were still not certain about their identity, torn between West Indian, Panamanian, and U.S. loyalties. Sidney Young deplored the behavior of some young people, who called their parents illiterate and backward, while they themselves strove to be more Panamanian than the Latins. A visiting labor expert found that "the Panamanian of West Indian origin, anxious to preserve his own skin, is not too keen to ally himself with the cause of his West Indian parents. His aim in life is to get himself accepted as 100 percent Panamanian."[1]

Newspaperman George Westerman rejected the stereotype that portrayed the West Indian as a childlike creature who wanted only to gratify primal needs, a "shiftless and lazy, happy-go-lucky and carefree, sullen and resentful, inferior tropical worker who is disinterested even in schooling and training." In fact, he wrote, members of the new generation were loyal, steady workers, but sometimes they tried to overachieve and seemed cocky and aggressive, especially toward whites. This came from their disadvantaged position in the Zone and from the doubts many still felt regarding their Panamanian nationality. Those attitudes would change if they received treatment as human beings irrespective of their color, religion, or cultural heritage. Westerman's voice won growing respect, from Panamanians and Zonians alike, as he sought to carve out an identity for his generation.[2]

Nobody knew for certain the size of the West Indian community in the mid-1940s, but the native-born certainly outnumbered the immigrants by a huge margin. The British minister estimated that the community had 10,000–15,000 West Indians, 60,000–70,000 first-generation, and 20,000 second-generation Panamanians, for a total of about 100,000. By "community" he meant those who spoke English, worshiped in Protestant churches, and felt some attachment to British traditions. Only a small proportion actually claimed British citizenship, however, and few spoke of returning to the West Indies.[3]

The British government liquidated its responsibilities to the West Indian community after the war. From 1942 to 1944 the Foreign Office had kept a special labor agent in the Zone to mediate disputes between management and the 5,000 contract laborers from Jamaica. The experience had shown just how different the older group had become from their contemporaries in the islands. The embassy also ran a small propaganda operation after 1942 to bolster patriotic feelings among canal employees, who often thought, "This is a white man's war." But by early 1945, after improvements in Panamanian legislation, a Foreign Office analyst noted, "The lot of the British West Indians would be greatly improved if they accepted Panamanian nationality, since more jobs would then be open to them." Embassy staff scrapped plans for a cultural program and reduced the consular staff. They recognized that an era was ending and that the new generation was more Panamanian than British.[4]

Anglo-American collaboration during the war had an unexpected and positive result for Panamanian West Indians after the war. In 1943 several people associated with the British consulate in Colón wrote a denunciation of Zone and Panamanian treatment of the West Indians entitled *A Forgotten People*. The pamphlet, summarizing familiar complaints, found its way to the Anglo-American Caribbean Commission in Washington. That body had been set up in 1942 to coordinate defense in the area and later expanded to include France and the Netherlands. The U.S. chair of the commission, Charles Taussig, asked his consultant Paul Blanshard to look into the accusations raised in *A Forgotten People*. Blanshard had served with the foreign service in the Caribbean during the war and took up the investigation with relish. His report lambasted racial policies of the Zone and said that canal managers were "obviously uneasy about the hypocrisy." Blanshard set out to increase their discomfort.[5]

In early 1946, President Harry S. Truman consulted with Taussig, who told him that the racial policies of U.S. agencies in the Caribbean basin had created resentment among West Indian blacks. The Russians had shown interest in exploiting the situation by promoting anti-American sentiment among labor leaders. Discussing the matter later with high officials, Taussig said that the Canal Zone fit the pattern and could face serious disruptions should the communists gain a foothold in the region. Truman, showing more interest in the problem than Roosevelt, declared open season on Zone segregation policies.[6]

Between 1946 and 1950, a number of government agencies attacked the problem of labor and race relations in the Canal Zone, and the matter surfaced in several international meetings as well. American policy makers were guided by two general sets of concerns. Some, like Taussig and Spruille Braden of the State Department, worried that alleged injustices in the canal invited communist agents to foment labor strife. This might be called the cold war analysis. Others believed that the United States had a responsibility to conduct its affairs—especially those abroad—as correctly and humanely as possible. For these people, canal injustices should be eliminated to promote better relations with Latin America and to strengthen U.S. claims to moral leadership of the Western world. But whatever their underlying motives, virtually all observers in the late 1940s agreed that U.S. labor policies in the canal needed urgent reform.[7]

Of all the agencies to look into canal operations, the Department of Defense proved the most forceful. The army, which had always segregated units by race, began to experiment with integration during World War II. After the war, a top-level panel debated the issue and concluded that the military should indeed eliminate segregation. Race problems

[107]

lowered the morale and effectiveness of the armed forces. They tarnished the image of American society as conveyed by forces stationed abroad. Finally, they invited criticism from communists and others hostile to the United States.[8] Yet the enunciation of policy and actual implementation were two very different things, and racial integration of the army would take decades to complete.

Desegregation of the Canal Zone was complicated by decentralized authority. The secretary of the army oversaw canal administration, but the Department of the Army had no jurisdiction over the civilian agency. The army, navy, and air force did, however, have line authority over their various military installations in the Zone. The Zone's second largest employer was the army's Panama Canal Department, established in 1917. In addition, a number of private contractors kept crews busy on construction projects. Most of the delay in creating a desegregated work force with a uniform wage system was due to the difficulty of reaching consensus among the several Zone employers.

Between 1946 and 1954, the army moved to end segregation on bases in Panama but insisted on keeping the dual wage system. Canal authorities fought against any changes. They argued that U.S. laws and desegregation cases did not bind them to similar policies. Mehaffey decided that "the complete abolition of any segregation in the Canal Zone could not be granted immediately or in the near future without wrecking the Panama Canal." He claimed that integration would cause half his white employees to resign and the other half to work less efficiently. Prompted by a suggestion from George Westerman, however, he agreed to remove the gold and silver signs from public buildings and to eliminate the offensive terms. He stressed that segregated facilities would remain.[9] Mehaffey, who had served since 1933, probably had the best opportunity of any governor to dismantle the third-country labor system and to end segregation in the late 1940s but he did not do so. As he liked to say, his job was to move ships from one ocean to another, not reform society.

Truman had requested an investigation of discrimination complaints. The secretary of war asked Brigadier General (retired) Frank McSherry, experienced with labor relations in the army, to conduct one. His secret report of 1 June 1947 proved explosive. Admitting that widespread discrimination against non-U.S. employees existed, he recommended replacement of the two payrolls with a single wage system. His analysis of silver wages showed what had been true since the 1920s: on average, remuneration matched levels in surrounding areas, but the scale had low ceilings that discouraged the talented and ambitious among noncitizen employees. Segregation should be eliminated at about the same pace as in Washington, D.C. The personnel department, dominated by MTC bigots, needed an immediate overhaul. The navy, army, and canal should adopt uniform labor policies. Finally, McSherry recommended that a joint board meet in Washington to iron out interagency differences in the Canal Zone. These suggestions, if taken, would have been bitter medicine for Zone officials and American canal employees.[10]

McSherry believed that Mehaffey had improved silver living and working conditions more than any previous governor and perhaps all of them combined. Mehaffey had pushed hard to obtain raises, shorter hours, high schools, housing, recreation facilities, and fringe benefits for silver workers. But Mehaffey also fought to preserve segregation and administrative autonomy. He convinced the service chiefs in Washington to drop McSherry's idea of a joint board, so that he retained the power to adopt changes at his own pace. He also declared that he would not follow Truman's civil rights recommendations but would instead pace desegregation with that of Washington, D.C. Truman got his inquiry, then, but little in the way of reform. (One analyst believed that quick action on the McSherry plan might have saved the defense sites agreement that Panama rejected late that year.)[11]

In early 1948 Truman declared that he would press for a ten-point program to reduce racial discrimination in American society. In July he issued an executive order "reaffirming policy of full participation in the defense program by all persons, regardless of race, creed, color, or national origin." Blacks in the United States hailed this as a step toward eliminating Jim Crow practices from the services. Yet army commanders did not favor the measure—Eisenhower testified against it and Omar Bradley denied that it applied to uniformed personnel—so it remained for individual units to implement the order as they desired.[12]

In 1948, the canal governor, Francis Newcomer, appointed Executive Secretary Frank Wang as Fair Employment Practices officer but limited his jurisdiction to U.S. employees. Meanwhile Washington kept up pressure for reforms. Following an exposé by Westerman in the magazine *Common Ground*, Secretary of the Army Kenneth Royall at Truman's request visited the Zone in early 1948 to look into discrimination practices. He asked the commanding general and the governor to keep him informed of progress on McSherry's recommendations. They reported that they were changing the old gold and silver designations to U.S.-rate and local-rate, and were studying ways to merge the two into a single wage system. They did not see much hope for abolishing segregation, however. In fact, the canal's director of personnel even wrote to a U.S. company that manufactured machines for grading paint colors to see if they could be used for differentiating skin colors more scientifically than the human eye. Several months later, Secretary of State Marshall urged the incoming secretary of the army to continue the implementation of the McSherry report.[13]

The last major assault on canal discrimination came from the U.S. Department of Commerce, which sent its deputy director of personnel to study conditions in 1949. George Vietheer had worked for the canal in the early 1940s and his department had become involved when Henry Wallace (who visited the Zone in 1943) received reports of Panamanian protests at an ILO meeting in Mexico. Wallace had contacted Spruille Braden, who assured him State was on top of things. Then when State proved impotent to mend the embarrassing gap between White House intentions and canal operations, the secretary of defense commissioned Vietheer to do a study, as an outsider familiar with inherited policy.[14]

Vietheer's month-long investigation generally covered the same ground as McSherry's and came to similar conclusions. He agreed that canal officials had been shortsighted in 1942 when they declined to put noncitizen employees under the Civil Service Retirement Act. Now they faced the complex and costly task of providing decent retirement for local-raters. He also urged that they get on with reclassifying many clerical positions so that they could be filled by Panamanians. In this he echoed the silverization proposals of 1921. Inequities would continue "just so long as U.S. agencies persist in maintaining an artificially high and uneconomic wage structure in the Canal Zone for positions that could just as well be filled by local workers at native rates of pay." In addition, personnel procedures violated the 1936 Hull note and showed "an almost wanton disregard of the law and . . . of sound principles of wage administration." He concluded, "The United States government has gotten itself into a nasty box in this matter [of discrimination, which] if allowed to drift . . . will continue to fester." Governor Newcomer's fifty-page rebuttal hardly lessened the sting of Vietheer's report.[15]

By late 1949, the canal administration had seemingly thwarted all attempts to reform the third-country labor system that by now was evolving into a simpler dual one. But Truman had another card up his sleeve. If he could not force canal officials to raise the standards of the local raters, he could force down those of U.S. employees through budget cuts. As early as 1947, the Bureau of the Budget had recommended consolidating the railroad and canal operations into one corporation or authority that would pay its own way. A closer look at the books convinced auditors that McSherry and Vietheer were right: canal accountants played around with profits and losses in such a way as to mask the extremely high salaries and benefits of some 5,000 U.S. employees. Virtually everything from housing to vacations was subsidized by the canal. This extravagance cost doubly: it made the canal uneconomical and created bad feelings among the local-rate workers, who did not enjoy the same benefits.[16]

Congress had already provided since 1948 for a board to oversee the operation of the canal, but Governor Newcomer managed to block its creation. He could not postpone the budget cuts, however, which began in late 1949. Then in January 1950 Truman issued an executive order with far-reaching implications. It transferred ownership of revenue-producing operations to the Panama Railroad so that the latter could

use the profits to cover running costs. Previously the railroad had transferred profits back to the canal, which used them as discretionary
funds.[17]

In September Congress went further in demanding economy and
accountability. It consolidated the former canal and railroad into a single
Panama Canal Company but detached purely governmental services from
ship operations. The company would be expected to cover all costs,
including depreciation; pay interest to the treasury on direct investment;
and reimburse the treasury for the annuity payments to Panama and for
costs of operating the Canal Zone government. In other words, the canal
should stop *receiving* money from the treasury and begin paying back
substantial amounts. The governor would have to reorganize and stream-
line the canal in order to reverse the cash flow.[18]

To show that he meant business, Truman appointed General Karl
Bendetsen, assistant secretary of the army, to end the excessive liberality
of the canal toward its U.S. employees. Bendetsen and the new board
called in the General Accounting Office for a thorough audit of Zone
operations. Both congressional appropriations committees also joined the
attack. Governor Newcomer tried to avoid cuts in U.S.-rate benefits by
proposing instead an increase in shipping tolls, which had changed little
since 1914. Congress seemed willing to consider the proposal. Shipping
companies, however, lobbied against higher tolls and actually sued the
government for *over*charging them to support luxurious accommodations
for canal staff. The suit failed, but so did Newcomer's efforts to raise
tolls.[19]

Bendetsen and his aide Colonel Beasley conducted a real shakeup.
When Newcomer objected to imposing rents on U.S.-rate employees, the
assistant secretary told him: "We should never presume to place ourselves beyond the administrative influence of our employer nor waste
time in resistance to that overlying authority." In February 1952 the
GAO reported the results of its year-long audit, and, as expected, it
criticized liberal fringe benefits and accounting sleight-of-hand. It also
called for further reclassification of U.S.-rate jobs to local rate, the new
version of the 1921 silverization proposal. Bendetsen pursued these measures relentlessly.[20]

The 1950–1951 reorganization and fiscal crackdown in part grew
out of Washington's frustration with resistance to labor reforms over the
previous years. But they were also dictated by a decline in the canal's
strategic role in American defenses. A chain of events beginning with the
first atomic explosions and culminating in the cold war reduced the canal
installations from a premier military site to an intelligence-gathering and
flag-showing point. Simultaneously, the government abandoned plans to
finish the third locks or build a sea-level canal. The canal had been vital
under the Monroe Doctrine but was merely useful under the Truman
Doctrine. The reorganization reflected that change.[21]

Local 713, Local 900, and the 1955 Treaty

Since the 1920 strike, canal administrators had effectively barred unionization of silver workers. They worked with Samuel Whyte's PCWIEA because it never challenged their authority. In 1939, however, Harry Stoudt, a seaman on one of the canal steamships, had stayed in the zone to begin organizing a union affiliated with the Congress of Industrial Organizations (CIO). In July he obtained recognition from the National Maritime Union (NMU). Zone officials appealed to the secretary of war, who stated that silver employees had the same rights as gold but that neither group could strike against the government. However, when Stoudt began denouncing poor living conditions and racial discrimination, the governor fired two local organizers (Noel Austin and Lionel Moore) and asked for authority to bar outside agitators. Secretary of War Woodring convinced President Roosevelt to issue an executive order to that effect, ending CIO organizing for the duration of the war.[22]

In 1945 the CIO made a new approach, this time through the secretary of war. Governor Mehaffey decided to allow them to organize, because he could not legally prevent it and because he feared that Lombardo Toledano might move into the vacuum if the CIO did not. Since 1943 the Mexican labor boss had shown great interest in the Panamanian labor movement and in using the canal to embarrass the United States. Meanwhile, leaders of the Canal Zone Workers Union, a 1943 offshoot of the Teachers Association, took over the PCWIEA in 1945 when Samuel Whyte retired and returned to his native Jamaica. They approached Philip Murray, president of the CIO, who recognized them as Local 713 of the United Public Workers of America (UPWA).[23]

Local 713's first New York representative, Ed Cheresh, was soon joined by the more militant Len Goldsmith and Jack Strobel. Local leaders were Ed Gaskin and Aston Parchment, of the old Teachers Association, and Cespedes Burke and Teodoro Nolan, of the PCWIEA. They selected Francisco Arauz as president in order to bridge the gap between those of West Indian and Spanish origins.[24] Their newspaper, *Ac-CIÓ-n*, ran articles in both English and Spanish.

Local 713 leaders hoped to overcome the inherent weakness in their position by forcing the transition from a third-country labor system to a dual one. The dual labor system that set immigrants against natives had long existed in the United States and was vulnerable to various attacks, including political and legal ones. In Local 713's favor was the fact that very few West Indians remained on the canal payroll, most having been replaced by first-generation black Panamanians. The 1946 constitution recognized their citizenship, and the postwar administration of Enrique Jiménez defended their cause in international organizations. As Panamanians, workers could claim equal opportunity and treatment under the Hull note of 1936. In a dual labor system in which nationality could not be used as a basis for discrimination, the workers could point to the huge disparities in wages and benefits as evidence that unjust practices continued. Therefore Local 713 leaders tried to unify Panamanians of West Indian and Spanish origin. They also favored a militant, combative style that would bring the Spanish Americans into their fold. Finally, they cooperated with the Panamanian government's efforts to press grievances against the United States.[25]

Mehaffey realized he might face a united non-U.S. labor front for the first time, but he counted on ethnic differences to prevent it. In his words, "The CIO union is made up of two essentially incompatible elements—Latin Americans and West Indian Negroes—and I believe that if it is allowed to go its way unmolested it will soon begin to lose strength and eventually perhaps fall apart." He had been in the Zone since 1933 and knew full well the kinds of problems the union faced. He preferred to fight Local 713 by improving local-rate benefits so that members would realize that loyalty paid off better than confrontation. And McSherry was undoubtedly right in saying that Mehaffey had done more than all previous governors to improve salaries and benefits.[26]

In the end militancy and association with communism brought down Local 713. Perhaps the UPWA representatives believed that combativeness would unify Panamanians. They organized marches and protests and hit hard on the issue of racial segregation. A mid-1946 pamphlet entitled *Men of Gold, and Men of Silver* declared, "In the Panama Canal Zone the color line still forms the basis for a pattern of discrimination which permeates every facet of life." Their placards in a Colón rally of early 1947 proclaimed: "We Can't Eat Sympathy"—"Jim Crow Has Gotta Go"—"Cut Out Discrimination"—"Down with Chicken Coop Quarters"—"Equal Pay for Equal Work"—"Children Need Food." They invited prominent politicians to address their rallies and often joined Panamanian labor federation marches. Some of the information used by the Panamanian government to attack canal policies obviously came from Local 713 files. This militancy frightened some older leaders of the West Indian community, who still remembered the strike of 1920.[27]

From early on, rumors of communist influence in UPWA and Local 713 circulated in Panama. Fears of just such a development had spurred Taussig, Braden, and others to urge improvements in labor and racial policies. In 1946 the Federal Bureau of Investigation called the UPWA a communist front organization, and the House Un-American Activities Committee investigated its role in the canal. In 1947 the earliest UPWA representative quit because of alleged leftist influence. That same year two new representatives, Max Brodsky and Joseph Sachs, arrived in Panama to replace Goldsmith and Robert Weinstein, and their approach raised protests from Panamanian leaders. These Jewish-sounding names probably worried descendants of the West Indians, who were used to

English or Spanish ones. Moreover, their brash, pushy style struck many as wrong, certainly in the context of canal labor relations.[28]

Mehaffey and his executive secretary, Frank Wang, knew that their employees would not become communists. McSherry did not mention communist influence in his 190-page report. And Congressman John McDowell (R-Pa.) concluded that the Panamanian employees of the canal could not be won over. Yet gradually leaders drifted away from Local 713, claiming that Brodsky and Sachs were communists or under communist influence. George Westerman, a principal leader of this breakaway group, years later stated that whether or not they were communists, the West Indian community could not afford the risk of leftist influence in Local 713. Abram Flaxer, president of the UPWA international, had come under heavy accusations in the United States, in what was fast becoming a new red scare. Mehaffey and Wang might have suggested this to Westerman, who covered the Zone for the *Panama Tribune*.[29]

By early 1948 the split widened, with Westerman, the *Panama Tribune*, and the original Local 713 leaders (Gaskin, Burke, Parchment) opposing Brodsky and Sachs. The latter then used physical threats to try to silence the dissidents, a style of unionism entirely at odds with the West Indian tradition.[30]

The turning point occurred in March, when the dissidents sponsored a resolution opposing communist influence and affirming loyalty to the United States. The resolution failed. In subsequent months, canal officials decided to counterattack. The U.S. district attorney issued subpoenas against Brodsky and Sachs, who thereafter had to stay out of the Zone. In 1949 Panama deported Brodsky, and Zone police eventually jailed Sachs on libel charges. Finally, throughout 1949 the State Department refused passports to new UPWA representatives assigned to Panama. One embassy official believed that this crackdown actually forced Local 713 leaders into the arms of Panamanian leftists.[31]

The split in the canal union reflected a larger breach between the conservative wing of the CIO and Flaxer's liberal wing, which were fighting for influence in Latin American labor movements. Flaxer appeared to be working closely with Lombardo Toledano's organization, the Labor Confederation of Latin America (CTAL). Soon, the AFL joined the struggle too.[32]

The government's Point Four aid program, designed to stem the spread of communism, had begun to put money into a pro-American hemispheric labor movement. The AFL, considered safer than the CIO, had been chosen for this role and had set up the Interamerican Confederation of Workers (CIT) in 1948. In January 1949 the AFL sent a delegation to the canal ostensibly to look into charges of discrimination but in fact to capture representation of local-rate employees. They saw the canal workers as important for success in Latin America and there-

fore fought the CIO for control. The January delegation included prominent political figures from Colombia, Costa Rica, and Puerto Rico. Taking many of their data from a recent pamphlet by Westerman, they
condemned racial discrimination in what should be a showcase of democracy. They recommended that the U.S. rate locals in the Zone organize
noncitizen employees. The MTC and CLU leaders, still fighting to maintain their ascendancy over local raters, did not take up the suggestion.[33]

At one point, the embassy political officer, Ed Clark, called Westerman in and offered him $10,000 to help swing the Local 713 dissidents
over to the AFL/CIT side. Westerman refused because of loyalty to the
CIO and because for so many decades the AFL had ignored their requests to organize the silver workers. He could not see how local-raters
could be adequately represented by the same federation that had always
defended the MTC and CLU.[34]

In July 1949 the CIO sent its own delegation to the Zone, composed
of conservative leaders. They openly criticized the UPWA and Local 713
and were studiously ignored by the latter. They met with Westerman
and other dissidents, however, and tried to prevent what they regarded
as an AFL raid on their membership. They condemned the racial discrimination and low salaries of noncitizens but also warned against allowing the movement to fall under communist influence.[35]

The CIO leadership in Washington finally broke the impasse by
expelling the UPWA in early 1950 for its alleged communist leanings.
This allowed the Government and Civic Employees Organizing Committee to take jurisdiction and to set up a new union in the canal, Local 900.
Westerman served as broker for the transition he had largely caused.
Governor Newcomer acted with restraint yet managed to kill off Local
713 by October. Several CIO officials visited Panama in mid-1950 to
advise Local 900 leaders and left behind Ed Welsh, a black American, as
their international representative. Not surprisingly, the dissidents of
1948–1950 assumed control of Local 900. Ed Gaskin became president
and received official recognition in July.[36]

Gaskin expected to get along with Newcomer better than had Local
713 leaders, since ideological differences were reduced. He also assumed,
as did black leaders in the United States, that segregation would soon
end because of civil rights decisions made by the U.S. courts. The warm
support given by the State Department convinced Gaskin that major
breakthroughs awaited them. He did not realize that the reorganization
under way would reduce funding and prevent canal administrators from
granting improvements. The grinding disappointments of the next five
years nearly ruined Gaskin's career.

In August and September, Gaskin sent Newcomer long statements
of Local 900's expectations. He listed sixteen aspirations that summarized years of unsuccessful struggle: (1) a single wage scale that would
erase the differences between U.S.-rate and local-rate employees and end

once and for all the old Caribbean wage scale; (2) the U.S. minimum wage for local-rate employees; (3) automatic step increases in grade (as was done for U.S.-rate employees); (4) equal pay for equal work, by reclassifying jobs without regard to nationality or race of incumbent; (5) differential pay for night work; (6) seniority rules for reductions-in-force and rehiring; (7) regular grievance procedures to protect against over-bearing supervisors; (8) increases in disability relief, with a minimum of sixty dollars per month; (9) six months' notification of permanent retire-ment; (10) quarters for retirees pending repatriation; (11) free outpatient medical care for dependents; (12) longer repayment schedules for major medical costs; (13) separate sick leave and vacation; (14) more and better housing; (15) payment by check; (16) elimination of racial segregation and discrimination.[37]

Newcomer's response chilled Gaskin and left little hope for im-proved labor-management relations. Point-by-point, the governor re-jected the requests. Local 900's international representative, Ed Welsh, told news reporters that Newcomer's denial lacked "human sympathy and justice" and represented "a complete negation of the fundamental principles of democratic thought and action." In a conference several weeks later, the governor explained that the reorganization of the canal meant no more appropriations. Everything would henceforth have to be paid out of tolls and other revenues. He also pressed Welsh, a tall, imposing man, for an apology. When Welsh refused, Newcomer urged Washington to take him off the Zone assignment.[38]

The following May, Newcomer and Local 900 officials had a six-hour meeting in which the governor proved more flexible. But relations soon froze over again when Gaskin took a trip to the United States and criticized canal treatment of local-rate employees. The State Department, having sponsored the trip, apparently encouraged him to speak out. A New York paper quoted him as saying: "The system of segregation and discrimination is a terrible blot on the conscience of America." Upon his return, canal officials threatened Gaskin with reprimands. Gaskin, thirty-three at the time, stood by his statements.[39]

Gaskin and other Local 900 leaders drew strength from emotions and experiences they had growing up in the Zone. They had suffered from poor schooling as children yet had enjoyed the intellectual stimula-tion of La Boca Normal. When they graduated from La Boca, they were given salaries *lower* than those prevailing three years before. Their ideals came from U.S. textbooks. No one told them that the books left out many aspects of American life. They grew up with segregation and de-meaning treatment by whites. The British colonial tradition, while in many ways as racist as the American, nonetheless did not prepare the West Indians and their children for the personal humiliations of Canal Zone life. Also, time and again promised improvements did not material-ize, as one governor after another broke the pledges of his predecessor.

Behind each governor they could see the mocking smiles of MTC leaders who controlled day-to-day personnel policy. And the injustice continued. Thirty years afterward, some of these same men still felt rage boil up when discussing the union struggles of the 1940s and 1950s.[40]

If Zone immobility angered labor leaders, it also frustrated the State Department, which had exercised only sporadic influence since the 1910s. Zone authorities could defy presidents and disregard treaties, so the foreign service posed no threat at all. Milton Eisenhower wrote after a 1958 trip:

> Our ambassador in Panama has no control over Zone affairs and has too little influence on Zone-Panama relations. He can report his views and recommendations to the Secretary of State, who in turn can report to the President. The President may then call in the Secretary of the Army, who supervises the Governor of the Zone. While this circuitous process is under way, the Governor of the Zone is most likely talking with high Panamanian officials, including the President of the Republic. He is probably visiting with Panamanian businessmen. . . . In some respects, the governor, in his capacity as president of the Canal Company, feels he is more responsible to Congress—to which he must go each year for appropriations—than he is to the Secretary of the Army and the President.

This picture was largely accurate, yet the Washington-Panama relationship had already begun to change.

In December 1951 the White House had convened a meeting on canal labor relations. State used the occasion to reinforce Bendetsen's and Beasley's resolve to carry out long-awaited reforms. Several months later Truman broke the normal line of succession when he appointed an outsider, Seybold, as canal governor. Traditionally, the chief engineer of maintenance became governor, but the man in line (Vogel) had angered U.S. canal employees by going along with Bendetsen's austerity measures. Too late, the employees learned that Seybold would play hatchet man with their and the local-raters' salaries and benefits. Finally, treaty negotiations regarding the canal began in September 1953, greatly increasing the influence the State Department could exercise over Zone affairs.[41]

When Panamanian President Remón opened treaty discussions with the Eisenhower administration, Ed Gaskin announced that Local 900 supported Remón's efforts. Gaskin also issued a lengthy position paper with labor's demands on the canal. He reiterated the points rejected by Newcomer two years earlier. The following January, Gaskin raised the stakes by organizing a massive rally of Zone workers to hear President Remón speak about his efforts on their behalf in treaty negotiations. Gaskin then denounced the Zone administration in the strongest language yet. Canal labor relations and recognition of sovereignty over the Zone stood at the top of the Panamanian negotiators' agenda.[42]

In the fifteen months spent working out the 1955 treaty, the State

Department tried valiantly to include canal labor reforms. State had consistently argued that such changes cost little and could bring great improvement in U.S.-Panamanian relations. Eisenhower was told that the dual wage system was the "greatest single irritant in relations between the United States and Panama." Yet two things obstructed such change: canal managers' reluctance to institute a single wage system and to put local-raters under the Civil Service retirement system; and the Department of Defense policy of paying local wages to foreigners employed on overseas bases. Secretary of State Dulles urged his counterpart in Defense to be flexible, as canal labor was "the most crucial point under consideration." Lack of progress might even abort the negotiations. Defense agreed in mid-1954 to make an exception for its Zone employees, but canal management held out for several more months.[43] The secretary of state offered to raise the annuity payment to Panama while earmarking part of the money for low-cost housing for displaced Zone workers. Panamanian negotiators did not accept the trade and instead offered a draft that would guarantee equal wages, benefits, and employment opportunities to citizens of Panama and the United States working in the Zone. Canal officials eventually accepted such language in a memorandum of understandings ancillary to the treaty and contingent upon federal legislation.[44]

Panamanian canal employees paid a high price for this promise of reform. The treaty contained several measures that reduced workers' disposable income by as much as a quarter. Their income became subject to Panamanian taxes in 1956. Moreover, those who resided outside the Zone lost the right to shop in the nonprofit commissaries. Finally, several hundred employees lost their jobs due to the transfer of certain operations from the Zone government to Panama. The negative impact of these measures was exacerbated by Governor Seybold's policy (discussed in detail below) of moving Panamanian citizens out of the Zone. These changes were designed in part to stimulate business activity in Panama and to make up for a small increase in the annuity payment. To some extent, the descendants of the West Indians paid the cost of reconciling Panamanian demands and Zone resistance to them.[45]

From the Zone employees' point of view, the 1955 treaty was a disaster, and Gaskin eventually lost his position because of it. In mid-1954, realizing the adverse effect of the pending treaty on his constituents, Gaskin had testified before the House Committee on Appropriations that canal employees needed some relief. The committee stuck to its budget-cutting course. After the treaty was signed, Gaskin supported it as a step toward better relations between the two countries, even though it hurt the workers he represented. The latter blamed Gaskin for their troubles.

To make things worse, canal authorities retaliated against Gaskin for his cooperation with Remón in the treaty talks. They viewed it as a violation of a long-standing policy that canal unions would refrain from dealing with Panamanian officials. The personnel office encouraged a breakaway group to form a new union among employees of the armed forces. This became Local 907 of the American Federation of State, County, and Municipal Employees.[46] Governor Seybold also set up civic councils in the non-U.S. neighborhoods to channel complaints and to rob Local 900 of the credit for securing improvements. In effect, he established a new rival organization. Seybold then tightened the noose on Gaskin by denying him continued leave of absence for union work and forcing him to resign as school principal. Then the Zone divorce court imposed such heavy alimony payments on him that he had to drop union work and take a job with the canal electrical division. When Gaskin finally resigned in 1956, he was a broken man. He had given up his marriage and career and almost presided over the demise of his union. His extraordinary talents and drive were crushed in a subtle betrayal by canal officials.[47]

The 1955 treaty eventually brought some benefits for canal employees and Panamanians in general. In 1958 Congress passed PL 85-550, designed to create a uniform wage scale under the Canal Zone Merit System. It represented a compromise between adoption of the Civil Service System and retention of the old U.S.-rate and local-rate scales. For many years afterward, the personnel department evaded compliance, but the law committed the U.S. government to the principle of equal pay for equal work. In addition, the law prohibited racial or national distinctions in labor relations.[48]

The same year, again in compliance with treaty obligations, Congress included noncitizen employees under the Civil Service Retirement Act. Noncitizens had been contributing to the program for several years, and Congress appropriated enough funds to make them fully paid in. Meanwhile, some 4,300 persons who had retired under the Cash Disability Act continued to receive low annuities.[49]

More important than these gradual improvements, the 1955 treaty signaled once and for all that the canal administration did not recognize any special obligations to the children and grandchildren of the original West Indian workers. They were Panamanians and should look to their own government for services and protection. It ended the old paternalism of the whites and the loyalty of the blacks. That message also came through loud and clear in policies regarding ancillary services to Zone employees.

Social Services versus Depopulation: Education and Housing

Great advances occurred in canal colored schools after the war, due largely to the efforts of Lawrence Johnson and Osborne's group from La Boca Normal. In 1946 they built high schools on both sides of the Isthmus and by 1948 operated grades kindergarten through twelve.

Johnson, who became superintendent in 1948, appointed some white administrators and teachers in the high schools. More important, he encouraged black teachers to pursue higher studies in La Boca Normal and in the United States. From 1943 on La Boca offered in-service training that raised most to high school equivalency. In 1950 Johnson converted it into the La Boca Junior College. From 1948 on, the University of Nebraska conducted an extension program which, when combined with summer study in the United States, led to the bachelor's degree. Finally, a number of teachers on their own enrolled in the University of Panama or other colleges. Johnson gave promotions and raises on the basis of advanced study and recommended good teachers for college work. In fact, in 1949 he urged the personnel department to transfer to U.S. scale any teacher who met minimum requirements for the white schools. These changes did much to improve the long-neglected colored schools.[50]

The schools themselves evolved in the 1940s. The postwar baby boom hit the schools in the late 1940s, driving up enrollments in both the white and colored systems. The division between college-bound white children and trade-oriented blacks persisted, but Johnson had higher skills in mind for the latter. He raised the level of skills taught in high school and upgraded the academic disciplines as well. He set up a summer recreation program for colored children. The junior college curriculum consisted of wood and metal fabrication, motor service, printing, needlecraft, business, and homemaking. Johnson hoped that his graduates would move up into middle-level jobs with the canal. He also added Spanish to all the curricula in order to facilitate interaction between those of West Indian and Hispanic descent. Johnson did not contemplate integrated schools, but he clearly committed himself to equal ones.[51]

Teachers were the ultimate keys to improving colored schools, and they struggled to better themselves. Johnson's promise of U.S.-rate appointments for qualified persons spurred many to higher studies. Guillermina Jump, Aubrey Stewart, and Emily Butcher obtained master's degrees at Columbia University, as had Osborne. A dozen others were at work on degrees in the United States. Once they qualified, however, most chose *not* to work in the segregated environment of the Canal Zone. Of the group that trained in the early 1950s, only eight went back to the Zone schools. Others, like E. Gooden, Steward, and Ana Bennett got jobs in private schools in Panama, where their credentials, experience, and English skills were highly prized. In the long run, the largest number simply stayed in the United States. Indeed, the 1950s saw the beginning of a brain drain from the Panamanian–West Indian community.[52]

The improvements Johnson and Osborne effected in the black schools raised costs substantially at a time when enrollments also rose. Expenditures in white schools (minus capital outlays) rose from $0.5 to $1.2 million between 1945 and 1950, while those in colored schools climbed from $0.2 to $0.4 million. In the wake of the 1950 reorganization, the canal began charging tuition for dependents of nonresident employees attending schools. And the GAO audit suggested integrating the schools in order to save costs. In January 1953, however, Seybold began considering an even more radical method for saving money. He asked department heads what economies could be gained from a 75 percent drop in the noncitizen population of the Zone. Johnson uneasily responded that the colored schools taught some Panamanian social studies and history, as well as Spanish, so their students could probably transfer to Panamanian schools. Seybold, indeed, was developing a plan for shifting most of the educational and social services for noncitizen employees onto Panama if they were forced to raise substantially the annuity payments.[53]

Sometime in 1953, Johnson realized that Seybold had decided to overhaul the colored curriculum so that if necessary the children could make the move to the Panamanian system. Colored schools would become Latin American ones by gradually shifting to Spanish instruction and increasing the amount of material drawn from Panamanian sources. They would hire more teachers from Panama as well, because salaries there were lower than in the Zone. They would dispense with the costly vocational programs in the high schools and junior college, on the grounds that Panamanian high schools offered only academic subjects. Seybold's motive seemed to be economy. Johnson, however, felt betrayed by what came to be called the conversion, because he had spent his entire career (1931–1953) building up the vocational offerings for black students. These achievements, recorded in his 1949 doctoral dissertation at Stanford, would be thrown out as a cost-saving measure. He tried to resign but could not, so he took sick leave to the United States. He died of a heart attack shortly afterward. Several associates believed that the planned conversion of the schools killed him.[54]

If costs prompted Seybold to conceive the conversion plan, fears of racial integration forced him to implement it hastily in 1954. In previous years the U.S. Supreme Court had eroded the separate-but-equal doctrine that had permitted segregated schools, and the president and Department of Justice favored fuller integration. Eisenhower promised to push for continued integration in Washington, D.C., and in the armed forces, and he set a time limit of two years to desegregate schools on military bases.[55]

Supreme Court Justice William O. Douglas visited Panama at the invitation of the State Department and President Remón. He later said that the United States had an opportunity to create an American showcase in the Canal Zone but instead displayed discrimination "of the worst sort."[56] Sooner or later NAACP lawyers, who had spearheaded the legal movement against segregation, would find a case that could force the issue across the nation. Thurgood Marshall, head of the NAACP legal department, thought he had it in *Brown* v. *Board of Education*, scheduled to be heard in mid-1954. The momentum built up also convinced Canal Zone officials that unless they did something, racial integration would be forced on them by Washington.

In mid-January 1954, civil affairs chief Donovan, a long-time Zone employee and leader in the MTC, urged the governor to carry out the conversion to Latin American schools "to prepare the children to live in their own culture and not that of the United States." Members of the West Indian community and Panamanian authorities had long decried the largely American curriculum of the colored schools. However, the conversion would take time because few teachers spoke Spanish. Therefore Donovan recommended converting kindergarten and first grade in the fall and the other grades gradually over several years.[57]

On 12 January, however, Secretary of Defense Charles Wilson had ordered the integration of all schools on U.S. military bases. Seybold announced that the measure did not apply to them, since the Zone was administered by a government corporation and facilities were segregated on the basis of nationality rather than race. Westerman contacted Thurgood Marshall, who in turn urged Roy Wilkins of the NAACP to get Eisenhower to enforce the integration orders in the Zone. Westerman then told the public information officer what he had done and published an account in the *Panama Tribune*. Canal officials decided to carry out the conversion immediately in order to avoid racial integration. Seybold, still apparently more concerned about costs than integration, refused to budget any extra funds for the conversion. The lieutenant governor wrote Donovan, the civil affairs chief, "Despite the dreary fiscal outlook, we must go through with this changeover to Spanish instruction. If you have any doubts on the alternative, read the front page article in the 21 February *Panama Tribune*. It may be later than you think. So keep all hands on the main issue and determined to make this new program succeed—on a shoestring for one year if necessary."[58]

The 1954 conversion changed names and procedures without altering segregation by race. In this, it resembled the switch from gold-silver to U.S.-rate and local-rate terminology in 1948. Officials sped up conversion and disguised their motives. Grades K through six went to Spanish instruction in August 1954 and grades seven to eleven the following year. A few Panamanian teachers tutored the regular staff, which devoted full time to learning Spanish. La Boca Junior College closed in 1954. Officials then searched the files for correspondence requesting more Spanish and Panamanian history in the curriculum.[59]

Addressing a service club in March 1954, Seybold said that he had ordered conversion at the request of Panamanian and West Indian leaders, especially George Westerman. He also claimed to possess studies by U.S. consultants approving conversion pedagogically. He billed conversion as a way to promote personal, social, economic, and civic adjustment to the students' country of birth and to encourage "a genuine relationship between native Panamanians and Panamanians of West Indian origin." His annual report that year stated that "the conversion from English to Spanish as the primary language was brought about in response to public demand from within the Republic of Panama and from individuals and groups concerned within the Canal Zone." Seybold, then, put the best possible face on conversion. He did not admit that they decided to do it to avoid integration, that he had no studies to justify it, and that economy was a primary motive.[60]

Mixed reactions greeted the conversion plans. Westerman recognized that the changes would foster better relations with Latin Panamanians, yet he resented Seybold's attribution of responsibility to him. Parents and teachers objected to the rapidity of the conversion, which would jeopardize student achievement for several years. Some blamed Osborne for the conversion, even though he was away from the Zone at the time of the decision. Panamanians viewed the change as positive, of course, but they urged hiring more native speakers rather than relying on English-speaking incumbents. The vehement reactions and continued criticism for two more decades revealed the importance of schools in the West Indian subculture and the community's frustration at not being able to control them.[61]

In order to legitimate the conversion, the next governor commissioned a survey of the local-rate schools by three leading Panamanian educators, Max Arosemena, Rafael Moscote, and Temístocles Céspedes. Their report noted that U.S. history and civics still overshadowed Panamanian affairs. Teachers lacked textbooks in Spanish. Classes were too large. Most teachers, despite impressive efforts, did not speak Spanish fluently and taught it incorrectly. Elementary teachers' qualifications met Panamanian standards, but only a few high school teachers' did. They suggested calling the schools "Spanish-teaching," because they were not Latin American in any sense. Finally, they believed that the schools did "contribute effectively to incorporate into Panamanian nationality a good nucleus of potential citizens." The question of the West Indians' descendants' citizenship and identity raised in the 1930s had still not been answered.[62]

A few protests made their way to Washington. For example, a white high school teacher married to a Panamanian wrote to Senator Herbert Lehman, charging that the conversion subverted the Supreme Court's *Brown* v. *Board of Education* ruling that had set aside the separate-but-equal doctrine and paved the way for integration. Yet the conversion stuck, and once again canal administrators defied presidential intentions with apparent impunity. Indeed, from 1954 on, the canal fell behind Washington, D.C., in desegregation.[63]

Local-rate teachers—still mostly Panamanians of West Indian descent—made the best of a difficult and unpleasant task. Most were able to teach in Spanish, but a few continued in English. Some believed that they owed their students a cosmopolitan education. Panamanians of West Indian descent had volunteered for service in Korea and had thereby obtained U.S. citizenship. Others attended universities in the United States. To deny them an acquaintance with American society and culture was just as bad as the old system which ignored Panamanian heritage. As parents and teachers, they knew the students' curricular needs better than the governor, who had chosen conversion for economic, social, and political reasons tangential to their lives. Teachers created bilingual and bicultural schools in defiance of Zone policy, then. A principal would later explain, "In effect, the program of instruction which has evolved is made up of elements from the U.S. program of instruction and from that of the Republic of Panama, with a strong North American flavor." If the governor could subvert presidential orders, they could do the same with the governor's.[64]

Housing policy for noncitizen canal employees underwent several major changes after the war, creating a sense of instability and alienation. The Crane housing report of 1944, which recommended more and better housing for noncitizens, was followed by a six-month study under the direction of Wallace Teare, of the Federal Housing Authority (FHA). Teare worked on the assumptions that employee/residents were permanent members of the Zone community; their neighborhoods should reflect well on the American way of life; silver quarters should receive priority; and rents should be set on a fifty-year amortization schedule.

Teare began his report with an assessment of existing silver workers' housing. Only a sixth of the units had private toilets and "none are satisfactory by other commonly accepted modern standards." The worst example was the forty-eight-unit building known to locals as the "Titanic," with a ground density of sixty families per acre. Large portions of the silver housing had been built before 1907. Teare, who had also worked in Puerto Rico, oversaw construction of fifty-two demonstration houses in order to determine costs and acceptability of various designs. He favored detached units or duplexes, smaller water mains, cul-de-sac streets, and overhead electric supply. His designs incorporated some of the best ideas available in low-income tropical architecture.[65]

Officers of the PCWIEA had an opportunity to evaluate the demonstration housing in early 1946. Shortly afterward, another architect proposed simplified construction techniques that would permit more space per unit. Everything pointed to provision of quality housing for most employees in the Zone.[66]

In 1949 another FHA planner reviewed the local-rate housing and found a "very urgent need to provide for the construction of new units, demolition of some units, and remodeling of others." Soon after, the governor submitted a ten-year, $71 million proposal to the Bureau of the Budget, half of which would be used for local-rate housing. It projected a

45 percent increase in local-rate capacity, to accommodate 60 percent of the local-rate employees. In early 1950 the firm of Skidmore, Owings, and Merrill put together a complete housing program for the Zone.[67] Yet by the time these proposals reached Washington, neither the director of the budget nor Congress cared to expend large sums on the canal. They authorized $2.5 million in FY 1951, which provided only 760 low-cost dwellings.

In 1952 canal officials scaled down their housing request following the reorganization. Due to the high cost of complementary services, they planned to house only 40 percent of the local-rate employees, those essential for operating the canal on an emergency basis. Yet on the recommendation of the GAO, Congress decided to suspend all new construction, and the House Appropriations Committee even mandated a reduction of local-rate housing from 3,200 to 1,750 units over the next five years. Thus ended efforts begun in 1944 to quarter most noncitizen employees in the Zone.[68]

Officials referred to the reduction in Zone local-rate housing begun in 1953 as "depopulation." This policy, ordered by Washington, fit in with Seybold's plan to cut government services for noncitizens. Some local-raters believed that depopulation was a reprisal for the growing militancy of Local 900. Others noted that depopulation passed social costs (housing, schools, medical care, and police and fire protection) to Panama, offsetting gains from the treaty negotiated in 1954 and 1955. Seybold favored it because it reduced costs and eliminated myriad petty administrative problems associated with the local-rate communities.

Seybold also decided to raise rents for local-rate housing in order to make Zone residence less attractive. He called in economist Hugh Norris to study family budgets. Norris found that canal employees who lived in the Zone earned 40–50 percent more than nonemployees who lived in Panama. Zone employees spent 8 percent of their earnings for rent, while the others spent 17 percent. Norris concluded that workers in Panama spent more than twice the share of income as the Zone workers for basic sustenance. He left no doubt about the greater desirability of Zone residence in all respects. On this basis, Seybold ordered a 20 percent increase in local-rate rentals for March 1955, and his successor raised them again in 1957.[69]

Leaders in the West Indian community remember Seybold with special anger. They describe him as ruthless, heartless, and a hatchet man. The fact that he cut the benefits of U.S. employees too did not lessen their dislike. The way they saw it, Washington used budget cuts to bring American employees to heel, but the latter passed most of the cuts on to the local-raters. In their view, they paid for the sins of their white oppressors.

The depopulation decision of late 1953 became public early the next year, when the *Panama Tribune* reported that "in its new economic program, [the Zone] was to accelerate the removal of the native workers resident in the Canal Zone into Panama territory and to suspend the social service facilities." The paper noted, however, that Panama had neither the schools nor the housing to receive thousands of local-rate families. Reaction became more negative when treaty negotiators announced that employees residing in Panama would no longer enjoy commissary rights and that they would begin to pay income tax to Panama.[70] All of these changes taken together—school conversion, depopulation, and the 1955 treaty—represented the worst news they had heard since the announcement of the 1941 constitution.

Nothing could be done to change the depopulation decision, and to oppose it as well as the treaty seemed unpatriotic. Therefore most leaders in the community followed Westerman's example in trying to make the best of the situation. He argued that as Panamanian citizens they should accept these changes gracefully.

Westerman conducted a study of housing in Panama in which he showed the urgent need for low-cost construction. He traced the situation back to 1945, when the social security agency invested $2 million in modern apartment buildings in the heart of the tenement district. The Arneson and later Solow plans for massive construction by the housing bank, however, fell through. For the next several years, little new construction had occurred, so that the Zone medical officer could describe Panama's housing as a "veritable powder keg." Migration to the terminal cities from rural areas exacerbated problems, forcing canal employees to compete with recent migrants for slum dwellings. The U.S. embassy described landlord-tenant problems in Panama as volatile, equal to the discrimination issue. And in 1950, the Tenants Board, created in 1932 after the second tenants' strike, collapsed under the weight of 2,000 eviction cases.[71]

Extension of utilities and services into outlying districts helped ease the problem somewhat. But study after study piled up on government desks without sparking any appreciable action. In eleven years the housing bank had built only 1,030 units, and the social security agency had extended a mere 651 mortgages to members. American authorities, worried about the health and political hazards of tenement overcrowding, proposed that new monies allocated to Panama under the 1955 treaty be earmarked for housing, but the Panamanian government refused. Westerman concluded that 10,000 new low- and middle-income homes were needed immediately.

Over the next ten years Westerman worked on a number of housing schemes in Panama, none of which came to fruition. Such plans would have helped to smooth the transition between canal and Panama residence, reassuring local-rate employees that the Panamanians cared about them. These proposals had political and cultural aspects too. Westerman had emerged as the leading figure of his generation, and he dedicated himself to smoothing the way for those forced to leave the canal due to the depopulation policy. Despite his efforts, though, housing starts lagged behind demand. The tenements remained and squatter settlements mushroomed in the hills and swampy lowlands of Panama City after 1955.[72]

Politics, Racism, and Integration

A dramatic rise in political activity among persons of West Indian descent accompanied the increased union activity, the new treaty, and the depopulation program of the postwar period. Already in 1944 Pancho Arias had laid claim to the criollo votes by defending West Indian immigrants and their children's citizenship rights and by promising a new constitution. President de la Guardia tried to do the same when he abrogated the old constitution in early 1945, but West Indians knew he had been responsible for many of their hardships since 1941. Don Pancho's Renovador party thus captured virtually all of the criollo vote in the late 1940s.[73]

Don Pancho Arias was born in 1887 into a wealthy Panama City family. He attended a military academy and a seminary in the United States and graduated from the University of Pennsylvania with a degree in finance. Afterward he served several years in the Panamanian legation in Washington. He dabbled in politics in the period after 1918 and achieved prominence by leading the 1931 coup d'état that paved the way for Harmodio Arias's election the following year. (They were not relatives and soon had a falling out.) In 1936 and 1940 he backed the Liberal party presidential candidates. In the latter year he suffered imprisonment for his activities, and Arnulfo persecuted him during 1941. By 1944 he had gained sufficient stature to mold a coalition of all the liberal factions, so that he became a leading contender for the presidency in the postwar era. That possibility ended in mid-1946, however, when he died of a heart attack while traveling in Colombia.[74]

Don Pancho had a "father complex," according to Westerman, a desire to be every Panamanian's favorite leader. He genuinely hoped to integrate the West Indians and other foreign groups into a cosmopolitan, dynamic society. He had paid his dues politically. He chose the correct (Allied) side in World War II. He was acceptable to the United States and to Britain. He might have become a president with the stature of a Betancourt in Venezuela or an Arévalo in Guatemala. His death deprived Panamanians of a statesman and the West Indian community of a genuine friend.[75]

Many candidates courted the criollo vote in subsequent years. In addition, West Indians and other foreigners regained the suffrage in municipal and provincial elections after 1946. The more united the criollo vote was, the larger its impact on politics. Domingo Díaz Arosemena succeeded Pancho Arias as leader of the Liberal coalition and inherited the loyalty of most criollo voters. In Colón, the young José Dominador Bazán, son of a prominent cattleman, worked closely with Don Pancho and inherited control of the Renovador party. He received some 90 percent of the West Indian vote in the 1948 Colón mayoral election and a substantial majority of the criollo vote as well. At first, most criollo voters simply followed those Panamanians who repudiated the Arnulfo and de la Guardia policies of the early 1940s.[76]

Felipe Escobar gave a typical pitch to the criollo voters in a 1946 radio broadcast. The new constitution had solved the legal problems of nationality, he said, correcting the "ghastly mistake" of 1941. Yet the emotional question remained, "nationality of heart, mind, habits, feelings, and behavior." The West Indian community still divided its loyalties between the West Indies, Panama, and the Zone. This sense of triple identity hindered their integration into Panamanian society, yet everyone recognized that the West Indians and criollos were there to stay.[77]

Some West Indian descendants launched political careers of their own after 1945. They usually helped in the campaigns and occupied lesser spots on party tickets. They did not win elective offices but instead received good appointments if their party won. A roster of these people in 1949 revealed one inspector of internal revenue, one department head in the ministry of agriculture, one employee in the foreign service, two officers in the national guard, and a half-dozen high school teachers.[78]

Serious leaders, such as Young and Westerman of the *Panama Tribune* and the labor union officials in the Zone, kept their distance from Panamanian politics. They sought positions halfway between Panama and the Zone and kept up their ties with the West Indies as well. They knew that if all leaders jumped into the political scramble, they would quickly become divided and powerless. Not all had made a permanent commitment to Panamanian nationality, a position that would not give them room to maneuver and to play off one side against the other. Finally, the fact that Arnulfo returned to political activity and won a surprising following among criollo voters put most serious leaders on the defensive.

After being deposed in 1941, Arnulfo had spent several years in exile in Buenos Aires. He began campaigning immediately upon his return in October 1945, and to the dismay of traditional leaders he succeeded in winning endorsements from prominent West Indians. Claudio Harrison, associated with Harmodio for years, came out for Arnulfo. So did Claudio Liverpool, who headed a Colón group called the United Criollo Society.[79]

In 1947 Arnulfo's party put out a broadside in English addressed to Colon's criollo voters. It denied that Arnulfo and his Panameñista credo were racist. Rather, they stood firmly for all Panamanians regardless of color. Yet, proclaimed the broadside, "The Panamanian of West Indian origin feels closer to the American for reasons of language, and economic influence, and in most cases, through the educational influence received in the schools of the Canal Zone, where they are at an early age made conscious of North American history and customs and even learn the national anthem of the great Colossus of the North." Their lack of identification with Panama came from the Liberals' casualness toward nationality and to their race prejudice. Arnulfo believed that the criollo "should and must enjoy all the guarantees and benefits of his country, but must first comply with his obligations to Panama, that is, embracing his Panamanian nationality and incorporating himself in the great Panamanian family. All this is only logical, and Dr. Arnulfo Arias only wanted this to be a voluntary act on the part of the Panamanians of West Indian origin." The broadside ended by blaming criollo troubles on Liberal racists who opposed West Indian citizenship, on slum landlords, and on North Americans, who "from the beginning of the canal have continuously exploited your labor, paying starvation wages for a high quality of labor."[80]

One former Arnulfista, Arcelio Hudson, broke ranks and warned criollos not to be fooled by Arnulfo's claims. The Panameñistas only wanted their votes and could not be trusted.[81] But the more the controversy, the more Arnulfo benefited. He and his party stood for nationalism and winning more concessions from the canal. Many persons of West Indian descent wanted to believe in Arnulfo and felt that the Panameñista party offered them acceptance as Panamanians. Voting for Arnulfo ended the terrible indecision about identity and made them 100 percent Panamanians.

Many first-generation black Panamanians had little formal education, having gone through the canal schools in the 1920s and 1930s. If their parents did not give them a strong sense of identity, they were especially apt to choose assimilation to Panamanian society in the 1940s and 1950s. These converts revered Arnulfo and "called his name blessed," according to Osborne.[82] Of course, serious leaders saw divisions in the community as threatening enough, and it seemed unthinkable that anyone should vote for Arnulfo so soon after the events of 1941.

The 1948 election provided a test for the various attempts to win criollo votes. The Renovador party in Colón and the Liberal party in Panamá campaigned heavily and attracted solid majorities. Alfredo Cragwell coordinated these efforts. Long-time socialist leader Pedro Rhodes ran on behalf of the Independent Workers party and refused to make any deals. Finally, Arnulfo mounted a campaign for criollo votes. One of his ads read, "We will rectify the errors that were made—to err is human—and all the citizens can be sure that our government will be for the people; . . . we are not interested in any group or sector in particular but in the welfare of the Isthmian conglomeration, because the strength of a nation lies in the masses irrespective of creed, religion, color, or race." The *Tribune* announced a policy of neutrality in the election, perhaps because Young and Westerman perceived that partisanship would erode their legitimacy. Therefore all major parties advertised in the *Panama Tribune,* an indication of the intense competition for criollo votes.[83]

Díaz Arosemena was declared elected, but a disturbingly large number of criollo votes went to Arnulfo. Looking back, Westerman noted that the West Indian community had never united behind an issue or platform but instead split at every election. They were simple pawns in the machinations of the Latin Panamanian politicians. Every major party ran criollo candidates, but only Fernando Bradley (Arnulfista) and Arcelio Hudson (Renovador) won seats, on the city councils of Panamá and Colón.[84]

In November 1949, Arnulfo staged a surprise comeback, when José A. Remón, head of the National Police (later the National Guard), decided to oust the incumbent in office and put him into the presidency. Arnulfo immediately gave assurances that he would not discriminate against or persecute any minority group. Indeed, he promised to provide night classes and other facilities for those "desirous and capable of exercizing full Panamanian citizenship." Within a year, however, he began pressing West Indians and their children to comply with chauvinist laws and in May 1951 even tried to replace the 1946 constitution with that of 1941. His behavior was so bizarre and erratic that the Assembly declared him deposed, and his fall was completed by the withdrawal of Remón's support.[85]

Arias's ouster led to the election of Remón in 1952. (See table 3.) Since 1941, Remón had dominated the National Guard, an institution on which the U.S. government came increasingly to rely for keeping political order and internal security in Panama. In many ways Remón's career paralleled those of Somoza in Nicaragua, Batista in Cuba, and Trujillo in the Dominican Republic. By 1943, a civil intelligence summary began, "Whoever controls the Policia Nacional writes Panama's political history." Remón had acted as power broker during the 1940s, but in 1951 he decided to become president himself. His talented wife Cecilia helped his transformation from police chief into politician, and he won election the following year.[86]

Remón declared himself opposed to racial discrimination in the Canal Zone, by which he meant the dual wage system. Some criollo leaders also pressed him for statements against racism in Panama in exchange for their electoral support. The fact that Remón awarded the country's highest honor, the Balboa medal, to Westerman suggests that the arrangement was mutually satisfactory.[87]

In early 1955 assailants murdered Remón, and Vice-President Ricardo (Dicky) Arias succeeded to the presidency. Dicky, the eldest son of Don Pancho, had considerable support from the criollo community. The government completed and ratified the treaty Remón had negotiated, but Dicky tried to persuade criollos to drop their hostility to it.

[130]

Table 3. Election Returns by Major Political Alliances, 1952–1964

	1952	*1956*	*1960*	*1964*
National Patriotic Coalition (PRv, MLN, PNR, PRA, UP)	133,215 (Remón)	177,633 (de la Guardia)	85,961	—
Civilian Alliance (PLN, FP, PRI)	78,094	81,737	—	—
National Opposition Union (PLN, MLN, PR)	—	—	100,042 (Chiari)	129,933 (Robles)
Panameñistas	—	—	—	119,201 (Arnulfo)
Others	20,539	47,400	55,455	68,037
Total	231,848	306,770	241,458	317,171

Sources: Panama Election Factbook: May 12, 1968 (Washington, D.C.: Operations and Policy Research, 1968), pp. 15, 31; *Panama Tribune,* 22 April 1967.
   Key: FP = Patriotic Front
         MLN = National Liberation Movement
         PLN = National Liberal party
         PR = Republican party
         PRA = Authentic Revolutionary party
         PRI = Independent Revolutionary party
         PRv = Renovador
         UP = Popular Union

Westerman wrote a great deal in favor of the treaty and encouraged his people to accept the changes as a patriotic duty.[88]

In mid-1955 the Renovador and splinter liberal parties again came together, in the National Patriotic Coalition (CPN). At a convention they selected as presidential candidate Ernesto de la Guardia, Jr., fifty-one-year-old manager of the country's largest brewery and a major figure in Liberal politics. Westerman, who had been de la Guardia's office manager for some years, immediately became adviser for criollo vote-gathering. He won over important criollo politicians by getting Dicky to appoint them to good jobs. For example, former Arnulfista Claudio Liverpool was appointed district court judge in Rio Abajo. De la Guardia issued a strong statement favoring citizenship rights for children of West Indian parents and promised to set up special offices in Colón and Bocas del Toro to facilitate issuance of papers for criollos. He also pledged more schools and housing for displaced canal employees: "The problems of the canal workers have as much concern of the government as any other major problem whose solution must be sought at a national level in the interest of the entire country." The *Panama Tribune* abandoned its nonpartisan stance and endorsed de la Guardia.[89] Arnulfo kept his Panameñista party out of the elections in the 1950s.

De la Guardia won easily in 1956 and he immediately appointed Westerman as ambassador to the United Nations, in addition to his duties as political adviser. The 1956–1960 presidential term marked the high point of Westerman's career and of criollo influence in the national life of Panama. Westerman commuted between Panama, New York, and Washington, making contacts on behalf of the government and his people. Housing in Panama concerned him greatly. The tenement districts bulged at their seams and could not take in the thousands of canal employees being moved out. His 1955 study, while documenting the housing deficit, had also argued against any large concentration of new homes for canal employees. This would merely transfer Zone segregation to Panama and might inspire envy among Panamanians unable to afford decent housing. Westerman admitted that local-rate canal employees resented the 1955 treaty. Together with decisions on depopulation, schools, and income tax, the treaty sacrificed their interests to those of the Panamanian business community. Yet the changes were inevitable and had to be implemented, he said. In the long run, he believed they would contribute to economic development in Panama and to greater integration of the West Indian community.[90]

Westerman and CPN leaders managed to pass two pieces of legislation important to criollos. In 1956 they won approval for the Huertematte Law prohibiting racial discrimination and establishing fines for infractions. Westerman himself drafted the bill, using as a model a similar Brazilian law. Then in 1959 they pushed through a constitutional amendment to facilitate granting citizenship to children born in Panama to foreign parents. The measure, originally sponsored by Bazán, had to be approved by a later legislature, and Alfonso Giscombe of Colón finally won passage in January 1960.[91]

Westerman also achieved one major victory while serving in the UN. In 1958 and 1959 unrest grew in Panama, due to the current recession, unemployment, disappointing results of the 1955 treaty, and bitter campaigns in the press against Zone policies. In November 1959 riots erupted over an incident involving the display of flags in the Zone. Eisenhower decided to take some action to reduce the tension, and he seized upon suggestions offered by Westerman. The president announced a nine-point program to improve relations by upgrading local-rate working and living conditions. Among the points were: 10 percent raises for those at the bottom of the scale, for teachers, and for disability compensation recipients; an expanded apprenticeship program and greater upward mobility for Panamanians; and replacement of substandard local-rate housing in the Zone and the construction of 500 new units in Panama.[92] The effect was to slow down depopulation and improve conditions somewhat over the next several years. The flag riots of

1959, however, were to prove merely a rehearsal for the major riots of January 1964.

At the same time, Westerman sponsored appointments of criollo politicians, and by 1960 he could point to several dozen in important posts throughout the government. Percival Toppin became the first full-time *corregidor* of the West Indian district of Calidonia; William Gibson, consul in Jamaica; Basilio Duff, governor of Bocas; Eduardo Charles, acting mayor of Panama; Hector Spencer and Norman Williams, department heads in the treasury ministry; Alejandro Stephens, deputy station commander of the National Guard in Colón; and many others. In addition, a half-dozen men and women of West Indian descent won elective posts during the de la Guardia administration.[93] Westerman himself, ambassador to the UN and presidential advisor, held the highest office of all.

Latin politicians ran the CPN, however, and the criollos tagged along. The influence of the latter rose because of two coincidences: Westerman's ties to de la Guardia and the pro–West Indian attitudes of most CPN leaders. Had these same politicians been divided among several parties, the criollo vote would have been split and had little force. Since alliances of convenience held the CPN together rather than any commitment to criollos, it was only a matter of time until it broke up and ended the highly favorable circumstances of 1956–1960.

Dicky Arias, heir to his father's Renovador party, claimed the CPN presidential nomination. In order to retain criollo support, he issued the customary attack on racial discrimination. Yet he failed to get the backing of the president, who might have served as mediator, and he passed over Bazán and the powerful Delvalle clan in making up his ticket. Bazán and his Colón supporters then bolted the party to join the opposition candidate, Roberto Chiari, in exchange for nominating Bazán to the vice-presidency. The CPN split and so did the criollo vote.[94] Chiari, a dark horse, won the election.

The 1960 election shattered criollo unity and foreshadowed even greater troubles. Westerman, who bought the *Panama Tribune* after Young's death in 1959, estimated that in Panamá province alone 31,500 criollo voters had gone to the polls. Nevertheless, they were so divided they elected only one criollo to the national assembly, Alfonso Giscombe. Given their numbers in Colón and Bocas, they should have elected several.[95] For the time being, criollos had lost most of their political influence.

The rise and decline of criollo politics after the war had several explanations. First, criollos banded together to protect the rights they had gained in the 1946 constitution. The threats of denationalization and deportation remained fresh and elicited a defensive response from the community. They lived in small geographical areas, facilitating communication. Perhaps most important, they enjoyed the sympathy of many Panamanian Liberals, who encouraged them to take political action. Yet as time went on, the memory of 1941 faded and their defensive posture relaxed. Competition arose among various leaders, breaking down unity. In particular, Panamanian-born leaders replaced those from the West Indies, and many tried to appear patriotic by ignoring their immigrant origins. Assimilation and integration were powerful attractions drawing people away from the West Indian community. Finally some politicians who cultivated criollo voters when they were united dropped them when they became divided. Integration was a mixed blessing, then, for the more secure criollos were the less influence they had as a group.

Some leaders looked back on politics in the 1940s and 1950s with bitterness. They recalled the era as one of crude politicking. Second-generation Panamanians, forgetting the hardships of their parents, lived high on the hog and played at politics like a game. They sold their votes and even went on excursions to the interior to vote for white candidates who cared nothing for their welfare. Life treated them well, and they saw no reason to stick together or to excel. Latin Panamanians did not discriminate solely on racial grounds, but they made it hard for nonwhites to excel in socioeconomic terms. Politics had distracted them from more serious concerns. Politicians had used criollos to get into office and then refused to reward them.[96]

If electoral exploitation had been the sole result of criollo politics in the 1950s, leaders would have had reason to be bitter. Yet considerable progress had occurred since 1946, the very progress that undermined group solidarity. Racism retreated quickly in the postwar years in response to a campaign by Westerman and the *Panama Tribune*. And dozens of Panamanians stepped forward to defend those of West Indian descent and to promote their integration into society. These aspects of Panamanian–West Indian relations tell a positive story, that ran counter to the negative experiences of the Canal Zone.

A 1945 letter published in the *Estrella* revealed the depth of antipathy felt by some Panamanians toward persons of West Indian descent:

> I believe it is useless to try to make even a halfway decent Panamanian citizen out of a West Indian Negro. . . . We all know that they take out papers . . . in order to compete against us for jobs, especially in the canal. . . . The West Indian Negro, even when born here, won't forget his native tongue [English] and will try to impose it; . . . his fetishism is the Panama Canal, the Panama Railroad, and the American boss. The West Indian is above all an employee of the Canal Zone and other foreign companies that need cheap, dependent labor. . . . The crime of the West Indian is not his being black, for that wasn't his fault, but rather his not being Panamanian in spite of his birth and upbringing here.[97]

Like most Latin Panamanians, the author refused to admit that racial aversion played a part in shaping his views.

Two sociologists took a more balanced position. Ramón Carillo argued that Panamanians did not have race biases before the Americans built the canal, but they developed a dislike of the West Indian blacks because the canal hired them before native workers. The Panamanians learned racist practices from the Zone whites. Now they displayed a strong color consciousness and had even legislated against blacks in the 1941 laws on commerce and employment. American sociologist John Biesanz, who conducted a poll among students in the late 1940s, found that those of West Indian descent generally liked their Latin compatriots (84 percent) due to their democratic, easygoing, tolerant, liberal, sincere, friendly qualities. Only a minority (20 percent) of the Latins, however, liked the West Indian descendants. The rest felt dislike (43 percent) or neutrality (37 percent).[98] Some form of aversion had definitely developed toward the blacks.

Over the next half-dozen years, leaders of the West Indian community publicized cases of Panamanian race bias, while campaigning simultaneously against the dual wage system of the Zone. They used contacts in the United States and Europe to bring moral pressure to bear on the Latins. For example, when the *Pittsburgh Courier* ran a story in 1945 about how the Panamanian government had protested the presence of a black army construction unit in 1942, the Panamanian ambassador asked the State Department to deny the story. When shown documentation, he expressed surprise and repudiated the incident. Meanwhile, the *Panama Tribune* publicized incidents of racial discrimination in Panamanian hotels and restaurants. The *Tribune*'s publisher Young pressed his Spanish-language newspaper colleagues to end the practice of identifying black criminal suspects by color, because they did not do so with mestizo or white ones. He achieved a breakthrough in 1947 when sister papers ran front-page pictures of prize fighter Joe Louis. Previously stories and photos of blacks had been relegated to special West Indian sections.[99] Yet the incidents in public facilities continued to occur.

Some Latin Panamanians spoke out against racial discrimination, just as some had opposed deportation agitation in 1933 and the constitution and laws of the early 1940s. Several Spanish language papers condemned incidents publicized by the *Panama Tribune*. The Catholic church reiterated its position against racism. Labor leader and politician Víctor Navas acclaimed Westerman's studies of race discrimination and urged his countrymen to recognize the contributions West Indians and their descendants had made. Writers like Gil Blas Tejeira and Eduardo Ritter Aislán condemned racism in their society.[100] Tejeira had attended secondary school in Kingston and always defended West Indian interests. The hero of his 1962 novel, *Pueblos Perdidos*, was named Pedro Prestán, after the black leader of the 1885 revolt in Colón.

After passage of the Huertematte Law in 1956, racial incidents diminished in Panama, although the problem of securing more and better jobs remained. Most banks and financial institutions hired whites only, a policy they communicated with want ads phrased, "Persons of good appearance only." More generally, businesses hired whites for clerical and sales jobs to avoid offending race-conscious clients. Finally, the government hired almost no blacks except those appointed for political purposes. The foreign service admitted only whites, and few jobs above the menial or manual ranks were open to blacks. Occasionally the *Panama Tribune* tried to embarrass the government by referring to this bias, but since it was not announced or explicit, little progress occurred.[101] Panamanians assumed that because English-speaking blacks had always fared well in canal employment, they did not need public sector jobs.

By the early 1960s, most vestiges of overt race discrimination had disappeared, and the debate shifted to issues of integration. Depopulation policies in the canal pushed thousands of employees into Panamá and Colón, where facilities did not exist to accommodate them. Classroom and housing shortages proved most urgent. The minister of education admitted in 1956 that 6,000 students had applied for 3,000 available places in the public schools. As a result, the British schools, which had almost disappeared during the 1940s, enjoyed a brief renaissance. The Panamanian government discouraged these schools, though, and at one point threatened to close them for noncompliance with official curriculum mandates.[102] Over the coming years and especially with U.S. aid after 1961, Panama gradually built sufficient schools for the children of the former Zone residents. Still, many thousands had missed years of school due to depopulation.

With U.S. aid, the government also built more low-cost residences on the outskirts of the cities. They overhauled the housing bank and gave it sufficient funds to finance hundreds of units. Discrimination played a part there too, because Latin Panamanians usually got government housing instead of former canal residents. Any construction for the low-cost market eased the pressure, but the move from the Zone into tenements and shantytowns proved an indignity too heavy for many to bear. They named one shantytown located on the Zone border "Hollywood," a sardonic comment on the American way of life in Panama.[103]

Colón itself gradually became one huge tenement district. The government had tried to revive the city with a free port where semiprocessed goods could be assembled duty-free and reexported to other markets. In the 1950s an oil refinery was sited there too. Yet nothing could stem the decline of the once-prosperous city, and Bazán—responsible for the free port and other businesses—frankly encouraged unemployed canal workers to get out if they could.

The deterioration of Colón symbolized the weakening of West Indian culture in Panama. In the late 1930s and early 1940s Colón had vibrated with tourism, music, culture, and business. When tourists disembarked in one port, crossed the isthmus by train, and reembarked in the other, Colón got much of the business. Residents of Panamá traveled to Colón for artistic events or shopping. Musical groups on the Caribbean circuit regularly played at Colón. The biggest and most prosperous benevolent societies operated there, with branches in Panamá. Yet by the 1950s all that had changed, because political and economic power migrated to Panamá, the national and economic capital. The immigrant generations passed away and so did the town that hosted their cultural life.

An exodus of West Indian descendants to the United States began slowly but gained momentum in the 1950s. Some West Indians had gone to work or had sent their children to school in the United States in earlier decades, and by the 1950s a considerable number had relatives living there. The U.S. embassy sponsored about twenty college students a year, mostly of West Indian descent from the Zone towns. Hundreds more signed up for military service during the Korean war and thereby gained naturalization preference. By 1965 some 3,000 had enlisted from Panama. And the more who had residency in the United States, the more who could sponsor relatives as immigrants.[104] New York, especially Brooklyn, attracted about 75 percent of the immigrants. They created a little Panama alongside the little Cubas, little Puerto Ricos, and little Jamaicas. Since most spoke English and had exposure to American work practices, they faced few problems becoming integrated. The relaxed atmosphere of New York offered far more possibilities than the closed system of the Zone. Besides, being unemployed in Brooklyn seemed better than unemployed in Panama.

Westerman noted in 1958 that many of those leaving for the United States were the most talented members of the West Indian community. This brain drain deprived it of potential leaders, yet one could hardly blame those who left in search of better jobs and communities. By 1965 he estimated that 16,000 Panamanians of West Indian descent had gone on permanent visas and perhaps that many more on temporary status. The Panamanian community in New York alone numbered 15,000.[105]

The departure of so many Panamanians of West Indian descent testified to the hardships and low morale caused by the 1955 treaty. By raising the possibility of escape, another phase of the diaspora, the exodus also forced many people to choose between loyalty to Panama and to the United States. The majority elected to stay even under the worsened conditions caused by the treaty. This collective decision became an important step toward their integration into Panamanian society.[106]

The nature of their integration, however, remained unclear and even today generates heated debate. Latin Panamanians usually held that persons of West Indian descent had only to become hispanicized to be accepted. This meant cultural assimilation, accepting the norms and customs of the Latin majority. In support of this view, they could point to tens of thousands of persons who had passed successfully into Panamanian life. The typical route included hispanicizing one's first name, marrying a Latin spouse (West Indian males to Hispanic females), disavowing the United States, converting to Catholicism, using Spanish, and committing oneself to raising children according to Panamanian mores. It also included embracing the myth that race made no difference in Panama.[107]

In addition, this process of assimilation paradoxically incorporated the idea of whitening Panama's population. This led to widespread use of skin lighteners and hair straighteners, as well as to a preference for marrying persons with lighter skin. The argument in favor of assimilation rested on the assumption that Panamanian culture was superior to West Indian or perhaps even to American culture. It also implied that assimilation constituted a pledge of loyalty to the nation in its long struggle with the United States.[108]

Some leaders of the West Indian community objected that they should not be obliged to give up a rich Anglo-American heritage simply to be accepted by the Panamanians. Deracination would destroy the self-respect and pride of several generations. It would deprive the community of skills and attributes that helped them survive, such as proficiency in English; American work ethics; institutions such as benevolent societies, schools, churches, and charities; and family lineages reaching back to the islands. Assimilation even meant repudiating what many believed was a solid record of accomplishment in Panama. Assimilation, in short, was a one-way street that forced them to abandon their very identity as a people.[109]

A more subtle version of this argument noted that the West Indians had many skills to contribute to Panama's development. Their familiarity with American ways could help bring tourism and business to the isthmus. Their music had already enriched life there. They had higher indices of literacy and education than the Latins, since they were almost entirely urban. In some lines of work they got better positions than natives, even in Panama. Given time and the freedom to retain their culture, they could make other contributions as well. Thus assimilation *hurt* Panama by wasting human resources.

Social integration became the synthetic resolution of this debate. The two peoples—Latin Panamanian and West Indian—could blend together on an equal footing and trade cultural elements freely, in a spirit of reciprocation. Then a hybrid society might emerge, one different from and better adapted to the modern world than either parent. Moreover, hybridization could be achieved without violating liberal democratic norms, for each individual and family unit could decide how much of each culture to retain and discard. Ideally, a kind of social Darwinism would select the best mix of Latin and West Indian traditions by rewarding the individuals who excelled.[110]

Westerman and others dedicated themselves to achieving the ideal of integration, especially after the collapse of criollo politics in 1960. Several factors worked in their favor. The brain drain and declining morale of the 1950s lowered community defenses against interaction with the Latins. Also the rural people migrating to the terminal cities in those years

[138]

had not been exposed to the anti–West Indian propaganda of the 1930s and early 1940s and accepted the West Indian descendants. Indeed, Biesanz found that campesinos who lived in the same tenements and shantytowns actually saw the West Indian descendants as models of urban survival. In addition, many colonial blacks migrated from the countryside to the cities in the 1950s and weakened racial barriers erected against the West Indians. Latin Panamanians claimed the ability to distinguish between these groups, the colonial blacks being more attractive physically, but the latter's greater freedom of mobility helped erase the color line for all blacks.[111]

Schools became a powerful force for promoting integration over assimilation. Elementary-age children interacting without too much adult supervision gradually overcame their parents' biases. Each group learned from the other, and cultural blending occurred naturally. High schools in Panama, which had not become so crowded, provided an opportunity for Zone-educated children to learn Spanish and Panamanian ways. A number of interviewees spoke of high school in Panama as a time of great intercultural learning. The Biesanzes observed that parents with the highest expectations for their children made use of opportunities in the Zone as well as in Panama, which usually meant primary school in the former and secondary in the latter. These children became truly binational. Since some persons of West Indian descent also taught in the Panama secondary schools—for example, Bennett, Fortune, Hayes, Gooden, and Steward—the process tended to be two-way.[112]

The University of Panama also facilitated integration by bringing together some of the brightest members of each community. Soon after it began operating in 1935, for example, Ed Gaskin took courses there. Ana Bennett received her degree there in 1950, only to find that the Zone administration would not recognize her studies in Panama. She had become friends with Professor Francisco Céspedes, however, whose wife ran a private school and urged her to teach there. She enjoyed great rapport with her colleagues and soon became integrated into the intellectual community of Panama. By the 1950s a fairly large number of West Indian descendants attended the University of Panama and gained access to middle-class Hispanic circles.[113]

Misinformation, unequal schooling, and continued Canal Zone residence impeded integration, however. Latins continued to believe that the West Indian community had a higher birthrate than the nation as a whole and that it would eventually convert Panama into a black, English-speaking new country. But in fact, those descended from West Indian immigrants had smaller families and a lower birthrate and spoke mostly Spanish by then. Latins also believed that the West Indian descendants were disloyal to their country. A common accusation was, "British by loyalty, American by economic necessity, and Panamanian for expediency." In fact, few professed loyalty to England.[114]

Misinformation regarding race relations slowed integration too. Daniel Goldrich, conducting a survey among well-to-do youths in 1961, found that two-thirds believed that no race discrimination existed in Panama. In fact, elite youth had no direct experience with the large black population. In a study made two years later, Goldrich learned that the majority still held that view, but by then 44 percent admitted that some discrimination existed. Most students of race relations hold that little progress can take place without recognition of bias problems.[115]

Unequal education proved a hindrance too. The quality of noncitizen Zone schools slipped after 1954, despite heroic efforts on the part of teachers. Moreover, many well-to-do Panamanian children attended Zone white schools and took college degrees in the United States. Therefore, the generation of Panamanians of Hispanic descent that came of age in the 1960s was far ahead of their Zone-reared counterparts and thus had scant basis for social interaction. Finally, the 1960 Eisenhower decision to finance more housing for noncitizen Zone employees temporarily halted the movement of families into Panama, interrupting the single most important (if unpleasant) dynamic for social integration.

Protestant churches were a final source of resistance to integration. Although some West Indian descendants had converted to Catholicism, the majority in the 1950s still retained their Protestant faith and worshipped in English-speaking congregations. The Baptists, Episcopalians, and Methodists constituted the "big three" non-Catholic groups and defended their parishes vigorously. Most started schools to assure continued support and a new generation of parishioners. Only in the 1960s, when the government threatened to close schools that did not provide instruction in Spanish, did they shift to Panamanian curriculum.[116]

The Early 1960s

Both hope and unrest characterized U.S.-Panamanian relations in the early 1960s. On the one hand, Ike's nine-point program, if carried out, would improve Panamanians' chances in Zone employment. And the 1958 Inter-American Bank and the 1961 Alliance for Progress promised relief from grinding poverty and underdevelopment. Even though it was a sense of Soviet danger in the hemisphere that spurred American generosity, Panamanians could still expect ample funds because of the canal. On the other hand, discontent arose among Panamanians, who kept up pressure on the United States during these years. The 1959 riots, the Castro-like invasion by Tito Arias that year, and the vulnerability of the canal to sabotage all focused considerable American concern on Panama.[117]

Aquilino Boyd and Ernesto Castillero Pimentel, who led the 1959 flag riots, proposed a fifty-fifty split of canal profits between the United States and Panama. A similar arrangement had been accepted by American oil companies operating in Venezuela, and the analogy seemed apt. Roberto Chiari, elected president in 1960, announced that if the oligarchy did not undertake reforms, it might lose control of the country altogether. The Cuban revolution spawned new radical movements among university students. Dissatisfied already with the 1955 treaty, Panamanians insisted on even more concessions.[118]

Despite this unsettled atmosphere, canal administrators proved just as resistant to change as ever. Governor Carter got firm orders from President Kennedy to do everything he could to improve relations with Panama. But Carter met with solid opposition from his staff and had to be replaced halfway through the normal four-year term. The unwillingness of the personnel bureau to implement the single wage system mandated by PL 85-550 proved the biggest source of trouble. Procedures continued to favor white North Americans for the better jobs, despite a costly new apprenticeship program. By mid-1961 only 240 Panamanians held appointments on the U.S.-rate schedule, with wages comparable to those of Americans. And a large gap still separated the two schedules, with U.S.-rate wages four times local-rate wages. This undermined the Alliance for Progress in Panama, because the aid it dispensed could not overcome the effects of the canal on the country's plans for national development.[119]

Governor Carter himself, caught between pressures from Washington and obstinacy from his staff, resisted suggestions from Secretary of Labor Arthur Goldberg to formalize relations with employee unions. Goldberg had convinced President Kennedy to issue Executive Order 10988 to institute collective bargaining procedures with government personnel groups. EO 10988 mandated elections to determine which unions would enjoy exclusive representation and authorized a dues checkoff system. The order could be suspended in the interest of national security, an option the canal administration quickly invoked.

Governor Carter's letter to Goldberg argued that EO 10988 should not be applied in the Zone because it would ruin the third-country labor system. His letter echoed that of Mehaffey fifteen years earlier:

> A major division exists between our English-speaking group of West Indian heritage and our Spanish-speaking Latin group. Some friction exists between these two groups and in many cases the West Indian employees have clung to their British citizenship and generally resist efforts to amalgamate them into the cultural, political, and civil life of Panama. . . . It would be expecting too much for our foreign national employees, who are continuously subjected to buffeting from ultra-nationalistic, anti–United States political demagogues, to be able to bargain, negotiate, or arbitrate without yielding to political pressures in Panama to convert such labor negotiations into international political issues.[120]

The third-country labor system lived on in the eyes of canal management, if only to avoid intrusions by Washington reformers.

The use of non-U.S. and non-Panamanian labor to keep the work force in a weak position had one last flourish in 1962, when the International Longshoremen's Association (ILA) tried to represent canal dockworkers. The ILA made its move in January by provoking a four-day walkout. Secretary of Labor Goldberg apparently favored the ILA's attempts, but the new canal governor, Robert Fleming, did not. ILA headquarters then declared a boycott of Panamanian ports. The local stevedores' union, that had been in existence since 1892, protested the ILA's muscling in and called on the government of Panama to take action. They also requested affiliation with a rival international, the National Maritime Union (NMU). By mid-1962 the interested parties prevailed on George Meany to call off the ILA and agreed among themselves to let the NMU represent the stevedores.[121]

The stakes in this jurisdictional dispute proved high. The secretary of labor still hoped to apply EO 10988 to the Zone, and if he succeeded the ILA or the NMU stood a chance of winning majority representation among the noncitizen work force. Since the latter outnumbered the Americans in the MTC/CLU, they could control labor relations. Locals 900 and 907 had never been weaker, so a concerted effort by a U.S.-based union could produce a coup d'état.

Governor Fleming countered the threat by issuing his own regulations on "employee management cooperation." This allowed the personnel department to divide the canal organization into many small bargaining units, each of which would hold separate elections. Voluntary bargaining would continue between management and the several unions, and the results would be included in employee manuals, not a contract. Fleming thus sidestepped EO 10988.

Fleming had favored the NMU over the ILA because the former did not have the political power of the latter. Moreover, one more union would further divide the noncitizen work force and make his job easier. The NMU and locals 900 and 907 would expend all their energies fighting for control of local bargaining units. The Department of Defense, however, still favored application of EO 10988 on the grounds that they could better manage employee relations through a single union. Fleming rejected the idea because it would stimulate international and interracial conflicts. He wrote to an army official, "Our problem is not one of maintaining control but avoiding Panamanian challenges and political interference, as well as providing equal treatment to all national groups in all agencies in the Canal Zone." A single election for exclusive representation would pit American unions against noncitizen unions and invite disaster. The canal administration would continue to block exclusive representation until 1981.[122]

Just to make sure the NMU did not capture too much control, personnel officials took steps to revive and strengthen Local 900. In 1959 they had decided that teachers in the Latin American schools could go on the same pay scale (that of Washington, D.C.) as the U.S. school teachers. Johnson had initiated this policy in 1952, but it had been discontinued in 1956 on the grounds that the conversion rendered the two school systems entirely different. Transfer to D.C. scale, however, depended upon meeting minimum certification requirements there, including the B.A. degree for elementary teaching and the M.A. for secondary. Teachers had ten years to meet those standards. This concession was won by a group of younger teachers that had risen to leadership in Local 900, among them Audley Webster, Saturnín Maugé, and Maurice Haywood. At the time the administration implemented the measure, only 20 percent of the local-rate teachers could qualify.[123]

In 1961 officials decided to separate the two school systems altogether. A single superintendent oversaw the work of two assistant superintendents, one for U.S. and another for Latin American schools. Alfred Osborne was the logical choice for the latter position, because of his many years of administrative service. These two changes reinforced the tendency for teachers to dominate in the leadership of Local 900. But as the teachers themselves advanced rapidly, many of the men who worked the ships, docks, and machine shops did not. The NMU slowly won more and more members in the latter category, under the leadership of a naturalized U.S. citizen, René Lioeanjie. By the mid-1960s, local-rate canal employees were evenly divided between the NMU and Local 900.[124]

Finally, as if to ensure rivalry between employees of Hispanic and West Indian descent, the personnel bureau began consciously to hire more Latin Panamanians. In January 1963, the director Doolan wrote,

> With the advent of the Canal Zone Merit System (PL 85-550) and the greater opportunities extended under this treaty commitment to residents of Panama, the non-Negro Panamanian began to appear in increasingly large numbers. As our wage rates increased . . . more middle class Panamanians of Latin origin have been attracted to Canal Zone employment. They often predominate on Merit System registers even to the exclusion of U.S. citizens as well as Negroes. The brutal fact of life is that either because of cultural, sociological, as well as other factors, the Negro of British West Indian origin is not always competitive with the Latin Panamanian.[125]

Doolan might have noted that since all employees were Panamanians, he wanted to keep a relative parity between the two groups. He might also have noted that the poor showing of West Indian descendants in merit exams resulted from inadequate education obtained in the Zone schools. Eventually, he did admit a few years later, "As a political matter, we make few 'brownie points' in employing people from the [West Indian] communities, whereas, on the political level, employments from Panama further our relations with the Republic of Panama." He acknowledged that residents of the Zone communities "are older employees, the product of a generation of low skill training and minimum educational levels. They provide little in the way of promotional material." Doolan implicitly blamed an earlier generation of administrators for this state of affairs.[126]

In fact, Doolan was making the transition from a third-country national to a dual labor system. The former no longer worked because those of West Indian descent were Panamanians and enjoyed full civil rights. But if Doolan and the others could drive a wedge between descendants of West Indians and Latins and keep the various work sectors divided, the more familiar dual labor system would still function. The way administrators handled the NMU-ILA rivalry, the local-rate teachers, EO 10988, and discriminatory hiring indicated that this was indeed their intent.

Between 1945 and the early 1960s, tremendous changes occurred in the West Indian community, both in the Canal Zone and in Panama. The pace of change equaled that of the construction era. Many U.S. government agencies and the White House demanded reforms in the canal. The Zonians' unwillingness to budge and the canal's demotion in strategic importance brought on the 1950 reorganization and budget cuts. The Zonians passed on what burdens they could to Panama and dodged the question of school integration, but they could not avoid some major transformations.

Rapid change can spur imaginative responses or diehard opposition. During the construction era, Americans had created a blend of U.S., Hispanic, and West Indian institutions in the Canal Zone. It had flaws and inequities that might have been eliminated by later generations, if pressure had been sufficient. The rapid changes of the 1950s, however, called up heavy defenses on the part of the American employees. They enjoyed salaries and benefits far in excess of those at home. They commanded deference from nonwhite underlings similar to that customary in the U.S. South. Vested interests and self-protection caused the Zonians to enact racist and oppressive policies out of step with American society and sometimes in defiance of orders from Washington. By 1964 they seemed to be succeeding, having held off reform and pushed many of the problems onto Panama. The January 1964 riots, however, would change all that. No amount of retrenchment would save what some called "southern comfort" and others the "Zonian way of life."

7

In the Shadow of Treaty Negotiations, 1964–1981

IN JANUARY 1964 riots erupted in Panama City following a new flag incident in the Canal Zone. Lasting several days and claiming twenty-four lives, these riots proved a turning point in U.S.-Panamanian relations. Presidents Lyndon Johnson and Roberto Chiari began negotiations designed to replace the 1903 Hay—Bunau-Varilla Treaty with another acceptable to Panama and consonant with American interests. Draft treaties produced in 1967 remained unperfected, but in 1974 new negotiations began. They resulted in the 1977 Carter-Torrijos Treaty.[1]

Local-rate labor unions in the Canal Zone took advantage of negotiations to improve members' wages and benefits and to eliminate most racial segregation. U.S. government officials had to put canal affairs in good order so that Panama could not use discrimination charges in negotiations. By the late 1970s they had virtually eliminated the gap between U.S. and local rates.

The treaty negotiations unified Panamanians in their struggle to obtain more benefits from the canal. Just as in 1955, however, persons of West Indian descent working for the canal found their interests undermined by Panama's demands. This touched off a new loyalty conflict in the West Indian community. In politics it surfaced in the 1964 and 1968 elections. Intellectually, it provoked a fascinating debate over negritude and the Afro-American experience in Panama. Finally, the loyalty conflict raised fears of another exodus to the United States.

Treaty Progress

Most knowledgeable people in Panama and the United States recognized the injustice of the 1903 treaty, signed under irregular circumstances by a French national. The problem was how to abrogate it without arousing excessive opposition in the United States or greed in Panama. The Panama Canal had become a part of the U.S. national myth, a symbol of American strength and enterprise. The public did not realize that military planners had downgraded the canal to secondary status. They mistakenly viewed the canal as vital to American trade and defense. By the same token, Panamanian nationalists, disregarding the extreme attachment Americans had for the canal, pushed for unacceptable concessions. Only a major confrontation like the 1964 riots could have overcome the U.S. reluctance to begin negotiations.[2]

The 1964 riots culminated a long history of disagreements over the display of flags in the Zone. As a premier American outpost, the Zone sported more than its share, and flags were a standing affront to the sovereignty Panama claimed over the Zone. Since Panama retained residual sovereignty while the United States exercised sovereign rights, Panamanian patriots believed that both flags should be flown together. After the 1959 flag incident, a limited number of dual flagpoles helped calm Panamanian spirits. Descendants of West Indians in the Zone had no serious stake in such symbols, of course. Until the mid-1950s they had usually pledged allegiance to the American flag yet were constantly reminded that they were not Americans. Thus they played little part in the 1964 riots.[3]

President Chiari used the riots as an excuse to break relations with the United States and to press for more jobs and profits from the canal. His militancy, unusual in a member of the oligarchy, owed much to the circumstances of the early 1960s, when the Alliance for Progress and the Cuban Revolution awakened expectations of rapid change. Chiari's anti-Americanism offended a large part of the West Indian community, however. Many found his stance hypocritical and sympathized with the United States. It did not take much imagination to foresee Latin Panamanian attacks on West Indian descendants too, if the confrontation escalated. The riots put the latter in an uncomfortable position of divided loyalty.[4]

The 1964 election demonstrated the difficult choices West Indian descendants faced. Arnulfo Arias, who in the early 1940s and early 1950s had acted against their interests, ran for president on a conciliatory platform. He offered to unify all Panamanians in the quest for national integration, and he promised to smooth troubled relations with the United States. Westerman, believing that diplomatic pressure might pay off, supported Chiari's tactics and backed his candidate, Marcos Robles. Yet a large number of criollos voted for Arnulfo, who offered them acceptability and no radical changes in the canal treaty. Arnulfo received more votes than Robles, but the election board rigged the count to give the latter a victory. The criollos not only split their votes, as they had in 1960, but many even voted for their nemesis, Arnulfo.[5]

Canal employees of West Indian descent had much to fear from the new treaty talks that Robles initiated in 1965. The 1955 treaty had reduced their disposable income and given them few compensating benefits. They might again be caught in the middle and sacrificed to Panamanian demands. In mid-1965, West Indian leaders voiced concern that the talks were secret, and an informal poll of local-raters revealed apprehension over reductions in benefits. They knew that the canal now hired and promoted Latin Panamanians over those of West Indian descent because it gave the United States political advantages in negotiations. As the personnel director put it, "The use of Panamanian nationals is sound business. . . . the political-sociological merits . . . have had a favorable effect throughout the entire Panamanian population." West Indian descendants feared that they would be sold out entirely in the interest of better U.S.-Panamanian relations.[6]

The MTC/CLU also sensed danger in the treaty talks and for virtually the first time collaborated with the local-rate unions in lobbying. International negotiations, which could alter the carefully constructed Zone way of life, always threatened the U.S. citizen employees. In this case, the canal organization came under the scrutiny of the Pentagon, the State Department, and both houses of Congress. At this juncture, the U.S.-rate unions began to mount a common defense with their local-rate counterparts. This strategy continued largely intact through 1981, when a coalition of the two won elections for exclusive representation of most canal employees.[7]

By mid-1967, details of the draft treaties appeared in the *Panama Tribune*, and the debate intensified. The main treaty, to run until 1999, would place canal operations under a Panama Canal Commission, composed of nine Americans and Panamanians, all appointed by the U.S. president. Most of the Zone lands would be turned over to Panama, and Zone businesses would be phased out. Mixed U.S.-Panamanian courts would take jurisdiction over the Zone. Employment procedures would favor Panamanians by applying merit criteria regardless of nationality. The U.S.-rate schools would be transferred to the Department of Defense, whose dependents now predominated among students. The Latin American schools would be turned over to Panama upon request. Finally, the draft treaty provided for toll sharing by the two countries. These provisions seemed in keeping with President Johnson's instructions that the "primary objective of the new treaty will be to provide for an appropriate political, economic, and social integration of the area used in the canal operation with the rest of the Republic of Panama."[8]

Underlying the formal treaty proposals, however, were two labor policy choices contemplated by the Panamanian government. One concerned preferential treatment for Latin over West Indian Panamanians. But an even more threatening change would be the application of Panamanian wage scales and labor law. Panama's chief negotiators said that local-rate canal employees had become a privileged class that earned much more than their noncanal colleagues. Some measure of parity would be established by lowering canal wages. In the words of Congresswoman Leonor Sullivan, quoted in the *Panama Tribune,* "Some workers may suffer adversely in the changeover, but the interests of the nation must be considered above those of any special groups or sectors, and this truth must be faced honestly and patriotically." Labor leaders sensed that the negotiators had taken the easy way, just as they had in 1955. They had gotten the support of the oligarchy by including many concessions to commerce and industry in Panama.[9]

The local-rate unions mounted campaigns to protect their members. Saturnín Maugé, president of Local 900, urged the governor to ensure that U.S. Civil Service rules would apply in the Canal Zone and that noncitizen employees be allowed to retain their retirement benefits. Any employees living in quarters that were given to Panama should have the right to purchase them. Phaseout of nonessential activities should last five years to give the employees time to adjust. Reductions-in-force and new hires should be conducted in accordance with seniority rules. Any increase in benefits for Panama should be met with higher tolls rather than savings in labor costs. The NMU, which by 1967 rivaled Local 900 in membership and finances, urged even more protection for local-rate employees and claimed that it most effectively represented their interests.[10]

The two governments set aside the draft treaty in August, due largely to opposition in Panama. Maneuvering for the 1968 election had already begun, and the treaty provided too much ammunition for opponents of the Robles administration and its candidate, David Samudio. The Johnson administration also feared adverse criticism in the coming elections. Yet despite its tabling, the draft treaty remained a potent election issue in Panama. Adversaries charged that, if elected, Samudio would sign the treaty and distribute the spoils (former Zone lands and businesses) to the corrupt supporters of the administration.

Arnulfo Arias threw his hat into the ring again, posing as defender of the common man against exploitation by the oligarchs. He charged that Robles had a secret plan for implementing the treaty, one that would channel the benefits to the wealthy few. Arnulfo promised that if elected he would scrap the old draft and frame a new one more beneficial to the nation as a whole. Widespread discontent with the level of corruption in the government and political disagreement over Samudio's choice also played into Arnulfo's hands. He managed to get the backing of four minor parties in addition to his enormous Panameñista party.[11]

From the standpoint of the criollo vote, the 1968 presidential election proved the most divisive and controversial of all. Arnulfo realized that if the criollo vote had been solidly for him he might have won an undeniable victory in 1964. He set out to get criollo backing in 1968. His party convention included enough West Indian names to appear representative. He bought ads in the *Panama Tribune* featuring photographs that made him look darkskinned. His campaign stressed equality and social integration of all Panamanians. To cement criollo support, he made a deal with Westerman. In an exchange of letters and an interview, Arnulfo promised full and complete respect for human rights and equality of opportunity: "We shall endeavor to promote the principles of social justice for all without regard to race, color, creed or national ancestry." Westerman gave his endorsement to Arnulfo, and the West Indian community split apart violently.[12]

In his defense, Westerman said that his usual allies had already joined Arnulfo. Arnulfo seemed to have changed, mellowed. He now admitted the injustice of the 1941 constitution, which he said he adopted to prevent new immigration for the third locks project and to force West Indians to make a choice between U.S. and Panamanian loyalty. Now he recognized their valuable contribution to the nation and wanted them on his side. Besides, criollos had already voted for him in large numbers in 1964 and seemed likely to do so again. Opposition to the canal treaty ranked high among their reasons. Westerman decided to accept the inevitable and tried to extract some pre-election pledges.[13]

Opponents of Arnulfo objected to his past record and argued that a leopard could not change its spots: opportunist to the end, Arnulfo would desert criollos after the election. An Arnulfo victory would jeopardize their jobs, institutions, culture, and legal rights. This opinion prevailed among leaders of the West Indian community interviewed for this study. Few indications are available on how the rank and file voted, but Zone employees probably backed Arnulfo. Some leaders in the West Indian community vilified Westerman for his decision, and after the election his car was vandalized. He believed that the result decided more than simply an election. His own role as leader stood challenged.

Arnulfo did win and he did renege on his promises to criollo supporters. He controlled vote counting in such a way that not a single criollo made it to the Assembly. The full impact of his election never materialized, however, because eight days after his inauguration the National Guard overthrew him. From October 1968, Arnulfo, the draft treaty, and politics took a back seat to what General Omar Torrijos came to call the Revolutionary Process.[14]

An ambitious officer with a taste for power, Torrijos soon emerged as head of the National Guard junta. Voicing extreme nationalist slogans and leftist rhetoric, he set out to change the power structure once and for all. He appointed intellectuals from the university, representatives of minority groups, and National Guard officers to high posts. Traditional political parties and members of the oligarchy were conspicuously absent. Torrijos and his advisers denounced U.S. imperialism while establishing friendly relations with Cuba and the USSR. Treaty talks did not resume until 1971, and then only fitfully.

Torrijos posed as a man of the people, highlighting his rural origins. He attempted to elicit support from sectors previously marginal in public affairs: campesinos, the urban poor, Indians, and blacks. For a time he even cultivated students and organized labor. The contrast with traditional oligarchical politics could not have been sharper. He relied on charisma, frequent tours of the country, revolutionary imagery, and an unorthodox style to win acceptance for his administration.[15]

Torrijos embraced the black Panamanians of Latin and West Indian descent. A 1970 study published by his office called for integrating the West Indian descendants, many of whom still lived isolated in the ghettoes. He believed that an active publicity campaign, plus more education and jobs, would promote their assimilation into the cultural mainstream. Torrijos's closest advisers included Rómulo Betancourt, Juan Materno Vásquez, Rigoberto Paredes, and Adolfo Ahumada, all mulattoes. He promoted several black officers to high posts in the National Guard and recruited youths of West Indian descent as well. He wanted to show that all Panamanians had access to his government. Yet Torrijos also used a subtle game to keep subordinates occupied: he played off one against the other, exploiting natural rivalries of regional origin, race, and ideology. He did manage to dismantle the old political system, yet the new one he had in mind never quite coalesced.[16]

Treaty negotiations fueled Panamanian politics and change in the Canal Zone as well. No other issue so dominated life on the isthmus. The first problem was getting talks underway again. The Canal Executive Planning Staff, designed to chart long-term policy, operated on the assumption that the 1967 treaty would be resurrected and implemented eventually. But nobody in the canal organization did much to promote that process. And until the Vietnam war ended, little could be expected from the State Department and the Pentagon. The Nixon administration refused to accept the 1967 draft as a basis for talks.

The Panamanian government kept up pressure by declaring the Zone its tenth province. Torrijos called elections for a constitutional assembly in 1972 and expected to conduct balloting in the Zone. Canal regulations forbade campaign activities and election of employees to Panamanian posts. By this ploy, Torrijos put canal officials in the difficult position of favoring integration of local-rate employees into Panama but prohibiting their exercise of a basic right. The hardliners argued for a policy "of easing our Panamanian citizen residents into Panama, not bringing Panama to them." The secretary of the army, however, decided to allow low-key campaign activities on behalf of Zone residents, with the proviso that any employee elected would have to resign and relinquish living quarters. This compromise led to the election of several Canal Zone women to the Assembly.[17]

Panama also used international forums to embarrass the United States and get negotiations under way again. The election of 1972 and a new constitution gave the Torrijos regime more credibility abroad. Panama, occupying a temporary seat, presided over the UN Security Council that year and persuaded members to schedule their 1973 meeting in Panama. Panama then introduced a resolution favoring its sovereignty over the canal and abrogation of the 1903 treaty. Thirteen members approved, but the measure was killed by a rare U.S. veto. The point had been made, for as one Panamanian said, "The United States vetoed the measure . . . but the rest of the world vetoed the United States." The following September the Panamanian delegate at a human rights meeting in Italy denounced American exploitation of Panama under an illegitimate treaty. Most of Latin America supported Torrijos. In early 1974 the United States agreed to new talks along lines favorable to the Panamanian position.[18]

The 1967 treaty draft, the basis for new negotiations, evoked the same apprehensions and opposition as before. The Canal Executive Planning Staff, meanwhile, had been doing everything possible to move noncitizens out of the Zone. Officials came to view them as a fifth column and a threat to Zone life. In 1972 the governor had commissioned a thorough review of the problem, the so-called Latin American Communities Study. The title itself revealed something. The former silver and local-rate townsites, always physically removed from U.S.-rate housing, had been renamed Latin American communities. The segregation remained, and of course most people who lived there had little Latin about them. Begun by Lieutenant Governor Charles Guiness, the study was completed in 1979 by administrative assistant and ten-year veteran, Robert F. Jeffrey.[19]

Canal officials found themselves under attack by Panama and embarrassed by the noncitizen residents. Their response harked back to the early 1950s depopulation: eliminate the Latin American communities altogether. Why support an often unruly, unproductive, disloyal, and angry group of Panamanians in the Zone? Besides, they had become a liability, a steady source of complaints to Congress. The noncitizen residents of the Zone were skeletons in the closet that reminded the world of past injustices. Jeffrey prefaced his study by observing that the canal suffered from a "United Fruit syndrome," in which practices of earlier times haunted attempts at reform.[20]

Jeffrey invested considerable effort in researching the Latin American communities, and the study completed under his direction came as close as anything extant to a comprehensive history of the silver and local-rate employees of the Zone. He focused on the depopulation policies of the 1950s and 1960s, that had somehow not solved the problem. To be sure, the number of noncitizen employees in the Zone had fallen from 6,000 to 1,500 between 1950 and 1972, but those remaining had managed to entrench themselves and took up more staff time than any other sector of the work force. Jeffrey noted "an intense and deep feeling prevalent among them that any attempt on the part of the administration to disengage them from the Zone and to direct them to a life in the Republic is tantamount to displacing by force families from a homeland which is theirs by birthright." Jeffrey and most of the Canal Executive Planning Staff wanted to accelerate depopulation and make the Zone an exclusive American compound. Despite this bias, his work assembled much good information.[21]

When treaty talks resumed, so did the insistence on removing noncitizens. Zonians simply refused to integrate such facilities as schools, recreation sites, and housing. Yet they realized that they would be forced to do so either beforehand (to eliminate bad publicity) or under the treaty. They did not succeed in moving noncitizens out, however, because too much attention had focused on them. In the end, citizens and noncitizens in the Zone joined forces to oppose the treaty.[22]

The treaty that emerged in 1977 and was ratified the following year establishes procedures for gradual transfer of canal operations to Panama until 1999, at which time Panama will assume full responsibility. The Panama Canal Commission replaces the company and Canal Zone government, and an administrator replaces the former governor. After 1990 the administrator will be a Panamanian. A binational board of nine directors (five U.S. and four Panamanian) appointed by the U.S. president sets policy for the administrator. About two-thirds of the former Zone reverts to Panama, including all of the former Latin American communities, to be administered as a land trust until the end of the treaty in 1999. Panama administers the railroad, the docks and customhouses, and most public services. The canal itself constitutes the core of a narrow restricted area needed for ship operations and security. Panama now receives a percentage of the tolls and shares in the profits as well.

The treaty also provides for accelerated replacement of U.S. employees by Panamanians. The U.S. government had to override tremendous opposition from the MTC/CLU in order to establish this goal. The process has been helped since the mid-1960s by the induced retirement of old-timers. New U.S. appointees usually speak some Spanish and understand that they will eventually be rotated to other federal jobs.[23]

The secretary of defense continues to play a major role in canal administration, but since the late 1940s the Pentagon has attached more military importance to its bases in the Zone than to the waterway itself. The thirteen bases existing before the treaty are being consolidated into four, but the overall military presence in Panama remains about the same. Many of the ancillary services formerly provided by the canal are now operated by the Department of Defense, such as schools, postal service, hospitals, and commissaries. As treaty implementation proceeds, a sharper distinction will arise between canal and military activities, the former becoming more Panamanian in nature, the latter remaining American.

Noncitizen canal employees that were still residing in the Zone opposed the treaty for several reasons. First, they fought hard to improve their wages and benefits and did not wish to see them lowered as Panama takes over the canal. Second, they regarded themselves as partially American, with certain rights owing to long employment, education, and other ties with the United States. Third, they felt uneasiness with regard to Panama's intentions toward them as citizens. Would they be forced to move out of their housing, send their children to Panamanian schools, enroll in the social security system, pay new taxes, or assume some special obligations? The treaty specified only that employees should not suffer a diminution of benefits after treaty implementation. Thousands of local-rate employees, however, would transfer from the canal to the new Panamanian agency set up to operate the railroad and docks and to administer former Zone lands, including non-U.S. citizen housing areas. The agency, called the Panama Canal Authority, made no binding promises regarding retention of benefits. As John Augelli notes, the 1,500 non-U.S. employees in the Zone lost the most under the 1977 treaty. Some descendants of West Indians claimed it was the third time a treaty had sacrificed their interests in order to increase Panama's profits from the canal.[24]

The 1977 Panama Canal Treaty gained Senate approval in April 1978, after an arduous campaign on the part of the State Department and the White House. It proved one of the most important and hard-fought foreign policy decisions of the century. Despite its great length and detail, however, the treaty left much to be decided by subsequent congressional action. The principal labor issues concerned early retirement benefits, special immigration quotas for noncitizen employees, seniority, the wage system to be used by the Panama Canal Commission, and collective bargaining rights. These questions were addressed in the Panama Canal Act of 1979.[25]

The treaty and implementing legislation took effect on 1 October 1979, ending an era of strained relations with Panama and considerable lobbying on the part of canal employee unions. The noncitizen unions—Locals 900 and 907 and the NMU—managed to get their members covered by the generous early retirement provisions of the Panama Canal Act. Those over the age of forty-eight could receive benefits after eighteen years of service. When large blocks of positions were taken over by the Authority, several hundred local-rate employees took retirement rather than transfer to the Panamanian payroll. In addition, the unions won special U.S. immigration rights for up to 15,000 employees residing in the former Canal Zone or with long service, with virtually no waiting time or restrictions. This answered the charge that the U.S. government was turning its back on descendants of West Indians who had given decades of loyal service. These measures offered a degree of protection for local-rate employees, among whom West Indian descendants figured prominently.[26]

Despite these cushions, canal administrators projected reductions-in-force of between 3,000 and 4,000 employees, due to the treaty implementation. These would be due to discontinuing canal operations, as Panama took over the majority of the territory and public services. For a year prior to treaty implementation, Panamanian and canal officials met in the working group to plan for and coordinate the transition. They asked employees scheduled for firing about their preferences among retirement, transfer, and termination. They then mounted a complex system of posting job openings and "bumping," whereby a person with seniority could replace another whose position was retained. Although the system caused a great deal of insecurity and movement in the ranks, it did reduce the actual terminations of non-U.S. employees to about 300.[27]

Even those who managed to transfer did not escape altogether, because they then came under the Panama Area Wage Base (PAWB), a new system that went into effect under the treaty. Panamanian representatives to the working group favored a gradual reduction in wages so that they would eventually equal those in the rest of the country. Therefore they proposed the PAWB to replace the old Canal Zone Merit System. No employee could suffer a reduction in wages while in the same position, so some remained on the CZMS. Transfers and new hires, however, went onto the PAWB, which was 20–30 percent lower than the old local-rate scale. Since American employees remained on a U.S. scale, the PAWB began to open up the wage gap between U.S. and Panamanian citizens that the unions had fought so hard to close.

The PAWB resulted largely from Panamanian rather than canal planning, so Local 907, the most politically oriented local-rate union, opposed it most vehemently. Its president, Luis Anderson, debated against Planning Minister Nicolás Ardito Barletta in 1978, arguing that the economy needed the stimulus of higher wages from the canal. He calculated that layoffs and lower wages would cause a loss of from $3 to $5 billion over the life of the treaty. Panama seemed to be killing the goose (canal labor) that laid the golden eggs (wages spent in Panama).[28] Local 900 and the NMU also opposed the PAWB, to no avail. They feared that new or demoted employees would blame them for allowing its creation. Their objections had to be voiced diplomatically, however, because Torrijos declared that he would brook no opposition that might jeopardize approval of the treaty in Washington.

The final controversy affecting the local-rate unions concerned applicability of U.S. or Panamanian labor laws. The Panamanian government claimed that its labor code should prevail, in order to set a lower minimum wage, establish collective bargaining, stimulate enrollment in Panama's social security system, and harmonize hours, holidays, grievance procedures, and so forth. The Panama Canal Act, however, extended Title VII of the 1978 Civil Service Reform Act to all employees of the Panama Canal Commission, regardless of nationality. The effects of this clash are still being worked out.

The background of the labor jurisdiction dispute stretched all the way back to construction days. Some American employees obtained civil service status, while the rest managed to tie their wages and benefits to federal employment without actually being civil servants. These same employees opposed giving U.S. wages and benefits to noncitizens, whose wages and benefits were set by administrative fiat. Given this tradition of two parallel employment systems in the Zone (which persisted even under the CZMS), personnel officials managed to exempt the canal from EO 10988, the 1962 rule allowing unions to bargain on behalf of federal employees.[29]

When President Nixon strengthened the collective bargaining mandate in EO 11491 (1970), the canal again won exemption. By that time, however, the NMU had surpassed Local 900 in membership and funds and sought elections to determine which group would win exclusive representation. The winner would gain jurisdiction not only over the loser's members but over U.S-rate employees as well. Personnel officials would not allow a noncitizen union to represent U.S. citizens, so they continued to block requests for exclusive representation elections. Local 900 leaders, to save their own skins, began to favor application of Panama's labor code which allowed plural representation.[30]

Treaty negotiations beginning in 1974 again raised the issue of applying EO 11491 or substituting some other system. By this time, a powerful coalition of local-rate and U.S.-rate unions had emerged, the NMU, the Canal Zone Pilots Union, and the MTC/CLU. This alliance, formed to protect labor's interests under the treaty, fought hard for EO 11491, which would strengthen their position by giving them exclusive representation and making collective bargaining mandatory. They agreed beforehand that the NMU would not compete with U.S.-rate unions for American members. The governor's special assistant for labor relations opposed the executive order, this time on the grounds that they should not initiate any changes that would run counter to the thrust of the U.S. bargaining stance. Since the latter aimed to give Panama growing administrative influence, personnel practices, especially those involving noncitizens, should move toward the Panamanian code.[31]

The treaty directed the Panama Canal Commission to establish a new wage system in which all employees enjoyed equal rights, yet it also guaranteed the benefits of incumbents at existing levels. This grandfather clause did continue the dual system, but it also anticipated its demise through attrition. The PCC industrial relations officer foresaw gradual transition to utilization of the Panama labor code for virtually all employees.

At this juncture, the Senate, due to obstructionism or neglect, decided to apply Title VII of the Civil Service Reform Act of 1978 to the entire canal work force. Senator Mathias of Maryland sponsored the measure at the request of U.S. unions. He simply did not care if it counteracted the PCC plans to phase in the Panamanian code. According to one administrator, the Senate erred in (1) applying Title VII to unions abroad contrary to all precedent, and (2) inviting a jurisdictional dispute with Panama. The latter fear soon materialized, when Panama detained members of the National Labor Relations Board upon their arrival to oversee elections in 1981. The contradiction has not been resolved.[32]

Local-rate unions split over the application of Title VII to the canal labor force. Leaders of Local 900, recognizing that they would lose an election to the NMU, argued against it, thus supporting the Panamanian position. The NMU, on the other hand, welcomed the decision and set out to win. In alliance with the pilots' union and the MTC/CLU, it campaigned heavily for exclusive representation. Rumor held that the NMU spent $250,000. It captured 64 percent of the votes overall and controlled all but a few specialized units within the organization. The NMU will lobby for application of Title VII until the treaty expires in 1999.[33]

In historical perspective, labor relations in the canal have moved from the horse-and-buggy days into the space age since the 1960s. For someone like George Westerman, who witnessed the 1920 strike, the change has been phenomenal. The West Indians began as an exploited minority in a third-country labor system. In the 1950s their descendants became Panamanians for all intents and purposes. Canal labor relations then became dual, with separate treatment for U.S. and non-U.S. citizens. Finally, by the late 1970s the remaining West Indian descendants living in the Zone were a privileged minority. The average local-rate wages rose from 20 percent of the U.S.-rate average in the 1950s to 50 percent in 1975. Under the treaty, local-raters lose some benefits and face gradual absorption into Panama's territory and population.[34]

Canal Segregation Yields to Integration

The United States had to conduct treaty negotiations under delicate circumstances throughout the 1970s. The protracted length of the talks added to the difficulties. The U.S. government wished to end a colonialist relationship with Panama yet faced the danger that adverse publicity about the canal might tarnish the American image abroad. Panama had since the 1940s done all it could to embarrass the United States in international bodies, and the very fact of treaty talks seemed a partial confession that Panama's charges were justified. The U.S. government decided, then, to eliminate as many sources of complaint as possible *prior* to talks. With canal affairs in order, the State Department could approach negotiations in a constructive rather than defensive manner. Such an approach seemed imperative due to Panama's unreliable participation. The success of the resultant agreements testifies to the skills of those responsible.

Even in the 1970s racism remained the most glaring sin of canal life. Management had done much to break down segregation, yet to outsiders the Zone looked like the Old South resurrected.[35] Just as in the 1940s and 1950s, segregation and dual labor rules played into Panama's hands, because the single term "discrimination" served to condemn both. In 1973, in particular, Panamanian diplomats compared the Zone with South Africa, a crude but effective device. Therefore the U.S. government renewed its efforts to end race segregation in the Zone. As usual, Westerman played a catalytic role.

In 1970 Ralph Abernathy of the Southern Christian Leadership Conference stopped in Panama during a tour of Latin America. He asked Westerman about the possibility of establishing a branch of his organization there. Some months later, three black members of Congress visited the canal, as part of their responsibilities as members of the Subcommittee on Education and Labor. Since the 1940s Westerman had cultivated black congressmen for occasional legislative favors. His first and longest contact was with Adam Clayton Powell, the redoubtable congressman from Harlem. By the mid-1960s Westerman knew six black members of the House and counted Gus Hawkins as a personal friend. In 1970 they managed to pass a bill authorizing widows of old-timers, largely West Indians, to continue collecting disability cash relief. The canal visit by three black congressmen grew out of this lobbying effort by Westerman, and for the next several years these men kept their eyes on the West Indian community there.[36]

A major discrimination case involving the Zone Elks Club started the 1970s attack on segregation. A white teacher whose husband was stationed in the Zone with the navy denounced the Elks' white-only membership policy to the Defense Department. Such a policy violated several federal laws, since the entire Zone was a government compound. The *Panama Tribune* gave the issue considerable play. By 1971 black servicemen calling themselves the Concerned Brothers joined the attack and requested support from the Black Caucus in the House. Late that year the International Elks convention allowed individual lodges to admit blacks, a concession designed to save the canal chapter. Still no action resulted, and some ugly racial incidents broke out in the Zone. Fights, marches, insubordination, AWOL defections, and lobbying brought tension to a peak. This period saw great disenchantment in the armed services in the wake of the Vietnam war, and racism threatened to undermine morale further. The case made its way to the deputy undersecretary of the army in mid-1972.[37]

When race problems erupted on U.S. bases around the world, the Department of Defense had responded with special programs to publicize minority rights and handle racial discrimination grievances. Black officers usually carried out these duties. The Canal Zone had become especially important because of the international implications. The government sent down a retired California judge to rule on the Elks lodge case, four years after the first protests. His decision was to withdraw the Elks' land license if they did not take steps to integrate within a month. The Elks admitted several blacks in order to comply and thus avoided closure.[38]

Meanwhile, the army's director of Equal Employment Opportunity programs flew in for an inspection in June. He criticized the lack of importance given to these programs. He considered the situation quite bad and said that "it was high time someone brought Zonians into the twentieth century." The canal practiced overt segregation of the West Indian descendants and covert discrimination against U.S. blacks in the armed services. He recommended an in-depth study.[39] Once more Washington—and especially the Pentagon—took careful aim at canal racism and determined to kill it.

Simultaneously Robert Leggett, chairman of the House Subcommittee on the Panama Canal, made an on-site inspection and came away with a different set of complaints. The noncitizen residents of the Zone criticized segregated housing and schools and claimed that officials wanted to send them all packing into Panama. Leggett made it clear that he would defend their interests in Congress. He did not try to be diplomatic, however, and he did not make much effort to understand the situation. He alienated white Zonians and caused a decline in canal employee morale. But whatever his actions, Leggett served notice that Congress itself wanted an end to segregation in the Zone. In a parting shot, he requested the GAO to conduct a thorough probe of canal wages and benefits and of possible violations of federal regulations there.[40]

The Pentagon then sent Minton Francis, deputy assistant secretary of defense, to assess canal race relations. Like most others, Francis lauded the army's internal program but heaped criticism on the Canal Zone civilians. He remarked that he had never seen as bad a situation. He recommended an immediate overhaul of personnel policies, integration of schools and housing, and a plebiscite to determine whether descendants of West Indians should be moved to Panama or be given U.S. citizenship. Back in Washington, Francis spoke vigorously and widely about his trip, and he later took credit for spurring the hearings by Leggett's committee. In fact, the canal's Latin American Communities Study backfired, by evoking the sympathy of leading black Americans for the West Indian descendants.[41]

Yet another blockbuster inquiry followed in mid-1974, conducted by Peter Pestillo, labor relations officer for General Electric on loan to the army. The preceding year pilots had carried out an undeclared strike, and Secretary of the Army Calloway asked Pestillo for a frank assessment of labor relations there. His two-week stay produced a bluntly worded secret report. He said that the poor labor-management climate resulted from rumors concerning treaty negotiations and labor's fear that they could lose everything by the "stroke of a diplomatic pen." All discontent focused on the canal administration, which ran virtually everything in the Zone. If they did not handle labor problems with more care, Pestillo warned, a big strike could occur. They must act firmly but wisely to keep workers on the job. He recommended keeping "them sullen but not mutinous."[42]

The "single most glaring deficiency," Pestillo found, was failure to give Panamanians equal opportunities, which he believed was

> more the product of a conscious racism on the part of senior canal company management than it is the result of lassitude, incompetence, or indifference. . . . Our policy over the years seemed to have been one of conscious subjugation of the Panamanians. . . . Full assimilation of the Panamanians is the right thing to do [and might slow down] the inexorable move toward Panamanian sovereignty. . . . Exploitation is a harsh term but not inappropriate in this setting.

These opinions, laced with some insulting descriptions of MTC/CLU labor leaders, constituted the worst indictment of canal management since the McSherry and Vietheer studies of the late 1940s. Unfortunately for labor relations, a copy of the Pestillo report got out and was published in the Panama press. Sullen moods turned mutinous, for it seemed that Washington wanted to castigate the Zonians.

Congress and the Pentagon kept up the pressure to reform canal labor and race relations concurrently with diplomatic talks. In early 1975 Congressman Ralph Metcalfe, a black, took over the Subcommittee on the Panama Canal and scheduled talks with labor groups. Continuing the approach initiated by Leggett, he focused on racial integration of schools and housing and promotion of more Panamanians into middle- and upper-management positions. Metcalfe, a friend of Westerman for some twenty years, attempted to be more accommodating to all sides, an attitude that earned him respect from Zone officials. When the GAO report came in, Metcalfe's subcommittee held hearings regarding possible enactment of its findings.[43]

The new governor, Parfitt, expressed his willingness to carry out many of the GAO recommendations and noted that some had already become policy. In particular, he had begun to reduce the number of positions designated as "security," to which only U.S. citizens could be appointed. This had been a way the personnel department kept Panamanians out of most of the better jobs. The GAO found the practice objectionable because only a few positions could be defined as genuinely critical to security. Moreover, barring Panamanians from these jobs stigmatized them as untrustworthy in their own country. Parfitt also said that revitalized training and apprenticeship programs tracked more Panamanians into skilled and supervisory positions. The EEO program was being strengthened with an upward mobility component for noncitizens. Finally, they had begun to recruit Panamanians for better jobs.[44]

Parfitt defended several existing policies, ones that the GAO had not termed illegal. He upheld the controversial tax factor, a deduction from noncitizens' salaries to compensate for lower Panamanian tax rates. Likewise he sustained the tropical differential or 15 percent bonus for U.S. citizens. Finally, he found the leave regulations (that gave longer vacations to U.S. citizens) fair because Americans had farther to travel and had to leave their familiar U.S. culture when they took jobs with the canal.

One of the most explosive issues the GAO raised concerned separate schools and housing for noncitizens. Since 90 percent of the noncitizen employees residing in the canal were black Panamanian descendants of the West Indians, distinctions by nationality meant that the schools and communities were almost perfectly segregated by race as well. The old defense that different customs warranted different facilities—which had served for seventy years—broke down. Parfitt admitted that they had to eliminate the *appearance* of racial segregation, whatever the motives for its institution. Several committees were studying the problem but no easy solutions had been found. In all, the GAO report and the congressional Panama Canal Subcommittee hearings increased the belief among Zonians that the impending treaty would destroy their way of life.

Metcalfe, refusing to let Parfitt off the hook, periodically requested information on the reforms. The lieutenant governor prepared an action list of thirteen points for implementation over the next ten months. Soon Assistant Secretary of the Army Victor Veysey put on more pressure. He imposed budget cuts to enforce reform in much the same way Secretary of War Weeks had done in 1921 and Bendetsen had done in 1951. Zonians regarded Veysey as a Santa Claus in reverse, with a bag of evil tricks to use against them.[45]

Faced with such a solid front in Washington, Parfitt prepared three decisions to comply with agreements reached with Metcalfe in July. First, he would eliminate the security designations from several hundred positions. This would allow Panamanians to hold many more jobs as police and firefighters. Second, he would eliminate nationality restrictions on housing so that all employees above a certain grade (NM-7) could apply on an equal basis. Finally, he proposed to end the dual school system by allowing students to transfer into either the U.S. or Panamanian schools. This last decision, called the schools merger, proved the most controversial and sparked a second strike among U.S. employees.[46]

Parfitt's staff had begun consultations with U.S. and noncitizen labor leaders in November regarding the merger plan. But the debate had already gone on for five years prior to his decision. By 1970 enrollments had dropped to uneconomical levels in the Latin American schools, because of the depopulation policy. Yet the less viable the schools, the more resolutely the Zone communities fought to preserve them or send the students to U.S. schools. The Canal Executive Planning Staff began devising ways to phase out the schools and send the students to Panamanian schools. Rumors of these plans only exacerbated fears and speculation. Local leaders then accused the administration of trying to do away with the schools to avoid integration, as their predecessors had done in 1954. The dispute polarized the two sides: officials wished to disband the Latin American schools, and teachers and parents wanted to integrate them with the U.S. schools.[47]

No easy solutions appeared, so the decision had been postponed year after year. Other problems seemed more pressing. U.S. school administrators (closely linked to the American Federation of Teachers, Local 29) refused to take in the noncitizen children (mostly third- and fourth-generation Panamanians of West Indian descent), arguing that they needed preparation for living in Panama, not the United States. They even more adamantly opposed incorporating the Latin American teachers into their schools. In fact, they became almost rabid on this point. Even though most Latin American teachers met their certification standards and were paid according to the Washington, D.C., scale, U.S. teachers regarded them as inferior. They insisted on two retention (seniority) lists so that the Latin Americans would be the first to go in reductions-in-force. They also tried to give the Latin American schools to Panama as part of the treaty. Most visitors from Washington saw the school problem as racial, which was largely true.

The Latin American teachers, mostly associated with Local 900, argued that many of their students were truly bicultural and that cutting them off from the United States would destroy half of their birthright. They noted that as many as a third of their graduates went to the United States for higher education, jobs, and military service and then stayed. They realized that the Latin American schools were a "dying entity" but argued that the students should move into the U.S. system. As for retention lists, they argued that they had served the schools faithfully for decades (much longer than U.S.-rate teachers). They had met the Washington, D.C., certification standards, usually by taking degrees in U.S. colleges. They deserved to be transferred to the U.S. schools. To buttress the seniority argument, they presented evidence that service in the Latin American schools counted for seniority according to the personnel manual used in Washington, D.C. It should count in the Zone as well. Many of the teachers' representatives possessed fine debating skills honed on decades of arguing with canal officials.

U.S. school administrators eventually lost their case, due partly to the racism underlying their position and to occasional lies and misstatements. Critics tarred them with the same brush used on segregated housing and the dual wage system. The lies, subtle to be sure, infuriated the local rate teachers and ensured that they would continue fighting. The superintendent of schools from 1973 to 1976, David Spier, affirmed on many occasions that the local-rate teachers were not qualified for U.S. school service despite their training: "The same standards of performance have not generally been demonstrated in the Latin American schools as in the U.S. schools. Only a relatively small percentage . . . could perform adequately." Later he objected to their "British West Indian" language, even though most were second-generation Panamanians. By 1975 he estimated that only ten of the eighty-eight local-rate teachers could be used in the U.S. schools, and then only for Spanish instruction. He had agreed by that point to take in the several hundred students, but not the teachers.[48]

Parfitt's decision to merge the schools brought protests and exaggerated claims of disaster to come. The president of the local wrote to the AFT international in New York to have it fight the decision. He erroneously stated that Spanish was the sole language of the local-rate schools, that Panama had insisted on separate schools in a treaty, that the curriculum and standards were Panamanian, and that "Canal Zone schools have never been racially segregated." The union leader went on, "Since most of the Panamanian teachers are blacks, Congressman Metcalfe—a black obsessed with racial issues real and imagined—has taken up their cause with bigoted zeal."[49] The vehemence of the AFT protest demonstrates the sensitivity of both Zone communities—U.S. citizens and Panamanians of West Indian descent—to issues of educational quality, cultural preservation, and racial mixing.

In retrospect, the years of strife seemed absurd. Only about 600 black Panamanian children transferred into U.S. schools, to be integrated with 11,000 U.S. students—that is, two or three per classroom. Surprisingly, about 35 percent of the younger students in Atlantic communities preferred to transfer into Panamanian private schools rather than to Zone schools. On the Pacific side, 16 percent chose that alternative.[50]

U.S. teachers insisted that their Latin American colleagues be recertified before being included in their ranks. Assistant Superintendent Latimer drew up a report showing only thirteen of the Latin American teachers to be qualifed, due largely to their low scores for English proficiency. This infuriated the teachers, many of whom had defended their positions eloquently before congressional committees. They were an exceptionally articulate group, in both English and Spanish. In October 1976, three specialists from U.S. universities flew down to review credentials. They found that all had bachelor's degrees and over half held master's degrees. Only one failed to meet standards and retired. The other sixty passed, most with several fields of competency.[51]

The Latin American schools closed officially in December 1977, their students and staff largely absorbed into the U.S. schools. Two years later, when the treaty went into effect, the school system was taken over by the Department of Defense. Thus ended a long, contentious, and discreditable aspect of U.S. canal operations in Panama.

Decline of the West Indian Subculture

Two months before the canal treaty went into effect, Ed Gaskin delivered a eulogy in honor of the West Indians of the construction era. Speaking for first-generation Panamanians, he paid tribute to the last generation of immigrants. Gaskin reflected on the progress they had seen over the previous half-century, especially under the new treaty.[52] They were no longer an oppressed minority group caught between two hostile societies, he said. Most were Panamanians with a strong dose of American culture and experience. A great many could opt for residency and naturalization in the United States.

These improvements for the West Indian community had taken their toll in the form of diminished group identity. The passing of the last old-timers broke the physical link with the West Indies. Few of the children had visited the islands or felt any attachment to them. And now that they had won acceptance by both Panama and the United States, they no longer needed their West Indian identity as a defense and a refuge. The subculture faded into memory as integration proceeded.

A 1971–1972 survey in two West Indian neighborhoods of Panama City revealed the extent to which solidarity had eroded. Only 8 percent of the respondents were born in the West Indies. Most spoke both English and Spanish, with greater bilingualism among younger people. Forty percent worked in the Canal Zone, while only 6 percent worked for the Panamanian government. Canal wages far exceeded those earned in other jobs. Younger persons had gone much farther in school, and about a quarter had completed university or vocational studies. The most striking finding was that a substantial majority were Catholics, in contrast with the Protestant faith of their parents. Religious leaders also noted that conversion to Catholicism had been a widespread means of assimilation.[53]

Attitudinal questions used in the survey revealed that respondents experienced difficulties getting along in Hispanic Panamanian society. For example, 40 percent thought that of all immigrant groups the West Indians had the hardest time gaining acceptance. Few believed that their group as a whole had achieved high economic or social standing. Fully 70 percent felt that Panamanians were prejudiced against them, mostly due to racial aversion and economic competition. Yet the very admission of these feelings indicated that the difficulties of assimilation and integration were being confronted.

The cessation of the West Indian press was another sign of subculture decline. In 1972 Westerman closed the *Panama Tribune*, which had been running in the red for years. The Panamanian government hastened its end by discouraging businesses from giving him their advertising. But with or without government harassment, the paper could not have continued much longer. Other papers shortened and then discontinued their

English-language sections as uneconomical. Then in 1981 the government-owned *La República* dropped its English section but considered replacing it with a cultural weekly, perhaps like the *Panama Tribune*. So the West Indian community lost what had once been an effective forum for cohesion and defense.[54]

Other institutions declined as well. Most of the old benevolent societies closed. The Independent United Order of Mechanics Friendly Society Lodge went bankrupt after forty years of operations (1918–1958). The Good Shepherd Benevolent Society collapsed three years later when the treasurer absconded with its funds. The Barbadian Progressive Society went into receivership after its investments in Barbados sugar estates went bad. The La Boca Mutual Beneficent and Friendly Association closed its doors in 1967, ending thirty-three years of service. Finally, the PCWIEA itself ended operations in 1968. Benevolent groups died naturally from declining numbers. Younger people failed to join because they lacked the need (they had coverage through the canal or Panama's social security agency) and no longer felt an attachment to the community.[55]

The cultural identity gap widened when second-generation Panamanians of West Indian descent reached maturity during the 1960s. Canal administrators first detected it in the form of juvenile delinquency. An investigation in 1962 turned up symptoms of social malaise in the Latin American communities: broken families, unemployed teenagers, absence of "self-identity and defiance to authority on the part of youth," marital conflicts, truancy, drunkenness, illegitimate births, cultural deprivation, and poor leadership. (On the other hand, mental illness was lower among noncitizens than among U.S. employees.) The canal created a social services program, directed by a Panamanian specialist, to address these problems.[56]

In 1966 a new study of delinquency concluded on a pessimistic note. Unemployment had now spawned a generation of "bachelors" and illegitimate children. Because noncitizen Zone housing was far more available for unmarried employees, a number of men claiming to be bachelors occupied these quarters, when they really had families in Panamá and Colón. They kept up Zone residency to remain eligible for commissary privileges. The study recommended forcing the men to live with their families. Finally, it noted a lack of leadership in the Latin American communities. Some members of the West Indian community acknowledged the generation gap but played down the importance of juvenile delinquency. They claimed that the real causes of malaise were secret plans to close their schools, move them into Panama, and terminate their fringe benefits. What could they expect when canal officials treated the youths as "castoffs and Zonian Antilleans"?[57]

Officials hit one problem on the head. The Latin American communities lacked leaders because the talented fled the oppressive atmosphere of the Zone or had their skills ground down by years of frustration.

Thousands of the best and most ambitious children of the West Indians had gone to the United States, where their talents found better rewards. The brain drain affected the communities of Panamá and Colón too, because Panamanians enjoyed easy access to residency in the United States. The cream of the second generation emigrated, leaving those behind with a sense of truncated culture and lost opportunities.

In the late 1960s, a new phenomenon troubled the older generation: black militancy. Young persons of West Indian descent picked up the language and styles of American blacks, including techniques of confrontation virtually unknown in Panama. These U.S. imports probably came with black servicemen stationed in army and navy bases. Canal youth wore Afro hairdos and Swahili robes and adopted other symbols of the black power movement. Westerman spoke out vigorously: "We reject any misguided militants who may emerge from black power sources abroad encouraging local youths to identify with them and develop anti-white sentiments, or to engage in disruptive efforts which could lead to violence and chaos in this country." Westerman's voice did not carry the authority it once had, though. Younger people dismissed him as an Uncle Tom.[58]

On a more serious level, young professionals formed two organizations in 1968, the Afro-Panamanian Union in Colón and the Afro-Panamanian Association in Panamá. Their aim was to act as pressure groups that could unify blacks of all backgrounds.[59] These groups held meetings for several years before fading from view, but they took an important step toward a unique cultural-political bargain in the 1970s. By calling themselves Afro-Panamanians, they changed the terms of the integration process. The name defined out of existence the Anglo-American component of their identify, that part the Latins found so objectionable. If they simply thought of themselves as dark-skinned persons with some heritage from Africa, they could easily be accepted into Latin society.

Torrijos and his advisers grasped the opportunity to redefine West Indian descendants as Afro-Panamanians. They appointed large numbers to the government and the National Guard in the early 1970s. Torrijos, for example, befriended a social worker in Rio Abajo, Hector Gadpaille, and urged him to run for the Assembly in 1972. He met Latin-Calypso singer Leroy Gittens, who had lived abroad for years, and persuaded him to return to Panama to lead his people. He met a young lawyer, Margot Hutchinson, and recruited her for public relations work in the National Guard. He reached out to dozens of others, telling them that they were as much a part of the Panamanian family as he was. He usually succeeded in winning over these people. He seemed sincere and personable—he was an able caudillo.[60]

A new complication arose, however, when blacks of West Indian and Latin descent debated race relations in Panamanian society. The former claimed that bias existed, especially in the actions of the economic elite. The latter, called colonial blacks because they were descended from slaves imported in colonial times, said that race prejudice did not exist. Rather, persons of West Indian descent experienced cultural exclusion because they insisted on retaining their English manners. The discussion that arose between these two groups did much to clear the way for integration.

Alberto Smith and Melva Lowe Ocran spoke for the first group. In a special issue of the Ministry of Education's cultural journal, they and others explored the question of national identity and integration. Smith, an architect with the army in the Zone, rejected the view that persons of West Indian descent were not more than Zonian Negroes who could never become good Panamanians. What most Latin writers claimed as pure Panamanian represented a myth of Hispanic American thinkers long out of touch with the modern world, an idealization like *hispanidad*. Smith said that canal employees and their descendants had invested as much in the nation as anyone else and should not be seen as unpatriotic because they spoke English. Moreover, he noted that racial discrimination existed, even to the extent of keeping children of West Indians out of public schools. He found racism in popular literature too. He concluded that miscegenation could not be stopped and was producing a new people in the Americas. The Panamanian of West Indian descent melted in with others in this process. He urged Latins to stop judging the criollos according to antiquated ideals of racial and cultural purity and to begin to accept and build upon the opportunities offered by a peaceful blending of peoples.[61]

Melva Lowe Ocran focused on language as a criterion for discrimination against persons of West Indian descent. She examined the strong official stance in favor of Spanish, especially as a means of cultural defense against the American influence from the Zone. The language, of course, carried with it a rich heritage from Spain. Yet emphasizing Spain's traditions excluded those of the Indian and African, so the policy of basing national identity narrowly on language could even be a form of cultural extinction for non-Hispanic groups. To pursue this policy would deprive the nation of valuable human resources.[62] These and other second-generation Panamanians urged their Latin counterparts to accept them as they were and to recognize their contributions—past and future—to the nation.

Juan Materno Vásquez, brilliant and articulate cabinet minister and later Supreme Court Justice, formulated a reply on behalf of a dozen or so black government officials who did not accept the charge that Latin Panamanians practiced racial discrimination. Materno Vásquez's 1974 booklet entitled *Pais por conquistar* had triggered much debate by insisting that all groups had to conform to the Hispanic culture. He responded to the Smith and Lowe Ocran essays by saying that Panama had fought long and hard to establish a separate national identity, based on Spanish language, Catholic religion, a distinctive folk culture, and the struggle against U.S. domination. According to this definition (and he cited several other authorities on the subject), those of West Indian descent could never fit in without changing their ways. Panama had gone more than halfway by enacting extremely liberal laws on citizenship and naturalization. He ended by inviting Smith and Lowe Ocran to rethink their position and to work toward integration as he defined it.[63]

A year later he hardened the attack, saying that black power and negritude had no place in Panama. The West Indian descendants could not claim any loyalty to the nation when they jumped at the chance to go to the United States. Nor could they contribute to the culture, because "the illiterate cannot communicate in writing. The ignorant cannot transmit wisdom." They had acted unpatriotically by opposing Panama's position in treaty negotiations. Their accusations of discrimination were insincere because they did not encompass plans to assimilate. He even dismissed the supposed contribution of building the canal, because their ancestors came as cheap laborers without any sense of permanence or belonging. Materno Vásquez spoke as a government representative but was not its sole voice by any means. To some he seemed an agent provocateur to keep blacks from becoming unified.[64]

Torrijos may have intentionally set blacks against blacks, because then he had a freer hand to deal with the canal negotiations. Black movements might prove useful in discrediting Zone society, but they could reflect badly on Panama too. Torrijos therefore encouraged diverse groups to compete in the political arena. One critic charged that "the oligarchy has utilized a racist nationalism which emphasizes language and color, both of which serve to divide the dangerous masses." Materno Vásquez, in this view, was a tool of white racism.[65]

Two new groups did form, perhaps at Torrijos's suggestion, called Acción Reivindicadora del Negro Panameño (ARENEP) and the Asociación de Profesionales, Obreros, y Dirigentes de Ascendencia Negra (APODAN). They were formed by Panamanians of West Indian descent to deal with questions of color and discrimination. These groups could mobilize public support for the government side in the plebiscite needed to ratify the impending treaty.

The name of the first organization, ARENEP, has a revealing history. After his return to Panama in 1974, Leroy Gittens gained attention by debating with Latins about the race issue on the radio. Soon two leaders from Rio Abajo recruited him to help form a group to be named Acción Reivindicadora del Chombo. They chose Gittens, an outgoing and well-known figure, as president. They also decided to emphasize the derogatory term *chombo* as a rebuke and in defiance of Latin discrimination. The government responded by sending out its top black officials to urge them to change the organization's potentially embarrassing name.

In a meeting attended by a large number of civil servants, the name was changed to Acción Reivindicadora del Negro Panameño. Gittens spoke with Torrijos, who did not like the possible challenge of a black movement. The latter persuaded Gittens to reach out to the employees of the Canal Zone. He should convince them that the government would respect their interests in treaty talks.[66]

Gittens mounted a whirlwind campaign in late 1977 to garner support for the treaty. He served as liaison for several black leaders from the United States, including Jesse Jackson, who visited Panama just after the plebiscite. Gittens took much of the language of Carter's human rights approach and adapted it to the West Indian community. Then, when Torrijos returned from talks in the United States, ARENEP strung banners at the airport proclaiming, "Chombos support the general!" ARENEP publicity appeared in the government newspaper, *La República*, successor to the *Panama-American*. This suggests that while Torrijos probably did not like the outbreak of ethnic and racial politics, he nevertheless channeled them in directions supportive of the government.

Gittens's most ambitious project, a consumer cooperative in the local-rate communities destined to be turned over to Panama, failed after six months. Residents of the former Zone areas, who were scheduled to lose commissary rights, lived far from shopping areas in Panama. Gittens reasoned that if ARENEP and the government could run a coop, they could ease the transition and overcome the residents' opposition to the treaty. He approached leaders of Locals 900 and 907 and the NMU, who showed little enthusiasm for the scheme. After he had spent much time and money on the project, Gittens realized that the local-raters of the Zone simply would not trust him because of his links to the government.

ARENEP enjoyed a brief renaissance in late 1978, when Torrijos held elections to choose a new figurehead president. Jimmy Lakas, a Greek-Panamanian from Colón, had, since the 1972 constitution, filled the role without distinction. Now that the treaty had been approved, Torrijos wanted to remove himself from the daily pressures of government. He had run the country for ten years, in addition to conducting negotiations with the United States for the past four. He chose for the office of president a handsome, articulate university law professor, Aristides Royo. Even though the results of the election could hardly be doubted, Royo nonetheless campaigned throughout the country. He appeared several times in Rio Abajo at meetings convoked by Gittens. They seemed to hit it off well, Royo much more at home with political byplay and rhetoric than Lakas or Torrijos.

Royo, perhaps reluctant to be associated too closely with ARENEP, sought support from upper-middle-class blacks. He made contact with attorney Raymundo Brathwaite, who arranged a luncheon at which prominent figures in the West Indian community would give the candidate their endorsement. As a result of this meeting, several participants formed a new black pressure group, APODAN. This group gave the image of favoring stable, constructive political action, and it obviously sought to counterbalance the militancy of ARENEP. For the next year, the two groups competed amicably for leadership of the black movement and for government favors. J. J. Harrison, veteran newspaperman and editor of *La República*, became president of APODAN in late 1978.[67]

Each of these organizations enjoyed some backing from the government, albeit veiled. Their existence marked a breakthrough in Panama, a grudging admission that blacks did form a community separate from the rest of the population. The price of this recognition, however, was a willingness to cooperate and respect the rules of the game. In particular, neither could criticize the canal treaty or subsequent implementation nor could they resort to militant tactics or confrontation. In a word, they had to be loyal.

By 1981 both ARENEP and APODAN had ceased activities except for an occasional press release, because the tense issues of the canal reorganization were settled. Ethnic and racial differences remained, of course, but they no longer complicated the country's international relations. The debate now became symbolic and academic. In 1980, for example, the granddaughter of a West Indian won the Miss Panama title. Government officials, dismayed by her dark color, failed to provide her with an automobile or the other usual perquisites. Derogatory remarks appeared in the press as well. A dozen or so prominent figures in the West Indian community, calling themselves the Grupo Doce, raised funds to help her in the Miss Universe contest, and she placed among the twelve finalists.[68] That the episode could even occur showed that the West Indian descendants had made great progress since the 1940s.

Scholarly debate on West Indians and on race and ethnic relations in Panama shifted to a series of conferences held between 1977 and 1981. Several descendants of West Indians participated in the First Congress on Black Culture in the Americas, held in Cali, Colombia.[69] In 1980 the Panamanian government hosted the Second Congress on Black Culture, so virtually everyone with an interest in the subject took part. Participants arrived from North and South America, as well as from Caribbean and Central American countries. Then, in 1981, several local groups sponsored the First Congress of the Panamanian Negro. The tenor of Panamanian contributions in these meetings remained moderate, opposed to racial and ethnic discrimination and favoring cultural pluralism. The government, especially when Royo enjoyed authority, could tolerate criticism if black leaders refrained from active protest.

Perhaps Alberto Smith came closest to a consensus position on the issue of race in a paper written in 1981. Starting from the sixteenth-century expansion of capitalism, he reasoned that black slaves had been an essential element of colonialism. Slavery established a new rung at the bottom of the social ladder. The extremes became polarized by color—whites on top, blacks on the bottom. In addition, it required destruction of African culture to eliminate resistance. In Panama, however, large numbers of slaves escaped and formed communities that eluded recapture by the Spanish. After independence they and most former slaves attained the condition of citizen, even though few exercised the right. Finally, more blacks arrived to build the railroad and canal.[70]

North Americans in Panama after 1904 resurrected the old systems of colonialism and racism that had gradually faded, continued Smith. The new levies of black laborers, however, also contributed to the development of the Panamanian nation by forming a market and an incipient middle class. They also enriched the culture of Panama with their various island traditions. Moreover, the West Indian community increasingly supported Panamanian interests in the struggle against U.S. imperialism. In particular, the Canal Zone unions fought for better pay and racial equality, a campaign that certainly benefited Latin Panamanians as well. If some canal workers left for the United States, many more stayed in Panama and fought for their rights. That exercise of civil rights constituted proof of their loyalty to Panama. Smith concluded that politics offered the surest means for Panamanian blacks of all backgrounds to continue to pursue their interests. They would have to combat racial discrimination as well as the myth of racial democracy. They should resist the temptation to import the tactics of the black movement in the United States.

Smith's analysis placed the Panamanian blacks squarely in the diaspora. In the preceding eighty years they had survived one form of struggle, and now they could reflect upon the millennial forces that had produced the struggle in the first place.

Only months before it went out of business, the *Panama Tribune* ran a story that must have touched the sentiments of all generations of readers. A group called the British Aid Society was soliciting contributions in order to give food packages, medical treatment, and clothing to indigent West Indian old-timers in Panama. Similar activities had gone on since the very start of West Indian immigration 120 years before. The community had always given generously, because they shared the insecurity of any expatriate group. Now only a handful of West Indians remained. Their children and grandchildren had become Panamanians and had lost contact with the islands. Those who went to the United States were even farther removed. The *Panama Tribune* would never again issue a call for help, because it passed away like the West Indian immigrants who had supported it for almost a half-century.[71]

The passage of time and the liquidation of the U.S. colonial role in Panama hastened the decline of the West Indian subculture there. In Panama and the Canal Zone, racial and cultural prejudices bowed to government pressure, allowing most descendants of West Indians to become integrated into the larger society. Differences and biases remained, of course, but the progress made since the 1940s seemed remarkable. The negotiations that produced the Carter-Torrijos Treaty helped promote West Indian integration. They forced Zone authorities to eliminate discriminatory practices that undermined the U.S. bargaining position. They also gave evidence that the United States would eventually give up its hegemonic position in Panama. Those who depended on U.S. authority had to adjust their lives accordingly. Many West Indian descendants faced a loyalty conflict just as their parents had in 1955. Most chose to stay. The character of their integration will be analyzed in the concluding chapter.

8

Conclusion

THE INSECURITY has ended for the West Indian descendants in Panama. The 1977 treaty affected some adversely, and a small number took the escape route to the United States. Yet the treaty set up a gradual transfer of canal operations to Panama and thereby made it easier to predict events for the next twenty years. Disagreements and conflicts will arise, but they should take place within the parameters of the treaty and the Panama Canal Act. The impending departure of a principal actor (the United States) simplifies the situation much as did the British Foreign Office withdrawal in the 1940s.

The New York colony of Panamanians of West Indian descent served as a litmus test for the integration process and for the treaty's impact on the community. They enthusiastically backed Panama in the treaty debate, evincing nationalistic pride that surprised their compatriots on the isthmus. They taught their children the Spanish language and Panamanian customs. They carried on a ratification campaign that impressed those Panamanians who had doubted their loyalty.

The diaspora moved to a new phase, because the treaty transformed migration from a community response to adversity (exodus) into an individual decision based on interest. Indeed, some reverse migration occurred, suggesting that migratory inducements had reached an equilibrium, with movements compensating one another. Some described the West Indian community as enjoying the best of two worlds. They could work and study in the United States and vacation in Panama, or work in Panama and retire in the United States. Many in fact held dual citizenship. The teachers' 1950s vision of their students becoming citizens of the world had not been far-fetched after all.

The Quality of Integration

Even as intellectuals debated whether black power and negritude were appropriate in Panama, others evaluated the quality of West Indian integration in the 1970s. Carlos Wilson, a Panamanian of West Indian descent who taught literature at Loyola-Marymount in Los Angeles, traced antipathy toward blacks throughout the history of Spanish literature and discovered strong evidence of it in Panamanian prose as well. He found differential acceptance of colonial and West Indian blacks reflected in literature. Yet few novelists admitted that race bias existed. Mirna Pérez-Venero's dissertation on race, color, and prejudice came to the same conclusion after studying the canal novels of Joaquín Beleño. She described a complex system of biases and rivalries among the various racial, ethnic, and national groups, fueled by the overarching antagonism between the United States and Panama over the canal.[1]

Still, few Panamanians recognized the existence of prejudice. A popular columnist, La Llorona, continually criticized the militants and proclaimed, "Nobody discriminates against anybody, and every day we see *chombos* talking with all manner of whites. And many good-looking black women marry whites. So what's the trouble?" Prominent historian Roberto de la Guardia wrote a satirical and mildly bigoted analysis of the race situation in his "Mecos—Chombos—Afros West Indians—Blacks—Latinamericans."[2] He proposed calling the West Indian descendants *melanoanglos* to denote their color and culture. He noted that a struggle had gone on over who would have the power to name this group. First, Panamanians and Zonians had fought for this authority, but now the melanoanglos themselves could not agree. Were they blacks, *chombos*, or Afro-Panamanians? De la Guardia made fun of their various attempts at self-identification, and in so doing he showed a lack of sympathy for the loyalty crises the group had experienced.

The popular impresario Roberto Morgan reflected on his generation's experience in Panama: blacks had grown up in a world economically secure but socially limited. Life had been carefree, yet they could never patronize the better stores or restaurants in Panama. By the late 1970s, however, they had gained almost complete acceptance. Young people's insistence on Afro hair styles and other black power symbols were not only unnecessary—because race prejudice barely existed—but also they put off Latins sympathetic to the West Indian community. To demonstrate the lack of a color bar, he listed fourteen blacks (Latin and West Indian) who occupied high positions in government and the private sector. He concluded with an exhortation to his people to be 100 percent Panamanian. Eight other Panamanians of West Indian descent (out of forty) interviewed for this study agreed with Morgan that no discrimination existed.[3]

University professor and newspaper columnist Camilo Pérez also took up the issue of racial bias and integration. In a series of articles prompted by ARENEP, he revealed that 95 percent of the actors in local television commercials were white. He urged the government to take measures to achieve a representative selection. The following year he met with Gittens to discuss the delicate problem of challenging race prejudice without undermining Panama's diplomatic position. U.S. opponents of treaty negotiations during the mid-1970s used anything negative about Panama to discredit the talks. Pérez suggested concentrating on individual and customary prejudices rather than systematic discrimination, which barely existed. The former was potent enough: the government savings bank and social security agency had no black employees, and in private enterprise few blacks held positions of responsibility. They did get a promise from president-elect Royo to eliminate photos on government employment applications.[4] This kind of action by Latin Panamanians revealed a maturity in racial attitudes and widening opportunities for integration as a two-way process.

The Panamanian government continued its attempts to win over citizens of West Indian descent. In 1980 the Cultural and Artistic Institute restored an old Baptist chapel in the West Indian district of Marañón and made it into the Afro-Antillean Museum. Community leaders contributed artifacts and oral histories. That same year the president's office financed a Spanish edition of a lengthy manuscript by George Westerman about the West Indian immigrants.[5] And that year the government sponsored the Second Congress on Black Culture in the Americas. The constitution of 1972 and the revised version of 1983 strengthen the evidence that the government of Panama wished to eradicate race discrimination. Both refused recognition to organizations based on racial or ethnic affiliation; prohibited wage distinctions based on sex, race, age, class, ideology, religion, or nationality; and barred parties based on sex, race, or religion.

The case of Woodrow Bryan, charismatic leader of the National Union of Panamanian Negroes, provided unusual evidence that Panama accepted West Indian descendants at last. After defeating Gadpaille for the Rio Abajo Assembly seat, he proclaimed that he would become Panama's first black president. This statement shocked many people and of course overlooked Mendoza's presidency in 1910. Yet his very utterance of an idea formerly repugnant to the white elite proved that the scope of ethnoracial dialogue had broadened considerably.[6] Panamanians had done much to bring about the racial equality which they proclaimed a part of their cutural heritage. The changing climate in Panama affected those who had gone to the United States too.

Migration of Panamanians of West Indian descent to the United States provided an index of integration at home. More people left in times of intensified prejudice and low employment opportunity. By the

1970s the expatriate community numbered some 20,000, still concentrated in New York but with significant numbers in other cities as well. Three had achieved national prominence in their respective fields but were rarely identified as Panamanians: educational reformer Kenneth Clark and baseball's Vida Blue and Rod Carew. Others moved in black leadership circles: insurance executive Cirillo McSween and college administrator Carlos Russell. Several had gained reputations in academia, business, and medicine. Since the upwardly mobile tended to emigrate, the expatriate community represented a select group with high achievement potential.

The treaty campaign of the late 1970s infused Panamanians in the United States with patriotism. They held parades, organized fundraisers, wrote members of Congress, and tried to persuade Americans to support the treaty. To be sure, the government sent up bright young persons of West Indian descent to stimulate protreaty activities. Yet the community mobilization appeared genuine. Moreover, it brought Panamanians of all backgrounds together in a common endeavor.[7]

Some Panamanians of West Indian descent have returned home, recruited by the government or private enterprise. Winston Welsh, a Ph.D. in mathematics, left New York to take employment with the Canal Authority. Orville Gooding, formerly with NASA, accepted a job as deputy minister of economic planning. Cynthia Franklin, a student of Marian Anderson, planned to establish a school of voice in Panama. Others felt the temptation to leave New York and take up a more relaxed life at home. As one person said, "You can learn and earn in the States, but Panama offers the really good life."[8]

Given the job attractions of the United States, some migration there will continue. Yet the exodus seems to have ended and with it the West Indian–Panamanian phase of the diaspora. As of April 1983, the U.S. consulate in Panama had issued only 1,666 special visas out of the total of 15,000 authorized by the Panama Canal Act.[9]

Liquidating Colonialism

Until very recently, the West Indians and their descendants have been pawns in a long struggle between the United States and Panama and within the United States itself. In 1903 Panamanians had felt compelled to accept the disadvantageous Hay–Bunau-Varilla Treaty with the United States as the price of separation from Colombia, and yet it made their country into a de facto U.S. colony, a status they opposed from the beginning. For nearly fifty years Panamanians viewed the canal as the main resource for promoting their nation's development. The United States blocked that aspiration in a variety of ways, especially by the development of the Zone as commercial entrepot. Moreover, Panamanians disliked the West Indians for taking jobs they asserted might have been theirs and for undermining their project of nation-building.

[175]

Race and ethnicity played a part too. In the early years of the century, Panamanians had envisioned a country peopled by white descendants of Europeans and a declining number of Indians. Prosperity and international recognition would flow from the canal. Their culture, Hispanic-American and essentially liberal, would combine the best of the Old World and the New. They would be cosmopolitan yet homogeneous. Instead, Panamanians found themselves inundated by blacks whose culture differed radically from theirs. They had no control over migration because the canal could import as many employees as necessary. The country remained poor and backward, a condition made less tolerable by the contrast with affluent life in the Canal Zone. The world looked down on the country because it was a protectorate of the United States, virtually without sovereignty.

The huge West Indian black community reminded the Panamanians constantly of their compromised aspirations and their impotence in dealing with the United States. The West Indians often became scapegoats. At times a clamor arose to deport them, as in 1926 and 1933. Their citizenship and civil rights stood in jeopardy in the 1930s and early 1940s. Many Panamanians imitated Zonian racism by calling the West Indians *chombos*, an offensive and derogatory term.

Yet throughout this unhappy era, some Panamanians defended the West Indians and reminded their countrymen that their national ideals included racial equality, democracy, and tolerance of diversity. Making the West Indians scapegoats violated these ideals and played into the hands of the Zonians. From 1944 on, this liberal view gained ascendancy over the chauvinism of earlier years.

Panamanian rejection of the West Indians was also caused by the third-country labor system. Early on, canal administrators had decided to rely primarily on West Indian laborers, who were powerless because they could not call upon either U.S. or Panamanian authorities to help them improve wages and benefits. Although most were British subjects, they could not expect much support from England due to the poverty and overpopulation of the West Indies. Reliance on West Indians allowed the canal to employ few native Panamanians. It also encouraged economic competition between the two groups and undermined their attempts to unionize. After 1944 West Indian descendants and Panamanians began to close the Anglo-Latin gap in order to work together against third-country labor exploitation. By the late 1950s they had succeeded, so that the system more resembled a split or dual one, with Americans on top and Panamanians underneath. The inequities of the split system were then more easily attacked. Elimination of the third-country labor system improved relations between Latin and West Indian Panamanians.

In the United States too, the racial and labor relations of the Canal Zone proved objectionable. American liberals continuously denounced segregation practices, though to little effect. Even when NAACP officials and other black leaders joined the assault, the canal managers protected segregation practices with a variety of subterfuges. The most blatant was the school conversion of 1954 to avoid applying the Supreme Court's *Brown* decision. From that moment on, the Zone fell behind Washington, D.C., in eliminating segregation. Yet racism became the Achilles' heel of the Zone, because in the 1970s American black leaders joined other reformers to destroy the Zonians' way of life. The army also found that racism undermined morale and since World War II had been slowly integrating its operations. By the 1970s, Zone race policies had to change.

The labor system also provoked debate in the United States, although no deep moral concerns surfaced as they did with the race issue. From the construction days on, members of Congress scrutinized canal operations to determine if the gold roll employees were receiving excessive wages and benefits. In 1921, the Connor Board investigation found that they were, and that unions controlled management. They recommended silverization, or replacement of most North Americans with native or West Indian workers. In the late 1940s, the McSherry and Vietheer reports criticized the disparities in wages and called for a more equitable single-wage scale. Even in the 1970s, the House Subcommittee on the Panama Canal and the GAO found that Americans enjoyed unfair advantages over noncitizen employees. To be sure, gradual improvements had almost eliminated the gap by the time the treaty was signed. But the practice of paying different wages for the same work had discredited Zone policies for far too long.

Why did the racial and labor systems of the Zone last so long when officials in Washington wanted them changed? How could Zonians defy the wishes of secretaries of the army or even presidents to reform Zone society? In the 1920s canal officials sat on Secretary of War Weeks's orders to implement silverization. In 1940–1941 they disregarded Roosevelt's advice not to recruit West Indians for the third locks work. In the late 1940s they refused to establish a single wage scale despite Truman's desires to end obvious inequities. Even when Congress mandated a single wage in PL 85-550, canal administrators managed to perpetuate old privileges for Americans.[10] In fact, their ability to defy Washington was one of the surprise discoveries of this study.

Several explanations account for the Canal Zone's successful resistance to orders for reform. First, the distance from Washington and the foreign setting gave the Zone special attributes that officials always cited when defending their policies. They spoke of Caribbean area wages, time-honored customs, overseas hardships, and tropical practices. They raised the fear that tinkering from Washington could jeopardize the efficiency of the canal, its defenses, or U.S. relations with Panama.

Second, the canal depended upon appropriations and hence came under congressional influence. Milton Eisenhower put his finger on the problem: jurisdiction was divided among too many agencies, the least effective of which was the State Department. Thus by the time necessary consultations had been held, the original urge for reform had diminished. Oftentimes a governor who attempted to carry out a policy had been replaced by the time it was implemented.

Third, the bureaucracy sustained policies inaugurated decades before, ignoring or denying circumstances that justified new ones. Nobody conspired to preserve the old ways. The administrative files themselves contained a view of the canal and its employees that justified the traditional ways. Even army officers rotated into the Zone, who were usually the most open-minded administrators there, fell victim to the files and preferred to follow "the way it has always been done."[11] In order to find some other modus operandi, officials would have had to spend a great deal of time in Panama and in the silver towns talking with laborers. And the few who did were ostracized by the civilian Zonians. Many abandoned reforms due to adverse responses from their staffs. Governors Jay Morrow (1921–1924) and William Carter (1960–1962) cut their tours short after encountering vicious opposition. Engineer of Maintenance Vogel, in line for the governorship in 1952, was blocked by Zonian opposition.

Fourth, the Canal Zone's strategic value provided reasons against changes. As long as the canal enjoyed top priority in military planning, authorities in Washington resisted the urge for reform, for fear that they might endanger the canal. Even after its demotion as a strategic defense site after 1945, Washington officials—and the public at large—continued to regard the Zone as untouchable. The myth of the canal's military value persisted into the 1970s and nearly caused the Senate to kill the Carter-Torrijos Treaty.

Finally, the labor system resisted change because it brought economic benefits to the United States. The third-country labor system cost less and afforded management more control than any other arrangement available. This meant that the fewest supervisors were required to oversee the maximum number of noncitizen workers. Time and again, personnel officials and governors explained the economics of the gold and silver system to congressmen, visitors, and union officials. They usually cited reasons of economy when turning down requests for higher wages and benefits. Any administrator takes pride in holding down costs, and canal officials were no exception. The split labor system after the 1950s was less economical than its predecessor, but it still saved a great deal over a unified wage scale.

Given all these reasons, it is not hard to understand why Canal Zone administrators opposed reforms over the years, usually successfully. The canal constituted the centerpiece of our colonial presence in Latin America, and to tamper with it—much less, give it up—was unacceptable to an American public conditioned to think of it as a symbol of national power. The Senate's approval of the Carter-Torrijos Treaty was a major step in the process of American decolonization of the region.

The fact that the treaty did win approval and has so far been implemented without major problems suggests that American foreign policy has gained maturity over recent years. Ronald Reagan, a powerful opponent of the treaty, defeated Jimmy Carter for the presidency in 1980, yet the new administration did not alter the agreement. Even Torrijos's death in 1981 did not disrupt the gradual incorporation of Panamanians into canal management. In fact, since 1979 diplomatic relations between the two countries have been calmer than at any other time in the past eighty years. Differences will undoubtedly occur in the future, but they should be soluble under the terms of the treaty and the 1979 Panama Canal Act.

Perhaps it is too soon to conclude that the West Indians and their descendants in Panama have become fully integrated into and accepted by Panamanian society. Yet the process has advanced enough to make such a future probable. The same confidence may be applied to the Carter-Torrijos Treaty. Seen in the long term, these two achievements are especially positive, given the hostility that has so often been the response to the West Indians of the isthmus and the perennially poor relations between the United States and Panama over the canal that was once a wonder of the world.

Abbreviations

Notes

Selected Bibliography

Index

Abbreviations

AFL	American Federation of Labor
AFT	American Federation of Teachers
APODAN	Association of Professionals, Workers, and Managers of Black Descent (Asociación de Profesionales, Obreros, y Dirigentes de Ascendencia Negra)
ARENEP	Panamanian Negro Defense Group (Acción Reivindicadora del Negro Panameño)
CFLU	Colón Federal Labor Union
CIO	Congress of Industrial Organizations
CIT	Interamerican Confederation of Workers (Confederación Interamericana de Trabajadores)
CPN	National Patriotic Coalition (Coalición Patriótica Nacional)
CTAL	Confederation of Latin American Workers (Confederación de Trabajadores de América Latina)
FHA	Federal Housing Authority
GAO	General Accounting Office
ILA	International Longshoremen's Association
INYC	Isthmian Negro Youth Congress
IWW	Industrial Workers of the World
MTC/CLU	Metal Trades Council/Central Labor Union
NAACP	National Association for the Advancement of Colored People
NMU	National Maritime Union
PAWB	Panama Area Wage Base
PCWIEA	Panama Canal West Indian Employees Association

Abbreviations

PPP	Panama for the Panamanians (Panamá Para los Panameños)
SRB	Silver Rates Board
UNIA	United Negro Improvement Association
UPWA	United Public Workers of America

Notes

Chapter 1: Introduction

1. The best surveys of this period are Lancelot S. Lewis, *The West Indian in Panama, 1850–1914* (Washington, D.C.: University Press of America, 1980); Velma Eudora Newton, "British West Indian Emigration to the Isthmus of Panama, 1850–1914," M.A. thesis, University of the West Indies, 1973; Olive Senior, "The Panama Railway," *Jamaica Journal* 14 (1980): 66–77; and Olive Senior, "The Colon People," 2 pts., *Jamaica Journal* 11–12 (1978): 62–71, 87–103.

2. George W. Westerman, *Los inmigrantes antillanos en Panamá* (Panamá: Impresora de la Nación, 1980); and Sadith Esther Paz, "The Status of West Indian Immigrants in Panama from 1850–1941," M.A. thesis, University of Massachusetts, Amherst, 1977, are good overviews.

3. The best introduction to racial and cultural interaction in the Caribbean basin is Harry Hoetink, *Slavery and Race Relations* (New York: Harper and Row, 1973), pt. 2.

4. The official version is Robert E. Wood, "The Working Force of the Panama Canal," in *The Panama Canal: An Engineering Treatise*, 2 vols., ed. George W. Goethals (New York: McGraw-Hill, 1916).

5. See Raymond Allan Davis, "West Indian Workers on the Panama Canal: A Split Labor Market Interpretation," Ph.D. diss., Stanford University, 1981, ch. 1.

6. Werner Cahnman, "The Mediterranean and Caribbean Regions—A comparison in Race and Culture Contrasts," *Social Forces* 22 (1943): 214.

7. Walter LaFeber, *The Panama Canal: The Crisis in Historical Perspective*, rev. ed. (New York: Oxford University Press, 1979) is an essential introduction.

8. William Archer, *Through Afro-America: An English Reading of the Race Problem*, 2d ed. (Westport, Conn.: Negro Universities Press, 1970), pp. 272–74.

[185]

9. Edwin Slosson and Garner Richardson, "Two Panama Life Stories," *Independent*, 19 April 1906, p. 923; John Biesanz and Mavis Biesanz, *The People of Panama* (New York: Columbia University Press, 1955), p. 214.

10. A. Beeby Thompson, "The Labour Problem of the Panama Canal," *Engineering*, 3 May 1907, p. 590.

11. CO to FO, 1 February 1908, in F0371/493/3821.

12. Olivier report, November 1911, in F0369/492/12126.

13. Kenneth E. Goldsberry, "The Strike of 1920: A Study of the Black Labor Movement in the Canal Zone," Panama Canal Collection, unpublished, pp. 45–46.

14. See, for example, the editorial in the *Panama Tribune*, 6 April 1930.

15. John Biesanz, "Cultural and Economic Factors in Panamanian Race Relations," *American Sociological Review* 14 (1949): 772–73; Willis Fletcher Johnson, *Four Centuries of the Panama Canal* (New York: Henry Holt, 1907), p. 356; John Biesanz and Luke M. Smith, "Race Relations in Panama and the Canal Zone," *American Journal of Sociology* 45 (July 1941): 7–14.

16. Biesanz, "Cultural and Economic Factors," pp. 775–76.

17. Alda Harper, *Tracing the Course of Growth and Development in Educational Policy for the Canal Zone Colored Schools, 1905–1955* (Ann Arbor: University of Michigan School of Education, 1979) is the best overview.

18. See especially George Westerman's 1970s essay, "For a More Unified Panamanian Nation," and "Fifty Years of West Indian Life in Panama, 1904–1954," unpublished, Westerman papers.

Chapter 2: West Indians in Panama Before 1903

1. Carlos Reid, *Memorias de un criollo bocatoreño—Light in Dark Places*, ed. Stanley Heckadon Moreno (Panamá: Asociación Panameña de Antropología, 1980), pp. 9–12, and chs. 6 and 12, *passim*.

2. Bonham Richardson, introduction to *Caribbean Migrants* (Knoxville: University of Tennessee Press, 1983), and "Freedom and Migration in the Leeward Caribbean, 1838–48," *Journal of Historical Geography* 6 (1980): 391–408; G.W. Roberts, "Emigration from the Island of Barbados," *Social and Economic Studies* 4 (1955): 245–50.

3. Olive Senior, "The Panama Railway," *Jamaica Journal* 14 (1980): 66–77.

4. Velma Eudora Newton, "British West Indian Emigration to the Isthmus of Panama, 1850–1914," M.A. thesis, University of the West Indies, 1973, p. 21; Olive Senior, "The Colon People," *Jamaica Journal* 11–12 (1978): 64. Statistics on migration are confusing. Those on departures from the islands overlook thousands who sailed from smaller islands or unpoliced ports, yet they count multiple exits of the same person. The figure 50,000 is from Mallet to Grey, 12 September 1906, in F0371/101/34896.

5. Charles D. Kepner, Jr., *Social Aspects of the Banana Industry* (New York: Columbia University Press, 1936); Humberto Ricord et al., *Panamá y la frutera* (Panamá: Editorial Universitaria, 1978); Frederick Upham Adams, *Conquest of the Tropics* (Garden City, N.Y.: Doubleday, Page, 1914), pp. 35–85. For a revealing diary of an Englishwoman in Bocas, see Winifred James, *Out of the Shadows* (London: Chapman and Hall, 1924), pp. 8–65.

6. Alfredo Figueroa Navarro, *Dominio y sociedad en el Panamá colombiano (1821–1903)* (Panamá: Impresora Panamá, 1978), ch. 7; Omar Jaén Suárez, *La población del Istmo de Panamá del siglo XVI al siglo XX* (Panamá: Instituto Nacional de Cultura, 1978), pp. 531–41.

7. Allen Glenn Morton, "The Private Schools of the British West Indians in Panama," Ph.D. diss., George Peabody College for Teachers, 1966, pp. 9–18; Senior, "The Colon People," p. 100.

8. George Westerman, "Fifty Years of West Indian Life in Panama, 1904–1954," unpublished, ch. 6, in Westerman papers; *Canal Record*, 1 January 1908, p. 139.

9. Senior, "The Colon People," pp. 94–98; Alfredo Castillero Calvo, *Los negros y mulatos libres en la historia social panameña* (Panamá: Impresora Panamá, 1969), pp. 1, 15–16; Roberto de la Guardia, *Los negros del Istmo de Panamá* (Panamá: Ediciones Instituto Nacional de Cultura, 1977), pp. 7–11.

10. Alex Perez-Venero, *Before the Five Frontiers: Panama, 1821–1903* (New York: AMS Press, 1978), ch. 5; Gustavo Adolfo Mellander, *The United States in Panamanian Politics: The Intriguing Formative Years* (Danville, Ill.: Interstate Printers and Publishers, 1971), p. 99.

11. Figueroa Navarro, *Dominio y sociedad*, pp. 337–44; Jaén Suárez, *La Población del Istmo*, pp. 448–51.

12. Pérez-Venero, *Before the Five Frontiers*, pp. 113–15; Eduardo Lemaitre, *Panamá y su separación de Colombia* (Bogotá: Biblioteca Banco Popular, 1972), pp. 152–56.

13. Gadpaille to Stevens, 5 July 1905, in PCC 2-E-2/Jamaica; Roberts, "Emigration from the Island of Barbados," pp. 256–57. The best accounts in English are David McCullough, *The Path Between the Seas* (New York: Simon and Schuster, 1977), bk. 1; and Gerstle Mack, *The Land Divided* (New York: Knopf, 1944), pt. 3.

14. The governors' reports, available in the *British Parliamentary Papers, Colonies General* (*BPP*), cover the subject but were drafted for public scrutiny and were not wholly candid. The quote is from Jamaica #14, 17 April 1883.

15. Ibid., Jamaica #112, 21 July 1890. Cf. Senior, "The Colon People," pp. 92–94.

16. McCullough, *The Path Between the Seas*, ch. 6. Any statistics are merely guesses, but this one is often cited.

17. Walter LaFeber argues this point forcefully in several books, including *The Panama Canal: The Crisis in Historical Perspective*, rev. ed. (New York: Oxford University Press, 1979), ch. 2.

18. David Healy, *U.S. Expansionism: The Imperialist Urge in the 1890s* (Madison: University of Wisconsin Press, 1970), p. 155.

19. Quoted in Thomas A. Bailey, *A Diplomatic History of the American People* (New York: Appleton, Century, Crofts, 1958), p. 245.

20. Howard K. Beale, *Theodore Roosevelt and the Rise of America to World Power* (New York: Collier Books, 1962), pp. 44–48. Even the anti-imperialists agreed on the question of race: see Healy, *U.S. Expansionism*, pp. 39–41, 123, 240–45; and Christopher Lasch, "The Anti-Imperialists, the Philippines, and the Inequality of Man," *Journal of Southern History* 24 (August 1958): 319–31.

Chapter 3: The Construction Era, 1904–1914

1. Robert E. Wood, "The Working Force of the Panama Canal," in *The Panama Canal: An Engineering Treatise*, ed. George W. Goethals (New York: McGraw-Hill, 1916), 2: 195–98; 1904–12, *passim*, in PCC 2-E-2/Jamaica, and PCC 2-E-1; Velma Eudora Newton, "British West Indian Emigration to the Isthmus of Panama, 1850–1914," M.A. thesis, University of the West Indies,

1973, pp. 148–55; *Canal Record,* 28 October 1914, pp. 91–92; Raymond Allan Davis, "West Indian Workers on the Panama Canal: A Split Labor Market Interpretation," Ph.D. diss., Stanford University, 1981, pp. 81–99.

2. Mallet to FO, 12 September 1906, in F0371/101/34896; U.S. Congress, Senate, *Hearings before the Committee on Interoceanic Canals . . . An Investigation of Matters Relating to the Panama Canal* (Washington, D.C.: Government Printing Office, 1906–07), pp. 680–81. Cf. ICC, *Annual Report,* 1905, pp. 9–11, and 1906, p. 5. For a representative description of the West Indians, see Frederick J. Haskin, *The Panama Canal* (Garden City, N.Y.: Doubleday, Page, 1913), ch. 13. Willis Fletcher Johnson, *Four Centuries of the Panama Canal* (New York: Henry Holt, 1907), pp. 354–59, discusses the labor question.

3. Taft to ICC Chairman Shonts, 13 April 1905, Moody to Taft, 5 June 1905, Shonts to Stevens, 29 November 1905, in PCC 2-E-1. U.S. Congress, Senate, *Hearings . . . Panama Canal,* p. 2575; Roosevelt to Taft, 27 July 1906, and Executive Order of 15 March 1907, in Taft papers, series 4A, LCMC; Magoon to Taft, 15 July 1904, in Taft papers, series 3, LCMC.

4. Stevens to Shonts, 4 May 1906 and 16 January 1907, Wood to Stevens, 22 October 1906, in PCC 2-E-1.

5. April and May 1907, *passim,* Gailliard to Stevens, 12 July 1907, Wood to Goethals, 20 May 1907 and 1 October 1913, in PCC 2-E-1.

6. U.S. Congress, House Committee on Appropriations, *Panama Canal—Skilled Labor, Extracts from Hearings, 1906–1914* (Washington, D.C.: Government Printing Office, 1915), pp. 107–10; U.S. Congress, Senate, *Hearings . . . Panama Canal,* pp. 2498–99.

7. Gerstle Mack, *The Land Divided* (New York: Knopf, 1944), ch. 44; Wood, "The Working Force," pp. 191–92.

8. Karner to Smith, 24 May and 3 July 1906, in PCC 2-E-2/Barbados; Gorgas circular, 11 April 1906, in PCC 2-E-1.

9. U.S. Congress, House Committee, *Panama Canal,* pp. 90–99; March 1906, *passim,* in PCC 2-E-2/Barbados.

10. JKB memo, accounting department, 13 August, 1908, in PCC 2-D-40.

11. U.S. Congress, House Committee, *Panama Canal,* p. 109; 1908–09, *passim,* in PCC 2-D-40; 1912–13, *passim,* in PCC 2-E-2/Barbados.

12. Newton, "British West Indian Emigration," p. 165; Mallet to FO, 30 October 1912, in F0371/1417/50353.

13. Magoon to Stevens, 14 November 1905, Belle Flanagan to Franklin Bell, 13 September 1908, in PCC 2-E-1; U.S. Congress, Senate, *Hearings . . . Panama Canal,* pp. 931–81.

14. H. S. Reed to Stevens, 16 March 1906, in PCC 11-E-6; Newton, "British West Indian Emigration," pp. 213–15; ICC, *Annual Report,* 1913, p. 373.

15. Sullivan to Magoon, 2 January 1906 and 1909 *passim,* in PCC 79-F-5; Mallet to FO, 9 November 1912, in F0371/1417/52667.

16. Newton, "British West Indian Emigration," pp. 208–12; Smith to Karner, 23 March 1906, in PCC 2-E-2/Barbados; Stevens to Shonts, 16 February 1907, in PCC 2-E-1; quote from John Oswald Butcher, "Reminiscences of Life and Work During the Construction of the Panama Canal," unpublished, IHS. Cf. U.S. Congress, Senate, *Hearings . . . Panama Canal,* pp. 2500–03, 2758–60; ICC, *Annual Report,* 1905, p. 8.

17. See Gorgas's report in ICC, *Annual Report,* 1913, pp. 526–29, and testimony in U.S. Congress, House Committee, *Panama Canal,* pp. 90–99, 107–10, 139–41, 221–25.

18. Tucker to Shannon, 1 September 1906 and Shannon to Williams, 10 April 1907, in PCC 2-F-14; Burnett to Stevens and Stevens to Burnett, 15 and 16

February 1907, in PCC 2-C-55; George Westerman, "Fifty Years of West Indian Life in Panama, 1904–1954," unpublished, Westerman papers, ch. 3.

19. Slifer to Gaillard, 12 and 15 February 1908, in PCC 2-F-14; "Privileges of Americans on Silver Roll," ca. 1916, in PCC 2-C-55; Davis, "West Indian Workers," pp. 4–9.

20. See 1908–10, *passim*, in PCC 2-E-11; and note 48 below.

21. October–December 1909, *passim*, in PCC 2-F-14.

22. Goethals to Smith, 25 September 1912, in PCC 2-P-49.

23. 1909–14 in PCC C/2-E-11/A; 1913–14, in PCC 2-E-11/P; 1909–13, in PCC 2-P-49/P; PCWIEA, *Annual Report*, 1936, pp. 13–17.

24. Goethals to secretary of war, 13 September 1910, Judson to Goethals, 22 October 1913, Goethals to Judson, 12 June 1912, in Goethals papers, LCMC.

25. Harry A. Franck, *Zone Policeman 88: A Close Range Study of the Panama Canal and Its Workers*, 2d ed. (New York: Arno, 1970), p. 119; U.S. Congress, Senate, *Hearings . . . Panama Canal*, pp. 52–53.

26. School children in 1909 were 35 percent southern, and in 1932 employees were 28 percent southern: see George Ninas report, 16 July 1913, in PCC 91-A-37; Alberto Wilson to Evans, 30 April 1932, in PCC 2-C-124; Wood, "The Working Force," p. 194; John Biesanz, "Cultural and Economic Factors in Panamanian Race Relations," *American Sociological Review* 14 (1949): 23; Franck, *Zone Policeman*, pp. 225–26.

27. Morrow to Connor, 19 July 1921, in PCC 28-B-5; *Panama Tribune*, 23 October 1955; Lewis interview, 8 August 1981.

28. Gaillard to Jackson Smith, 11 February 1907, Wood to Henry Smith, 24 July 1907, McIlvaine to Washington office, 18 July 1928, and 1907–12, *passim*, in PCC 2-C-55; Franck, *Zone Policeman*, p. 119.

29. Sullivan to Bolich, 4 August 1906, in PCC 2-F-14.

30. Burnett to Thomas O'Connell, 9 November 1905, in PCC 2-E-2/Jamaica; Burnett to Karner, 23 March 1906, in PCC 2-E-2/Barbados; Mallet to FO, 2 September 1907, in F0371/300/31889; Mallet to FO, 9 November 1912, in F0371/1417/52667.

31. Franck, *Zone Policeman*, p. 145; Slosson and Richardson, "Two Panama Life Stories," *Independent*, 19 April 1906, p. 922.

32. ICC, *Annual Report*, 1913, p. 486, and 1915, pp. 446–47.

33. Mallet to FO, 12 June 1911 and 2 May 1916, in F0371/1176/27051 and F0368/1086/175925, Bennett to FO, 1 March 1920, in F0371/4536/A986; U.S. Congress, Senate, *Hearings . . . Panama Canal*, p. 2766.

34. See 1905–13, *passim*, in PCC 2-P-59; unidentified to Walker, 4 October 1904, in PCC 2-D-40; Rosseau to Thatcher, 7 January 1913, in PCC 2-E-11; U.S. Congress, Senate, *Hearings . . . Panama Canal*, pp. 2265–67, 2730–34.

35. William D. McCain, *The United States and the Republic of Panama* (Durham, N.C.: Duke University Press, 1937), chs. 3–4; Gustavo Adolfo Mellander, *The United States in Panamanian Politics: The Intriguing Formative Years* (Dansville, Ill.: Interstate Printers and Publishers, 1971), pp. 66–67.

36. "Affray between Jamaican laborers and Panama Police," in C0137/645/19405 and C0137/646/29539; *Foreign Relations of the United States*, 1905, pp. 709–12.

37. Mallet to FO, 12 June 1911 and 14 March 1919, in F0371/11761/27051 and F0371/3857/17158; Franck, *Zone Policeman*, p. 231.

38. Police chief to John Carr, reporter for *Outlook Magazine*, 17 April 1906, in PCC C/28-B-233; Newton, "British West Indian Emigrants," p. 206; Skinner to Shannon, 8 April 1907, in PCC 2-P-59.

39. Mallet to FO, 4 April 1914, in F0371/2058/18805; William Archer,

Through Afro-America: An English Reading of the Race Problem (Westport, Conn.: Negro Universities Press, 1970), p. 284; Wayne Bray, *The Common Law Zone in Panama: A Case Study in Reception* (San Juan, P.R.: Inter-American University Press, 1977), p. 104; A. Beeby Thompson, "The Labour Problem of the Panama Canal," *Engineering*, 3 May 1907, p. 590; U.S. Congress, Senate, *Hearings . . . Panama Canal*, p. 81; quotation from Harrigan Austin, "Reminiscences of Life and Work," unpublished, IHS.

40. Stevens to Shonts, 19 April 1906, Belding to Rousseau, 17 January 1907, and 1904–11, *passim*, in PCC 28-A-31; *Canal Record*, 4 December 1907, p. 107, and 1 January 1908, p. 139.

41. Lancelot S. Lewis, *The West Indian in Panama: Black Labor in Panama* (Washington, D.C.: University Press of America, 1980), p. 73; 1906–14, *passim*, in PCC 28-A-32/Alpha.

42. Rufus Lane to Magoon, 8 August 1906, and 1904–13, *passim*, in PCC 91-A-39; 1904–13, *passim*, in PCC 91-A-37; annual school reports, 1905–13, Webster papers; George W. Westerman, "School Segregation in the Panama Canal Zone," *Phylon* 3 (1954):276; "Press comments on the CZ Schools Changes, 1954," Westerman papers.

43. *Panama Journal*, 12 October 1908 and Moore to Chief of Record Bureau, 13 May 1943, in PCC 91-A-39; Alda Harper, *Tracing the Course of Growth and Development in Educational Policy for the Canal Zone Colored Schools, 1905–1955* (Ann Arbor: University of Michigan School of Education, 1979), ch. 2; Osborne biographical sketches in George W. Westerman, *Pioneers in Canal Zone Education* (Panama Canal Zone: n.p., 1949), pp. 13–20; Lowell C. Wilson et al., *Schooling in the Panama Canal Zone, 1904–1979* (Panama Canal Area: Phi Delta Kappa, 1980), pp. 106–10.

44. Harper, *Tracing the Course of Growth*, p. 59.

45. MCL memo, 20 July 1911, Thatcher to Goethals, 4 August 1911, O'Connor to Reed, 1 May 1907, in PCC 91-A-39.

46. Walter LaFeber, *The Panama Canal: The Crisis in Historical Perspective*, rev. ed. (New York: Oxford University Press, 1979), ch. 2; Mellander, *The United States in Panamanian Politics*, chs. 5–12, *passim;* 1904–15, *passim*, in PCC 80-F-9, PCC 79-F-5, PCC 58-A-1, PCC 94-A-3/T, and PCC 58-A-6; Mallet to FO, 1 February 1909, in F0368/315/9133; *Canal Record*, 18 December 1907, pp. 121–22; Antonio Burgos, *Panamá y su inmigración* (Panamá: Imprenta Nacional, 1913), pp. 104–07.

47. *Foreign Relations of the United States*, 1906, 2:1196.

48. Taft to Roosevelt, 16 May 1908, in Taft papers, semi-official, LCMC; Collins, "Relative Rights of citizens," 5 March 1919, U.S. chargé to Jackson Smith, 6 June 1919, and State Dept. to War Dept., 19 June 1919, in PCC 2-E-12.

49. See 1919, *passim*, in PCC 2-E-12.

50. Executive order 1888 (2 February 1914), in PCC 2-D-4.

51. HR 27250, *Congressional Record*, 9 February 1909, p. 2168, remitted in F0371/785/7443; Mallet to FO, 19 June 1913, in F0371/1703/33655; 1909–14, *passim*, in PCC 80-F-9.

52. Roosevelt to Taft, 19 December 1904, and 13 April 1905, in Taft papers, semiofficial, LCMC; Squiers, quoted in Mellander, *The United States in Panamanian Politics*, p. 124.

53. Mellander, *The United States in Panamanian Politics*, pp. 134–35.

54. Chalkley to FO, 14 March 1910, and Mallet to FO, 15 June 1910, in F0371/944/11516 and 25146; Thatcher to Goethals, 29 June 1910, in Goethals papers, LCMC.

55. Marsh to State Dept., 28 July 1910, Goethals to secretary of war, 13 September 1910, in Goethals papers, LCMC.

56. See State Dept. files 847 and 819.00 for 1910, RG 59, USNA.

57. Mallet to FO, 22 August 1910, in F0371/944/33140.

58. Goethals to Wilson, 4 December 1912, in PCC 2-C-124; Goethals to Witlock, 2 August 1912, in PCC 58-A-13.

59. Goethals to Boggs, 20 March 1915, in PCC 2-E-11.

Chapter 4: Consolidation of Zone Life and Panama's Reaction, 1914–1929

1. Major General [illegible] to Goethals, 9 October 1913, in PCC 2-C-124; Delaney to Goethals, 7 January 1914, in Goethals papers, LCMC; Olivier report, November 1911, in F0369/492/12126; U.S. Adjutant General's Office, *History of the Panama Canal Department*, 4 vols. (microfilm of typescript in PC, 1947), 1:15; Goethals visit to State Dept., 7 October 1916, in file 711.19/15, RG 59, USNA.

2. Schley to secretary of war, 1 August 1936, in PCC 65-J-3; Raymond Allan Davis, "West Indian Workers on the Panama Canal: A Split Labor Market Interpretation," Ph.D. diss., Stanford University, 1981, ch. 3.

3. Olivier report, November 1911, in F0369/492/12126.

4. Mallet to FO, 22 January 1912, in F0371/1417/7341; Mallet to FO, 15 April 1912 and 8 August 1913, in F0371/1703/40088 and 40448; Mallet to FO, 28 October 1912, and CO to FO, 18 September 1912, in F0371/1703/50350 and 39390; 1913, *passim*, in F0369/604.

5. Mallet reports for 1913, *passim*, in F0371/1703.

6. Mallet to FO, 12 January 1912, in F0371/1417/5404; George W. Goethals, *The Government of the Canal Zone* (Princeton, N.J.: Princeton University Press, 1915), p. 64.

7. Goethals, *The Government of the Canal Zone*, pp. 65–69, 92–93; George W. Westerman, "Fifty Years of West Indian Life in Panama, 1904–1954," unpublished, Westerman papers, pp. 64–65; "History of rental rates for Local Rate Quarters," 4 November 1914, and 1915–16, *passim*, in PCC 11-E-6; "Depopulation," *Canal Record*, 21 March 1917, pp. 387–89.

8. *Canal Record*, 6 October 1915, p. 56; Police Chief Barker to Goethals, 10 August 1914, Harding to Mallet, 15 July 1916, and Dunsmoor to acting executive secretary, 19 October 1915, in PCC 46-D-8; Westerman, "Fifty Years," pp. 64–65; Colonel Robert Wood, quoted in ICC, *Annual Report*, 1914, p. 271; Collins to SRB, 7 October 1921, in PCC 2-D-40.

9. Wilson to McIlvaine, 5 August 1916, and 1914–18, *passim*, in PCC 79-F-5, Jno. Smith to McIlvaine, 20 September 1921, and Gilkey to McIlvaine, 20 October 1921, in PCC 46-D-8.

10. Data from Collins memo of 7 October 1921, in PCC 2-D-40. Number of employees has been adjusted upward to account for those of private contractors. See ICC, *Annual Report*, 1915, pp. 238–39.

11. Gilkey to governor, 19 August 1919, file 10,634–672, War Dept., Military Intelligence Div., RG 165, USNA; Collins memo, 7 October 1921, in PCC 2-D-40; anon. to Harding, 6 September 1918, in PCC 2-P-70.

12. Wood to Harding, 10 May 1915, and 1915–16, *passim*, in PCC 11-E-6; Harding's congressional testimony, 16 January 1917, in PCC 13-Q-1.

13. U.S. Congress, House Committee on Appropriations, *Panama Canal— Skilled Labor, Extracts from Hearings, 1906–1914* (Washington, D.C.: Government Printing Office, 1915), p. 378.

14. Ibid., pp. 375–77.

15. Emilio Elizaga to H. A. A. Smith, 3 August 1918, in PCC C/28-B-233.

16. SRB minutes, 8 January 1919, in PCC 2-F-14.

17. Westerman, "Fifty Years," pp. 34–41; Davis, "West Indian Workers," pp. 106–24; Harding testimony, 8 January 1917, in PCC 13-Q-1; Mallet to FO, 27 October 1916, in F0368/1584/233173; *West Indian Progress*, 16 November 1916, and 1916, *passim*, in PCC 2-D-40; Harding to Goethals, 20 October 1916, Goethals papers, LCMC; file 2479520, Office of Adjutant General, RG 94, USNA.

18. See 1916–18, *passim*, in PCC 2-P-70.

19. A. Blanchfield Thompson, *Resume of the Silver Employees' Strike on the Canal Zone* (Panamá: author, 1920), pp. 7–8.

20. Murray to FO, 10 May 1919, in F0371/3857/89214; *Workman*, 12 April 1919.

21. Flint (Washington office) to Harding, 11 April 1919, PCC 2-P-70; *Workman*, 12 July 1919.

22. Hernando Franco Munoz, *Movimiento obrero panameño, 1914–1921* (Panamá: author, 1979), pp. 18–20; Gilkey to Harding, 18 August 1919, file 10,634–672, War Dept., Military Intelligence Div., RG 165, USNA; *Workman*, May 1919, *passim*.

23. Murray to FO, 10 May 1919, F0371/3857/89214; Kenneth E. Goldsberry, "The Strike of 1920: A Study of the Black Labor Movement in the Canal Zone," unpublished, Panama Canal Collection.

24. E.g., editorial, *Workman*, 16 August 1919.

25. List of 1 September 1919, in PCC C/2-P-59/20. This eight-part file contains the most complete documentation on the strike. See also *Workman*, 3 September 1919.

26. Williams to secretary of war, 24 July 1919, in PCC C/2-C-129.

27. See 1917–19, *passim*, in PCC 2-P-70.

28. Harding to quartermaster general, 27 September 1919, in PCC C/28-B-233; *Workman*, 4 October and 29 November 1919; 1919–20, *passim*, in PCC C/2-P-59/20.

29. *Workman*, 22 November 1919; Collins memo, 7 October 1921, in PCC 2-D-40; Graham to FO, 25 November 1921, in F0371/7233/A9 and A6093; Westerman, "Fifty Years," pp. 41–55.

30. Undated roster, ca. March 1920, in PCC C/2-P-59/20.

31. *Workman*, 27 December 1919, and 2 January 1920. President Lefevre stepped down from office on 30 January 1920.

32. SRB minutes, 2 January 1920, in PCC 2-D-40/B.

33. *Workman*, 17 and 24 January 1920.

34. February 1920, *passim*, in PCC-2-D-40/B; Collins memo, 7 October 1921, in PCC 2-D-40.

35. Flint (Washington office) to Harding, 30 September 1919, in PCC 2-P-70, Barker to Saunders, 5 August 1919, in PCC C/2-P-59/20; Flint to secretary of war and Randolf to military staff, Washington, 11 February 1920, file 10,6234/-672, War Dept., Military Intelligence Div., RG 165, USNA.

36. Official announcements appeared in the *Canal Record*.

37. *Workman*, 21 June 1920.

38. 1920, *passim*, in PCC C/2-E-11/A.

39. Bennett to FO, 1, 6, and 11 March 1920, in F0371/4536/A986, A1127, A2185.

40. The report is in Bennett to FO, 7 May 1921, in F0371/5594/A3911. Cf. Bennett's and Graham's correspondence of May–November 1920, in

F0371/4536/A3530, A5783, A8751; and Graham to commission, 21 May 1920, in PCC 2-D-40.

41. *Workman*, 26 June 1926; Olmedo Alfaro, *El peligro antillano en la América Central: La defensa de la raza*, 2d ed. (Panamá; Imprenta Nacional, 1926), pp. 13–15.

42. *Congressional Record*, 14 May 1921, pp. 1456–57; *Canal Record*, 22 June 1921, p. 697.

43. *Report of the Special Panama Canal Commission* (Washington, D.C.: Government Printing Office, 1922); Graham to FO, 8 July and 25 November 1921, in F0371/5602/A5449 and F0371/7233/A9.

44. Morrow to Connor, 19 July 1921, in PCC 28-B-5; Morrow to Weeks, 17 September 1921, in *Report of the Special Panama Canal Commission*, pp. 38–52; Morrow to Weeks, 3 October 1921, in PCC 28-B-5/B, Evans to Superintendent, 18 November 1921, in PCC 2-E-11.

45. Hushing to McConaughey, 22 October 1921, in PCC 2-E-11/P; A. J. Berres, AFL president, to President Harding, 8 December 1921, in PCC 2-E-11; Weeks to Morrow, 18 October 1921, in *Report of the Special Panama Canal Commission*, pp. 53–64.

46. Morrow to McConaughey, 26 November 1921, and 1921, *passim*, in PCC 2-E-11; *Workman*, 29 October, and 3 December 1921; Morrow testimony, U.S. Congress, Subcommittee of the House Committee on Appropriations, *War Department Appropriation Bill, 1923 . . . Panama Canal* (Washington, D.C.: Government Printing Office, 1922), pp. 454, 473–512, 522–23.

47. Graham to FO, 6–7 and 10 October 1921, in F0371/5602/A7406 and A8053; Graham to FO, 18 August 1922, in F0371/7233/A6093; Mallet to FO, n.d. [1916], in F0368/1086/175925.

48. Burgess to department heads, 16 November 1928, in PCC 2-D-40.

49. Extract from hearings on HR 10646, 29 June 1922, in PCC 2-E-11.

50. Flint to governor, 20 September 1921, in PCC 2-E-11/P; Wallis to FO, 15 and 20 January 1924, in F0371/9579/A1141 and A1143.

51. Jorge L. Paredes, in *Star and Herald*, 30 November 1919; Wallis to FO, 15 January 1924, in F0371/9579/A1141. Cf. Davis, "West Indian Workers," pp. 135–38, and Westerman, "Fifty Years," pp. 97–101.

52. Sadith Esther Paz, "The Status of West Indian Immigrants in Panama from 1850–1941," M.A. thesis, University of Massachusetts, Amherst, 1977, p. 38; "The Chombo Competition," *Workman*, 25 June 1921.

53. Special issue on the rent strikes, *Loteria* 213 (October–November 1973).

54. Alfaro, *El Peligro antillano*.

55. *Workman*, 11 September–23 October 1926; Panamá, Ministerio de Relaciones Exteriores, *Ley 13 de 1926 sobre inmigración* (Panamá: Imprenta Nacional, 1926); Paz, "The Status of West Indian Immigrants," pp. 62–63. Immigration laws since 1904 had excluded other groups as undesirables: Chinese, Syrians, Turks, and "North Africans of the Turkish race." This was the first time the list included West Indian blacks.

56. *Workman*, 30 October 1926; William D. McCain, *The United States and the Republic of Panama* (Durham, N.C.: Duke University Press, 1937), ch. 11.

57. *Gazeta Oficial*, 20 January 1927; legislative act of 19 October 1928, enclosed in Narciso Garay to McIlvaine, 17 October 1939, in PCC 80-F-9; 1917–35, *passim*, in PCC 94-N-3/C.

58. *Report of the Health Department of the Panama Canal for the Calendar Year 1930* (Mt. Hope: Canal Zone Press, 1931).

59. See Mallet to FO, 26 March 1918, in F0369/1011/71576, on repatriation of several dozen insane persons.

60. Murray to Mallet, 15 August 1916, in F0368/10861/175925.

61. *Report of Health Department*, pp. 20–23.

62. *Workman*, 20 January 1929.

63. *Workman*, 6 January 1923, 22 December 1926; Bennett to FO, 7 April 1921, in F0371/5602/A3197; *Panama Tribune*, 13 January 1929, 18 May 1930.

64. Mallet to governor of Jamaica, 17 July 1918, in F0369/1011/137904; 11 January–1 July 1919 *passim*, in F0371/3856.

65. *Workman*, 28 June 1919; Westerman interview, 1 February 1981; Gittens interview, 5 July 1981; Velma Eudora Newton, "British West Indian Emigration to the Isthmus of Panama, 1850–1914," M.A. thesis, University of the West Indies, 1973, p. 243; *Workman*, 5 March 1927.

66. *Canal Record*, 3 March 1920, pp. 240–41; *Report of the Special Panama Canal Commission*, p. 16; annual reports of the schools, 1923 and 1928–30, in Webster papers; Alda Harper, *Tracing the Course of Growth and Development in Educational Policy for the Zone Colored Schools, 1905–1955* (Ann Arbor: University of Michigan School of Education, 1979), ch. 3.

67. Harper, *Tracing the Course of Growth*, pp. 84–89; "Statistical Summaries," Webster papers.

68. Mallet to FO, 4 October 1911, in F0371/1176/42972.

69. *Workman*, 6 January 1923; Allen Glenn Morton, "The Private Schools of the British West Indians in Panama," Ph.D. diss., George Peabody College for Teachers, 1966, pp. 65–108, *passim*.

70. Westerman, "Fifty Years," ch. 7; 1920–29, *passim*, in PCC 28-A-31; Charles Barton, "Towards the Development of Panama: The Afro-Panamanian Contribution," unpublished, ch. 6.

71. Westerman, "Fifty Years," pp. 55–63; March–October 1924, *passim*, in PCC 2-P-70; *Panama Tribune*, 31 March, and 7 April 1929.

72. PCWIEA, *Annual Report*, 1926, 1933; *Panama Tribune* 3 September 1966; Davis, "West Indian Workers," pp. 128–33; Barton interview, 11 August 1981.

73. *Workman*, 10 May 1919; *Panama Tribune*, 7 April 1929, 22 March 1931, 11 September 1932, 25 September 1932; Westerman, "Fifty Years," pp. 138–42.

74. Jamaica Provident and Benevolent Society file, 1927–33, *passim*, in PCC 28-A-12/Alpha; John Biesanz and Mavis Biesanz, *The People of Panama* (New York: Columbia University Press, 1955), pp. 376–78.

75. War Dept., Military Intelligence Div., file 10218-418, RG 165, USNA; *Workman*, April and May 1921, *passim*; Robert G. Weisbord, *Ebony Kinship: Africa, Africans, and the Afro-American* (Westport, Conn.: Greenwood Press, 1973), p. 60.

76. *Workman*, 8 October, 10 December 1927; *Panama Tribune*, 27 April 1930.

77. George Westerman, "Glimpses of West Indian Life . . . and Isthmian Negro Press," Westerman papers; *Workman*, 13 February 1926; *Panama Tribune*, 2 March 1947; Westerman, "Fifty Years," pp. 162–64.

78. *Panama Tribune*, 21 August 1932, 11 November 1928; Westerman interview, 1 February 1981.

79. Mallet to FO, 17 September 1918, in F0371/3485/170211; *Panama Tribune*, 2 March 1947; *Panama American*, 29 November 1936; Westerman, "Fifty Years," pp. 164–66.

80. *Panama Tribune*, 4 May 1930, 13 September 1969, 20 January 1929; Chesney McDonald interviews, 10, 13 July 1981.

81. *Workman*, 15 October 1927, 20 March 1926; Giscome interview, 15 July 1981.

Chapter 5: Depression, War, and Chauvinism: 1930–1945

1. *Panama Tribune*, 17 July 1932, 4 June, 16 July 1933; Flint (Washington office) to Burgess, 6 February 1931, in PCC C/2-E-12, SRB, 28 July 1932, in PCC 2-D-40; Almon R. Wright, "The United States and Panama, 1933–1949," U.S. Department of State, research report 499, August 1952, pp. 29–34.

2. *Workman*, 29 March 1930; *Panama Tribune*, 5 January 1930.

3. Burgess to Denison, 18 January 1930, in PCC 2-D-40; *Panama Tribune*, 10 May 1931; PC, *Annual Report*, 1931, pp. 70–78; George W. Westerman, "Fifty Years of West Indian Life in Panama, 1904–1954," unpublished, Westerman papers, pp. 65–67.

4. N. L. Englehardt, *Report of the Survey of the Schools of the Panama Canal Zone* (Mt. Hope: Canal Zone Press, 1930), pp. 33–42, 101–06, 168–71, 194–211, quotation from p. 170.

5. SRB minutes, 28 June and 22 November 1930, and Whyte to Burgess, 18 November 1930, in PCC 2-D-40.

6. *Panama Tribune*, 23 May, 28 June 1931; John Major, "FDR and Panama," *Historical Journal*, forthcoming.

7. McIlvaine to governor, 4 September 1931, and G. Jacques, "Abstract of Correspondence relative . . . recruiting . . . repatriation," 28 June 1933, in PCC 46-D-8.

8. Jamaica Provident and Benevolent Society file, 18 October 1932, in PCC 28-A-12/Alpha.

9. July–August 1932, *passim*, in PCC C/2-E-12; Alfaro to secretary of state, 12 June 1933, and Lea to Schley, 1 November 1933, in PCC 46-D-8; *Panama Tribune*, 15 October 1933; Major, "FDR and Panama."

10. Excerpt from memo of conference of department heads, 28 October 1933, 30 June 1934, in PCC 46-D-8; 1933, *passim*, in FO371/16584.

11. Crosby to FO, 16 August 1934, in FO371/17540/A7201; *Star and Herald*, 13 March 1935.

12. *Panama Tribune*, 17 January, 4, 11 June, 17 September 1933; PC, *Annual Report*, 1935, p. 112, 1936, p. 86; Schley to British Chargé Cleugh, 14 August 1934, and Whyte to Schley, 24 August 1934, in PCC 46-D-8.

13. Board minutes, 1929–30, *passim*, PCC 2-B-30/B; Manuelita O'Sullivan, "The Disability Relief Program," October 1959, in PCC 2-B-30; PC, *Annual Report*, 1933, p. 78.

14. Secretary of War Dern to House Speaker, 10 January 1935, in PCC 2-P-70; "Superannuation disability pay for alien canal employees, 1935–36," Westerman papers; PCWIEA, *Annual Report*, 1936, pp. 8–9; Bing Howell, "The Anatomy of Discrimination in the Canal Zone vis-à-vis Stated United States Policy from 1940–1977," Ph.D. diss., UCLA, 1979, pp. 53–54.

15. See 1937–38, *passim*, in PCC 2-P-70.

16. McIlvaine to Young, 23 August 1938, in PCC 2-P-70; 1938–41, *passim*, in PCC 2-B-30/S. In 1966 the disability ceiling was raised to sixty-five dollars a month: *Panama Tribune*, 9 December 1967.

17. *Panama Tribune*, 21, 19, 26 April 1931. The rule was discontinued in December: Rogers to FO, 22 December 1931, in FO371/15847/A205.

18. Crosby to FO, 8 September 1932, in FO371/15847/A6566.

19. Westerman, "Fifty Years," pp. 101–14; Charles Barton, "Towards the Development of Panama: The Afro-Panamanian Contribution," unpublished, ch. 11; Abel Villegas Arango to *Panama Tribune*, 19 February 1930, published 23 February 1930.

20. *Panama Tribune*, 23 February, 2, 9, 23, 30 March, and 22 June 1930.

21. Ibid., 22 April 1945, 23 May 1948, 1 December 1929; *Panama American*, 11 October 1936; "Leading Personalities, 1930," in F0371/14250/A1722.

22. *Panama Tribune*, January–April 1932, *passim*.

23. Crosby to FO, 20 February 1932, in F0371/15849/A1720, A2285; Eastman report, 27 February 1932, in file 2657-M-246, War Dept., Military Intelligence Div., RG 165, USNA; *Star and Herald*, 12 February 1932.

24. PCC 80-H-3/1936, *passim;* 1936, *passim*, in PCC 80-H-10; *Star and Herald*, 25 October 1936.

25. Crosby to FO, 27 September 1932, in F0371/15849/A7189.

26. *Panama Tribune*, 24 July 1932, 21 August 1932.

27. Ibid., July–November 1932, *passim;* Demetrio Porras, "El movimiento inquilinario," *Loteria* 213 (October–November 1973): 169–98; Crosby to FO, 11, 20, and 25 August 1932, in F0371/15849/A5365, A5658, A5955; G-2 report no. 1824 of 4 November 1932, regional files 1933–44, War Dept., Military Intelligence Div., RG 165, USNA.

28. Crosby to FO, 28 November 1932, in F0371/15849/A8537, 23 December 1932, in F0371/16583/A353, 15 and 27 June 1933, in F0371/16584/A5119 and A5325; Adam to FO, 18 July 1935, in F0371/18713/A7145.

29. *Panama Tribune*, 6 and 20 August, 3 September 1933.

30. PC, *Annual Report*, 1935, p. 112; January 1933–January 1934, *passim*, in PCC 2-E-11; quote from Smith to McIlvaine, 26 January 1933, and 1933, *passim*, in PCC 2-E-12.

31. *Panama Tribune*, 11, 29 June 1933; *Panama American*, 18 June, 9 July 1933; Crosby to FO, 15 June 1933, in F0371/16584/A5119.

32. *Panama Tribune*, 2 July 1933; *Panama American*, 31 December 1970.

33. Marriot to FO, 10 August 1933, in F0371/16584/A6359; *Panama Tribune*, 16 July 1933.

34. Robert Jeffrey, "Latin American Communities Study," unpublished, in PCC 0/BLD6, p. 7; "History of Rental Rates for Local Rate Quarters," 4 November 1954, in PCC 11-E-6, Milligan report, 28 March 1935, in PCC 11-E-5.

35. Report of J. L. Byrd, health officer, 22 September 1942, in PCC 11-E-5.

36. PC, *Annual Report*, 1941, p. 91; *Panama American*, 11 April 1937, 15 January 1939.

37. See 1931, *passim*, in PCC 2-D-131; 1932–33, *passim*, in PCC C/2-E-11/A; Crosby to FO, 8 September 1931, in F0371/15105/A5802; *Panama Tribune*, 6, 20 March 1932, 1 October 1933; 1931–32, *passim*, in PCC 2-E-11; Raymond Allan Davis, "West Indian Workers on the Panama Canal: A Split Labor Market Interpretation," Ph.D. diss., Stanford University, 1981, pp. 145–49.

38. Item 11, file 3827, War Dept., War Plans Division, in numerical file 1920–44, RG 165, USNA; 1935, *passim*, in PCC 2-E-11/L; *Panama Tribune*, 31 January 1932.

39. Seymour Paul to Railey, 25 January 1936, in PCC 28-B-44; governor to secretary of war, 3 December 1934, in official file 25-i, FDR Library; Wahl to secretary of war, 16 February 1938, in PCC C/2-P-46/L.

40. Railey report, 8 June 1936, enclosures 7, 10, in PCC C/28-B-48.

41. Alfaro, quoted in Wilson to Schley, 6 December 1934, in PCC C/2-E-12, also in U.S. Dept. of State, *Foreign Relations of the United States*, 1934, 5:603–08.

42. Wilson comment on draft treaty, 26 September 1934, in file 918.74/303A; legal adviser's comment, 4 October 1934, in file 711.1928/273 ½, RG 59, USNA.

43. Schley to Wilson, 8 and 11 December 1934, in PCC C/2-E-12.

44. Adams to FO, 15 October 1935, in F0420/287/A9270; meetings 16, 78,

92, 99, 100, 101 of file 711.1928/436 ½, RG 59, USNA, also in PCC 94-A-3/1936; Howell, "The Anatomy of Discrimination," pp. 47–49.

45. McIlvaine to superintendent of the mechanical division, 9 April 1934, in PCC 80-F-9.

46. "General Relations, agreement . . . 18 May 1942," in PCC 80-A-3. The best account of the treaty negotiations is found in Major, "FDR and Panama."

47. *Foreign Relations of the United States*, 1947, pp. 953–57; Adam to FO, 18 May 1939, in F0371/22821/A3988, Dodd to FO, 13 April 1940 and Lothian (Washington) to FO, 16 April 1940, in F0371/24244/A2762 and A2819; Dawson to Garay, 19 and 24 June 1940, file entitled "Discriminación racial y económica contra empleados panameños en la ZC," in Westerman papers; January–August 1940, *passim*, in official file 25-i, FDR Library; Davis, "West Indian Workers," pp. 149–56; Wright, "The United States and Panama," pp. 187–93.

48. Adam to FO, 18 May 1939, in F0371/22821/A3988, and *passim*.

49. Garay to Dawson, 6 January 1940, in PCC 2-E-1; letter from Octavio Vallarino to Garay, *Panama American*, 10 January 1940.

50. Stayer, Kramer, and Vietheer to governor, 24 January 1940, in PCC 2-E-2/Jamaica; Dodd to FO, 4 April 1940, in F0371/24244/A2925; PC, *Annual Report*, 1940, pp. 67–68.

51. Major, "FDR and Panama."

52. Early June 1941 memo from the government of Panama, in PCC FOR-1; 1940, *passim*, in PCC 2-E-1 and 2-E-2/Jamaica.

53. Dodd to FO, 7 October 1940, in F0371/24219/A4842; *Panama American*, 2 October 1940.

54. Memo of conversation, 17 October 1940, PCC 2-E-1; item 5, in file 3827, War Dept., War Plans, RG 165, USNA; Dodd to FO, 17 October 1940 and Butler (Washington) to FO, 15 November 1940, in F0371/24244/A3133 and A4642.

55. Dunsmoor to acting executive secretary, 19 October 1945, in PCC 46-D-8. Rubén Carles, Jr., *La evolución de la política de empleo y salarios en la Zona del Canal y el desarrollo ecónomico de Panama* (San Pedro Sula, Honduras: n.p., 1970), p. 51, gives the number of recruits by nationality.

56. See 1936–39, *passim*, in PCC C/28-B-233; U.S. Adjutant General's Office, *History of the Panama Canal Department*, 4 vols. (microfilm copy of typescript in PC, 1947), 2:77; Wilson to Mehaffey, 7 March 1942, in PCC 2-P-68.

57. See 1940–41, *passim*, and especially Paul to Lombard, 18 June 1940, in PCC C/28-B-233; "ID cards for Clubhouse and commissary privileges, 1940," Westerman papers; Wang to governor, 30 December 1944, in PCC 2-C-55; Wang to Lombard, 27 March 1941, in PCC 28-A-31.

58. See 1941, *passim*, in PCC 2-E-8.

59. Edgerton to Cramer (Fair Employment Practices Committee), 1 May 1941, in PCC 2-P-68; Major, "FDR and Panama."

60. Arthur Springarm–FDR correspondence, September–October 1941, in PCC C/28-B-233.

61. *Panama Tribune*, 15 June, 6, 13 July 1930; Westerman, "Fifty Years," pp. 77–90.

62. *Panama Tribune*, 21 February 1932; Osborne interviews, 15, 22 July 1981.

63. Barker to Osborne, 7 March 1932, in PCC 11-E-6; Barker to executive secretary, 4 March 1932, in PCC 2-C-55.

64. Williams to governor, 31 December 1936, in PCC 91-A-40; Lloyd Blauch, "The Division of Schools," July 1936, in PCC 91-A-37; Johnson to Williams, 24 October 1940, in PCC 91-A-39.

65. E. A. Gaskin, "Brief submitted to . . . governor," 28 September 1967, in Gaskin papers; *Panama American,* 11 July 1938; *Panama Tribune,* 29 July 1961.

66. Alfred E. Osborne, Leonor Jump, and P. S. Martin, *General Objectives of the Canal Zone Colored Schools: Curriculum Monograph A* (Balboa Heights, C.Z., 1938, mimeographed).

67. Webster interviews, 9, 13, 30 July 1981.

68. Charles F. Reid, *Education in the Territories and Outlying Possessions of the United States* (New York: Columbia University Teachers College, 1941), pp. 431–42; 1940–42, *passim,* in PCC 91-A-39; *Panama American,* 29 November 1940, 12 July 1969; Webster interview, 13 July 1981; Wang to governor, 5 April 1941, in PCC 91-E-3/41.

69. Parchment et al. to governor, 3 October 1942, in PCC 91-A-39; George W. Westerman, *A Plea for Higher Education of Negroes on the Canal Zone,* 1942, pamphlet in the Panama Canal Collection; "La Boca School Library, 1943," Westerman papers; "Reports and Research Studies, annual, 1943," Webster papers; Westerman interview, 6 July 1981; Gaskin interview, 20 July 1981.

70. *Panama American,* 20 January, 23, 30 November 1940, and 3 May 1941; Westerman interview, 6 July 1981; Davis, "West Indian Workers," 142–44; Cecil Smith to Barker Benfield, 30 April 1944, in F0371/38672/AN3441; INYC, *Bulletin,* 1942–46, *passim; Panama Tribune,* 17 February 1946; report of chief of naval operations, 5 July 1943, Intelligence Div., RG 38, USNA; and 1942–46, *passim,* in PCC 28-A-12/Alpha INYC.

71. Edgerton to Stimson, 29 May 1943, Whyte et al. to Roosevelt, 22 April 1943, and Thatcher to Edgerton, 9 November 1943, in PCC 91-A-39.

72. *Panama Tribune,* 29 July 1961; cf. Gaskin to Studebaker, 1 October 1943, in PCC 91-A-39.

73. Donald Lee DeWitt, "Social and Educational Thought in the Development of the Republic of Panama, 1903–1946," Ph.D. diss., University of Arizona, 1972, pp. 182–88; J. Conte Porras, *Arnulfo Arias Madrid* (Panamá: n.p., 1980), pp. 86–95; Gil Blas Tejeira, *Biografía de Ricardo Adolfo de la Guardia* (Panamá: n.p., 1971), pp. 34–35; Westerman, "Fifty Years," pp. 114–20.

74. Westerman et al., "Memorials" of 25 and 31 October 1940, in PCC 80-F-9; files entitled "Denationalization Act of 1941," and "Liga Cívica Nacional," 19 July 1944, in Westerman papers; *Panama Tribune,* 16 May 1964 and 18 December 1949; Dodd to FO, 20 September, and 12, 31 October 1940, in F0371/24219/A5095 and F0371/24244/A4283.

75. Dodd to FO, 20 December 1940, in F0371/26090/A323. On Harmodio's relationship with Arnulfo, see Dodd to FO, 20 September and 12 October 1940, in F0371/24244/A4283.

76. *El Tiempo,* 30 June 1942.

77. Howell, "The Anatomy of Discrimination," pp. 50–52; 1942–1945, *passim,* in PCC C/2-D-40.

78. Westerman, "Fifty Years," pp. 122–25.

79. Dodd to FO, January–June 1941, in F0371/26090, 26091, 26092, 26101, 26104, *passim;* George W. Westerman, *A Minority Group in Panama,* 3d ed. (Panamá: Liga Cívica Nacional, 1950), pp. 18–19.

80. Dodd to FO, 17 June 1941, in F0371/26090/A4657.

81. Irving to FO, 6, 19 January 1944, in F0371/38384/AS563 and F0371/38391/AS886; Dodd to FO, 20 October 1943, in F0371/34036/A9986.

82. Westerman interview, 16 April 1981; PC, *Annual Report,* 1942, pp. 113–14; file 350.5, War Dept., general and special staff, decimal file 1943–45, RG 165, USNA; file 811.2319/791, RG 59, USNA; 1941–42, *passim,* in PCC 79-F-5.

83. Austin to Wallace, petition of 23 March 1943, and Wilson to Edgerton, 26 March 1943, in PCC 2-P-70; Edgerton to Wilson, 9 April 1943, in PCC C/2-P-70.

84. *Star and Herald*, 21 March 1943; 1941–42, *passim*, in PCC 2-P-68.

85. Chamorro to Roosevelt, 19 July 1943, in *Calle 6*, 2 October 1943; Wilson to Edgerton, 27 August 1943, enclosure, in PCC C/28-B-233; Lombardo Toledano to Roosevelt, 3 October 1943, and enclosures, in PCC 2-P-68; Major, "FDR and Panama."

86. Malvina Thompson to Stimson, 17 December 1943, Burdick to Mehaffey, 19 February 1944, Collinge to Williams, 6 March 1944, in PCC 91-A-39; Major, "FDR and Panama."

87. Stettinius to Stimson, 4 June 1944, in file 336/Panama, War Dept., general and special staff, operations division, RG 165, USNA; de la Rosa et al. to Perkins, 6 May 1944, in PCC 2-P-68.

88. Roosevelt to Mehaffey, 16 May 1944, in PCC 2-P-68; Mehaffey to Stayer, 10 July 1944, in Mehaffey papers, LCMC; John Major, " 'Pro Mundi Beneficio'? The Panama Canal as an International Issue, 1943–8," *Review of International Studies* 9 (1983):22.

89. In official file 25-i, February–August 1944, FDR Library; Crane to Mehaffey, 3 October 1944, in PCC 11-E-6.

90. Major, " 'Pro Mundi Beneficio'?" pp. 22–23, and "FDR and Panama"; Mehaffey to Washington office, 6 January, 26 February 1945, in PCC 2-P-68.

91. Irving to FO, 20 July and 4 December 1944, in F0371/38672/AN3259 and AN4700; Westerman et al., "Solicitud de reforma . . .," 19 July 1944 file entitled "Miscellaneous," Westerman papers; Eleodoro Ventocilla, *Don Pancho Arias* (Panamá: Ministerio de Educación, 1955); *Panama Tribune*, 22 April 1945.

92. *Panama Tribune*, 12 September, 11 January 1948; broadside from the *Panama Tribune*, August 1944, in PCC 80-F-9; *Panama Tribune*, 2 January 1945; *Gazeta Oficial* 431 (8 October 1945); Eduardo Bailey, "The Presidential Decrees," pamphlet of 11 January 1945, in PCC C/80-H-10.

Chapter 6: The First Generation Comes of Age: 1945–1964

1. *Panama Tribune*, 14 October and 26 August 1945, and 5 October 1947; PC, *Annual Report*, 1957, p. 30; Tennyson, labor attaché in Mexico, 15 November 1949, in PCC 2-P-11.

2. *Panama Tribune*, 2 April 1950; Raymond Allan Davis, "West Indian Workers on the Panama Canal: A Split Labor Market Interpretation," Ph.D. diss., Stanford University, 1981, pp. 169–71.

3. Irving to FO, 20 July 1944, in F0371/38672/AN3259.

4. Smith to Benfield, 30 April 1944, and 1944, *passim*, in F0371/38672/AN3441; cover note, in F0371/45064/AS469; 1945, *passim*, in F0371/44438; *Panama Tribune*, 29 May 1949.

5. CO to FO, 7 December 1943, in F0371/34185/A11132 and A9839, Irving to Butler, 16 March 1944, in F0371/38672/AN1224, and F0371/51549/51551, *passim;* report of 19 March 1945, in file 291.21, case 54, War Dept., general and special staff, RG 165, USNA; Blanchard, *Democracy and Empire in the Caribbean* (New York: Macmillan, 1947), pp. 238–44; "Jim Crow at the Canal," *Survey Graphic*, May 1947, pp. 288–313; John Major, " 'Pro Mundi Beneficio'? The Panama Canal as an International Issue, 1943–8," *Review of International Studies* 9 (1983): 23.

6. *Foreign Relations of the United States*, 1946, pp. 1149–51; State Dept. file 711.19/1-2346, RG 59, USNA.

7. *Foreign Relations of the United States*, 1946, pp. 42–49, 54–64; 1947, pp. 948–67; Major, " *'Pro Mundi Beneficio'*?" pp. 23–32; Almon Wright, "The United States and Panama, 1933–1949," U.S. Dept. of State, Research Report 499 (1952), mimeographed, pp. 267–82; Raymond Allan Davis, "West Indian Workers on the Panama Canal: A Split Market Interpretation," Ph.D. diss., Stanford University, 1981, pp. 177–83; Bing Howell, "The Anatomy of Discrimination in the Canal Zone vis-à-vis Stated United States Policy from 1940–1977," Ph.D. diss., UCLA, 1979, pp. 59–70.

8. File 291.2 (26 January 1946), War Dept., general and special staff, operations div., RG 165, USNA.

9. "Notes of Meeting at Foreign Office," 23 July 1946, in PCC C/80-A-3; Bentz to governor, 3 June 1946, Mehaffey to Hines, 18 September 1946, in PCC 2-P-68; circular G442, 24 November 1948, and August–September 1946, *passim*, in PCC C/28-B-233; Mehaffey to executive secretary, 20 July 1946, in PCC 2-P-70.

10. Frank McSherry, "Report to the Governor of the Panama Canal" typescript, Washington, D.C., 1947, esp. pp. 1–9, 59–98, 167–70, enclosure in PCC 2-E-11; John Ohly to Mehaffey, 14 November 1946, in Mehaffey papers, LCMC, and *Foreign Relations of the United States*, 1947, pp. 950–53.

11. McSherry, "Report," pp. 30–32; *Panama Tribune*, 2 November 1947, and 1947, *passim*, in PCC 2-P-68; Major, " 'Pro Mundi Beneficio'?" n. 52.

12. *Panama Tribune*, 8 February, 18 April, and 1 August 1948; executive order 9980, 26 July 1948, in PCC 2-E-8.

13. *Panama Tribune*, 29 August, and 12 September 1948; Newcomer to Washington office, 29 March 1949, in PCC 2-E-8; *Panama American*, 13 February 1948; *Star and Herald*, 18 October 1948; Royall to Mehaffey, 29 March 1948, in PCC 2-P-71, Paul to Pittsburgh, 28 May 1948, in PCC C/28-B-233; 1948, *passim*, in PCC C/2-D-4/PB; Howell, "The Anatomy of Discrimination," pp. 85–87.

14. George Vietheer, "Labor Conditions in the Canal Zone," Washington, D.C., 31 October 1949, enclosure, in PCC C/2-D-4/PC; *Panama Tribune*, 8 May 1949; file 291.2, army staff, plans and operations decimal file, 1946–48, RG 319, USNA.

15. Quotations from Vietheer, "Labor Conditions," pp. 139, 173, 154; Newcomer, "Comments relative to the Vietheer Report," enclosure, in PCC C/2-D-4/PC. Cf. report of Sen. Johnson, in State Dept. file 611.19/2-1650, RG 59, USNA.

16. Mehaffey to Rossbottom, 11 February 1947, and Pfitzer to Newcomer, 31 August 1949, in PCC 65-J-3/M.

17. *Panama Tribune*, 28 August 1949; executive order 10102, 31 January 1950; *Federal Register*, 3 February 1950, pp. 595–97.

18. PL 841, *Federal Register*, 26 September 1950, pp. 1038–43; PC, *Annual Report*, 1950, pp. 51–52, 1955, p. 2; *Panama Tribune*, 5 February 1950, and 28 May 1960.

19. Bendetsen to file, 16 May 1951, and memo of conference of department heads, 29 June 1951, in PCC 65-J-3/M; "Basis for appt. of members of the board of directors of the Panama Canal," 16 April 1959, in PCC 65-J-3; *Marine Review*, 29 June 1951, pp. 46–47.

20. Bendetsen to Newcomer, 2 November 1951, in PCC 65-J-3; Seybold to Chair, House Appropriations Committee, November 1953, and 1953, *passim*, in PCC C/65-J-3/M; *Panama Tribune*, 30 March 1952.

21. John Major, "Wasting Asset: The U.S. Re-Assessment of the Panama Canal, 1945–1949," *Journal of Strategic Studies* 3 (1980):140–42.

22. See 1939–40, *passim*, in PCC 2-P-71; Curran to Geyer, 6 April 1940, in PCC 28-B-28; Adam to FO, 28 October 1939, in F0371/22822/A8784; PCWIEA, *Annual Report*, 1940, pp. 2–3; *Panama Tribune*, 9 January 1940; Davis, "West Indian Workers," pp. 160–65.

23. Davis, "West Indian Workers," pp. 165–77.

24. Gaskin interview, 20 July 1981.

25. Report by Mr. House, in Irvin to FO, 4 May 1946, in F0371/52123/AS2684.

26. Mehaffey to John Wood, chair of House Un-American Activities Committee, 25 October 1946, in PCC 2-P-71.

27. Pamphlet of 13 July 1946, in PCC C/28-B-233; Turner to police chief, 20 July 1947, and 1946–47, *passim*, in PCC 2-P-71.

28. *Panama Tribune*, 2 November, 1947, 11 January, and 22 February 1948; 1947, *passim*, in PCC 2-P-71; Davis, "West Indian Workers," pp. 167–68; J. Parnell Thomas, "Reds in the Panama Canal Zone," *Liberty* 25 (May 1948), pp. 14–15, 47, 54.

29. *Nation*, 8 August 1947; U.S. Adjutant General's Office, *History of the Panama Canal Department*, 4 vols. (microfilm copy of typescript in PC, 1947), 4:79–84; Westerman interview, 1 February 1981.

30. "CIO correspondence," Westerman papers; *Panama American*, 29 February 1948.

31. George W. Westerman, *Blocking Them at the Canal* (Panamá: n.p., 1952), pp. 20–21; State Dept. file 811F.5043, 1949, *passim*, RG 59, USNA; *Panama Tribune*, 9 January, and 8 May 1949; David McMorris quarterly labor report, 29 October 1949, in PCC 2-P-11; 1949 communist pamphlets, enclosures, in PCC 2-P-72.

32. See 1948–49, *passim*, in PCC 2-P-71.

33. George W. Westerman, "Working Conditions on the Panama Canal Zone as of August 1949," unpublished, Westerman papers; George W. Westerman, *A Study of Socioeconomic Conflict on the Panama Canal Zone* (Panamá: Liga Cívica Nacional, 1948); "Extract of UPI Miami report," 8 February 1949, in PCC C/2-P-12; *Panama Tribune*, 13 February 1949.

34. Westerman interviews, 11–12 May, and 3 February 1981; Ed Clark, in State Dept. file 711.19/6-4-49, RG 59, USNA.

35. Sam Roe to police chief, 7 July 1949, in PCC 2-P-71; *Panama Tribune*, 17 July, and 20 November 1949; Carlos Hall, "Alleged Failure of U.S. to meet Treaty Obligations," in State Dept. file 711.1928/7-2049, RG 59, USNA.

36. "CIO Correspondence," 1950, *passim*, Westerman papers; 1950, *passim*, in PCC 2-P-71 and PCC 2-P-72; 1950, *passim*, in State Dept. files 819.062 and 811F.062/3-1850, RG 59, USNA; *Panama Tribune*, 5 March, 16 April, 28 May, 16 July, and 15 October 1950.

37. Gaskin to Newcomer, 8 September 1950, in PCC 2-P-72; cf. memo of conversation with Westerman, in State Dept. file 819.062/9-1150, RG 59, USNA.

38. Newcomer to Gaskin, 27 November 1950, in PCC 2-P-72; Sinclair interview, 24 July 1981; meeting notes, 24 January 1951, and Newcomer to Murray, 25 January 1951, in PCC 2-P-72; memo of conversation, in State Dept. file 819.06/8-750, RG 59, USNA.

39. *New York World-Telegram*, 10 July 1951; 1950–51, *passim*, in PCC 2-P-72; Gaskin interview, 20 July 1981; memos of conversation, in State Dept. files 881F.06/5-3151, and 811F.606/11-2151, RG 59, USNA.

40. Interviews with Harold Williams, 10 July, Kirvin, 20 July, Sinclair, 24 July, and Gaskin, 20 July 1981.

41. Milton Eisenhower, *The Wine is Bitter* (Garden City, N.Y.: Doubleday, 1963), pp. 225–26; State Dept. files 811F.06/12-2051, and 811F.061/12-2051, RG 59, USNA; *Panama Tribune*, 27 April 1952.

42. *Panama Tribune*, 10 May, 14 June, 11 October 1953, and 24 February 1954; "Labor developments," in State Dept. file 811.06/11-752, RG 59, USNA; "Summarized statement on socioeconomic problems," August 1953, and address in National Stadium, 24 January 1954, in Gaskin papers; Capehart report of 1954 (no. 1082), U.S. Congress, Senate Committee on Banking and Currency, *Study of Latin American Countries* (Washington, D.C.: Government Printing Office, 1954), pp. 459–85.

43. April 1953 correspondence in file 611.19; Bedell Smith to Eisenhower, in file 611.192/1554; Dulles to Wilson, in file 611.19/6-554; Holland to Dulles, in file 611.193/7-3054, State Dept., RG 59, USNA.

44. State Dept. file 611.1913 contains the record of negotiations; Chaplin to Holland, in file 611.19/6-1154; Dulles to Chaplin, in file 611.1931/8-1254 and 8-2654; meeting notes, in file 611.1913/10-754 and 10-2754; Chaplin to State Dept., in file 611.1913/10-2954, State Dept., RG 59, USNA.

45. *Panama Tribune*, 14 March 1954; "Testimony by E. F. Gaskin," July 1954, in Gaskin papers; Gerardo Maloney and George Priestly, "El grupo antillano en el proceso político panameño," *Tareas* 33 (September–November 1975): 23.

46. Memminger to State Dept., in file 819.062/9-1754, State Dept., RG 59, USNA; Norman Johnson, 13 September 1954, in PCC 2-P-72; Robert Jeffrey, "Latin American Communities Study," in PCC O/BLD 6, pp. 105–07; 1953, *passim*, in PCC 28-B-48/N.

47. *Panama Tribune*, 22 January, 19, 26 February, and 26 August 1956; 1955, *passim*, in PCC 2-P-72; Westerman to Ernesto de la Guardia, 19 July 1957, in file entitled "Memoranda para el presidente," Westerman papers; Durant article in *Star and Herald*, 21 February 1956; interviews with Sinclair, 24 July, Harold Williams, 10 July, and Malcolm, 15 July 1981.

48. *Panama Tribune*, 13 July, 3 August, 14 December 1958, 11 January, 22 February, 1, 22 March, 25 July 1959, and 6 February 1960; directors' meeting, 5 July 1951, enclosures, "Report 1869," House Committee, 85th Cong., 2d sess., in PCC 2-D-2.

49. See 1959–60, *passim*, in PCC 2-B-30.

50. George W. Westerman, *Pioneers in Canal Zone Education* (Panama Canal Zone: n.p., 1949), pp. 1–8; *Panama Tribune*, 21 May 1950, Johnson to special adviser, 25 March 1949, in PCC 2-P-71; Johnson to acting executive secretary, 19 March 1949, in PCC C/2-D-40; Gaskin, "Brief," 28 September 1967, and Gaskin to Yancy, 18 August 1950, in Gaskin papers; Alda Harper, *Tracing the Course of Growth and Development in Educational Policy for the Canal Zone Colored Schools, 1905–1955* (Ann Arbor: University of Michigan School of Education, 1979), pp. 157–84, *passim*; George W. Westerman, "School Segregation on the Panama Canal Zone," *Phylon* 3 (1954): 276–86; 1945–49, *passim*, in PCC 49-A-39; Lawrence Johnson, "The Upward Extension of the Canal Zone Schools for Native Colored Children," Ph.D. diss., Stanford University, 1949.

51. *Panama Tribune*, 21 September 1952, 3 July 1965; "Committee Requesting black instructors for proposed Jr. College, 1950," Westerman papers; Lowell C. Wilson et al., *Schooling in the Panama Canal Zone, 1904–1979* (Panama Canal Area: Phi Delta Kappa, 1980), pp. 122–25; Michael E. Smith, "The Growth and Development of the Canal Zone College," Ph.D. diss., North Texas State University, 1973, pp. 90–94.

52. Those who returned to the Zone schools were Owen Shirley, Sadie

Springer, Myrtle Mulcare, Horace Parker, Carla Whatley, Robert Beecher, Emily Butcher, and Charles Barton (interviews with Barton, 11 August, Webster, 9 July, Bennett, 17 July 1981); Harper, *Tracing the Course of Growth*, pp. 164–66, 189–98; "Scholarship proposals for Canal Zone noncitizen teachers," unpublished, Westerman papers.

53. Webster interview, 13 July 1981; meeting of 15 January 1953, in PCC 65-H-2/Civil Affairs Bureau.

54. "Press comments re changes in the CZ colored Schools, 1954," Westerman papers; interviews with Osborne, 15 July, Gaskin, 20 July, and Webster, 9, 13 July 1981.

55. *Panama Tribune*, 11 January, 8 February, and 20 September 1953.

56. "Justice Douglas, 1953," Westerman papers.

57. Donovan to Seybold, 19 January 1954, in Webster papers; cf. Doolan to Seybold, 13 January 1954, in PCC 91-A-39.

58. Interviews with Westerman, 6 July and 3 February 1981; "Brief," 28 September 1967, in Gaskin papers; *Panama Tribune*, 21 February 1954; *Nation*, 21 February 1954; Paxton to Donovan, 23 February 1954, in Webster papers; Chaplin to Muccio, in file 611.1913/2-2754, State Dept., RG 59, USNA.

59. Norman Johnson memo, 19 April 1954, and 1954, *passim*, in PCC 91-B-2.

60. Seybold speech to Rotarians, 18 March 1954, in Westerman papers; PC, *Annual Report*, p. 106; Zone memo of 4 June 1954, in file 811F.43/6-1854, State Dept., RG 59, USNA.

61. "Press comments re changes in CZ colored Schools, 1954," "Segregación escolar en la zona del canal," and "CZ Junior College and Conversion of Colored Schools," Westerman papers; 1954, *passim*, in PCC 91-A-39 and 91-B-2; interviews with Gaskin, 20 July, and Webster, 9 and 13 July 1981; Wilson et al., *Schooling in the Canal Zone*, pp. 125–26.

62. "Report submitted to Zone Governor W. E. Potter," 9 November 1956, enclosure, in PCC 91-A-39.

63. Anon. to Lehman, 31 December 1955; Roderick to governor, 27 June 1956, in Webster papers; Schull to Washington office, 11 June 1956, in PCC 91-A-39.

64. Interviews with Henry, 7 July, Webster, 13 July, and Kirvin, 20 July 1981; quote from "Problems of the Latin American Communities of the Canal Zone," 3 June 1971, in Webster papers.

65. "A Housing Program for the Panama Canal," July 1945, enclosure, in PCC 28-B-44; George W. Westerman, "Fifty Years of West Indian Life in Panama, 1904–1954," unpublished, Westerman papers, pp. 72–76.

66. Graham Lewis to Mehaffey, 12 February 1946, Mehaffey to Lewis, 28 February 1946, and Stephen Arneson, "Modular House for Panama Canal," 1 July 1946, in PCC 2-B-44; George Westerman, *Urban Housing in Panama* (Panamá: Institute for Economic Development, 1955), pp. 35–39.

67. Alstrup to governor, 18 May 1949, and Gray, secretary of the army, to Frank Pace, director of the budget, 22 July 1949, in PCC 11-E-6; Skidmore, Owings, Merrill report, 15 February 1950, in PCC 13-Q-1/C; file 611.1913/4-2450, State Dept., RG 59, USNA.

68. "Housing replacement program," 31 March 1952, in PCC 13-Q-6/C; *Panama Tribune*, 31 January 1954; Jeffrey, "Latin American Communities Study," pp. 14–16; board meetings, 23 December 1953, 25 January 1954, in PCC 28-B-48/N; Seybold to Chair, House Appropriations Committee, November 1952, in PCC-65-J-3/M; memo of conversation, file 811F.02/1-2552, State Dept., RG 59, USNA.

69. Norris report, 6 July 1954, and 1955–56, *passim*, in PCC 11-E-6: *Panama Tribune*, 23 January 1955; Davis, "West Indian Workers," pp. 194–98.

70. *Panama Tribune*, 14 March 1954; PC, *Annual Report*, 1953, p. 23.

71. Westerman, *Urban Housing*, pp. 10–12, 18; *Panama Tribune*, 1 April 1945, 10 July 1949, 9 April 1950.

72. Westerman to Ernesto de la Guardia, 10 July 1957, in file entitled "Memoranda para el Presidente," and "American Guiana Development Corp.," Westerman papers; *Panama Tribune*, 8 April, 23 December 1956, and 27 October 1957. In 1966–67 I served as adviser in a U.S. foreign aid program attempting to alleviate problems in Panama's urban slums.

73. Irving to FO, January–June 1945, in F0371/45064, *passim*, and 5 January 1946, in F0371/52122/AS459; 1945–46, *passim*, in PCC C/80-H-10.

74. *Panama Tribune*, 29 April 1945.

75. Interviews with Westerman, 16 April, and Bazán, 26 July 1981.

76. *Panama Tribune*, 27 September 1953, 6 July 1947; Roe to police chief, 7 February 1945, in PCC C/80-H-10; Bazán, interview, 26 July 1981.

77. Broadcast, Radio Miramar, 4 November 1946, in file entitled "Miscellaneous items of West Indian History," Westerman papers.

78. *Panama Tribune*, 18 December 1949.

79. *Star and Herald*, 23 March 1945.

80. Broadside, 12 June 1947, in PCC C/80-H-10.

81. *Panama Tribune*, 22 January 1947.

82. Allen Glenn Morton, "The Private Schools of the British West Indians in Panama," Ph.D. diss., George Peabody College for Teachers, 1966, p. 100.

83. *Panama Tribune*, 18 January 1948; Lapeira to police chief, 28 April, 1948, in PCC C/80-H-3/1948.

84. *Nation*, 8 May 1948; *Panama Tribune*, 27 September 1953, 27 November 1949, and May–June, 1948, *passim*.

85. *Panama Tribune*, 11, 27 December 1949, 22 January 1950, and March–May 1951, *passim;* Walter LaFeber, *The Panama Canal: The Crisis in Historical Perspective*, rev. ed. (New York: Oxford University Press, 1979), pp. 106–13; Larry LaRae Pippin, *The Remon Era: An Analysis of a Decade of Events in Panama, 1947–1957* (Stanford, Calif.: Institute of Hispanic American and Luso-Brazilian Studies, 1964), p. 81; J. Conte Porras, *Arnulfo Arias Madrid* (Panama: author, 1980), pp. 123–67; *Panama Election Factbook* (Washington, D.C.: Operations and Policy Research, 1968), p. 9.

86. Irving to FO, 9 March 1944, in F0371/38384/AS1776; Steve C. Ropp, *Panamanian Politics* (New York: Praeger, 1982), pp. 26–27; Pippin, *The Remon Era*, chs. 6–7.

87. Pippin, *The Remon Era*, ch. 9; *Panama Tribune*, 6 September, 4 October 1953, and February-May 1952, *passim;* La Hora, 29 November 1952; *Panama American*, 20 October 1953.

88. *Panama Tribune*, 23 January 1955, and 1955, *passim*.

89. Ibid., 12 June, 5 July, 4 September, 4 December 1955, and 6 May 1956; Bazán to Dicky Arias, 25 March 1955, "Westerman charges unfair discrimination," Westerman papers.

90. Westerman, *Urban Housing*, pp. 38–39; Westerman to de la Guardia, 19 July 1957, file "Memoranda para el presidente," Westerman papers; *Panama Tribune*, 8 April, 27 May, 26 August, 2 September, 4 November, 23 December 1956, 10 February, and 27 October 1957.

91. *Nation*, 8 and 12 February 1956; *Panama Tribune*, 2 February, 5 October 1958, 11 January, 1, 22 February 1959, 5 November 1960, 14 January, 4, 11, 25 February 1961, and 28 November 1964.

92. LaFeber, *The Panama Canal*, pp. 124–30; cable, 19 April 1960, in Jeffrey, "Latin American Communities Study;" Carter to Chargé Shillock, 25 July 1960, in PCC REP 7; Board meeting, 9 April 1960, and Senator James Murray to Wm. Fulbright, 22 April 1960, in PCC 28-B-44.

93. "Memoranda para el presidente," "De la Guardia, recomendaciones," Westerman papers; *Panama Tribune*, 22 March 1959, 2 April 1960.

94. *Panama Tribune*, 15 August 1959, and February–May 1960, *passim*; Bazán, interview, 26 July 1981; Westerman interview, 26 April 1981.

95. *Panama Tribune*, 18 June 1960, 18 December 1956.

96. *Estrella de Panama*, 12 June 1979; Maloney and Priestly, "El grupo antillano," pp. 25–26; Leslie Williams, interview, 27 July 1981.

97. Efrain Candanedo C. to *Estrella de Panama*, 23 July 1945. Cf. Westerman's article, *Star and Herald*, 21 May 1946.

98. Ramón Carillo, "Viewpoints of a Panamanian," *Boletín del Instituto de Investigaciones Sociales y Económicas* 2 (July 1945): 713–65; John Biesanz, "Cultural and Economic Factors in Panamanian Race Relations," *American Sociological Review* 14 (1949): 778, and 772–79, *passim*.

99. *Panama Tribune*, 25 November 1945, 26 August 1946; "Glimpses of West Indian Life . . . Negro Press" and "List of discrimination cases," Westerman papers.

100. "Discrimination Skychief incident," Westerman papers; *Panama Tribune*, 13 November 1949, 28 January 1951, 19 August 1945, 24 February, 2 March, 1952.

101. *Panama Tribune*, 23 December 1961, 16 February 1963; Westerman speech in ibid., 17, 24 August 1963.

102. Ibid., 11 March 1956, 28 October 1961; Charles Barton, "Towards the Development of Panama: The Afro-Panamanian Contribution," unpublished, ch. 12.

103. PC, *Annual Report*, 1956, p. 105.

104. *Panama Tribune*, 11 January 1953, April 1953, *passim*, and 30 December 1967.

105. Ibid., 9 November 1963; interviews with Appin, 31 July, and Silvestri, 30 July 1981; "For a more unified Panamanian nation," Westerman papers; Henry testimony in meeting of civic councils with Ellsworth Bunker, 27 November 1973, in PCC REP 7.

106. Alfredo Castillero Calvo, *La sociedad panameña* (Panamá: Dirección de Planificación, 1970), pp. 106–10.

107. Westerman, "Fifty Years," pp. 134–38; interviews with Castillero Pimentel, 31 March, Figueroa, 13 April, and Pacheco, 31 January 1981.

108. John Biesanz and Mavis Biesanz, *The People of Panama* (New York: Columbia University Press, 1955), p. 227; advertisements in the *Panama Tribune* and the *Workman*. On the definition of integration, see Jorge A. Arosemena, "Los panameños negros descendientes de antillanos: ¿Un caso de marginalidad social?" *Estudios sociales centroamericanos* 5 (1976): 9–34.

109. Henry interview, 7 July 1981; A. Faulkner Watts, "Perspectivas sobre el Afro-panameño," *Lotería* 234 (August 1975): 36–48; *Panama Tribune*, 17 August 1963.

110. See, for example, Carlos D. Castro G., "Notas para una sociología del negro antillano," *Lotería* 202 (September 1972): 6–23; Biesanz and Biesanz, *The People of Panama*, p. 216; Otilia Tejeira, "El problema antillano en Panamá," in ibid., pp. 321–22.

111. Biesanz and Biesanz, *The People of Panama*, pp. 224–25; Webster interviews, 9, 13, and 30 July 1981.

112. Westerman, "Fifty Years," pp. 126–34; Biesanz and Biesanz, *The People of Panama*, p. 346; Barton, "Towards the Development of Panama," p. 70.

113. Interviews with Bennett, 17 July, and Weatherborne, 17 July 1981.

114. Castro, "Notas para una sociología," p. 23; Biesanz, "Cultural and Economic Factors," pp. 777–78.

115. Daniel Goldrich, *Sons of the Establishment* (Chicago: Rand McNally, 1966), pp. 46–47, 105.

116. Interviews with Ford, 3 July, Hayes, 6 August, and Scarlett, 7 July 1981.

117. Eisenhower, *The Wine is Bitter*, pp. 213–17, 225–28.

118. LaFeber, *The Panama Canal*, pp. 132–35.

119. Webster interview, 9 July 1981; PC, *Annual Report*, 1961, p. 33, and 1964, p. 33; Board of directors meeting minutes, 5 June 1961, unnumbered files, PCC.

120. Carter to Goldberg, 6 October 1961, PCC PER 4-5.

121. Governor to board, 19 January 1962, in PCC O/PER 4-6; 1962, *passim*, in PCC O/Alpha/ILA; Witman to governor, 20 July 1962, in PCC PER 4.

122. Fleming to deputy undersecretary of the army (Haugerud), 13 May 1963, in PCC PER 4-5; Lioeanjie interview, 1 May 1981.

123. Webster interview, 9 July 1981; *Panama Tribune*, 18 January 1959; Doolan report, 2 February 1971, in PCC SCH 1-2; Esser to Latin American teachers, 16 December 1960, file 9.2, and Temistocles Céspedes, Victor Gómez, Rafael Moscote, "Report of the Survey Committee appointed to evaluate the Latin American Schools [1962]," in Webster papers.

124. Civil affairs director to governor, 31 January 1961, in PCC ADM 7-6-6; Doolan to W. Gill, 8 November 1967, in PCC PER 4-5.

125. Doolan to information officer, 31 January 1963, in PCC O/PER 5-9.

126. Doolan to lieutenant governor, 15 May 1970, in PCC O/PER 5-9.

Chapter 7: In the Shadow of Treaty Negotiations, 1964–1981

1. The best overviews of this era are Sheldon B. Liss, *The Canal: Aspects of United States-Panamanian Relations* (Notre Dame, Ind.: University of Notre Dame Press, 1967); David N. Farnsworth and James W. McKenney, *U.S.-Panama Relations, 1903–1973* (Boulder, Colo.: Westview Press, 1983); and William J. Jorden, *Panama Odyssey* (Austin: University of Texas Press, 1984).

2. Walter LaFeber, *The Panama Canal: The Crisis in Historical Perspective*, rev. ed. (New York: Oxford University Press, 1979), pp. 142–45.

3. See PCC 28-B-150, *passim; Panama Tribune*, 11 March 1967.

4. Bazán interview, 26 July 1981.

5. *Panama Tribune*, 16 May 1964; 1964, *passim*, in PCC O/PER 4-9.

6. *Panama Tribune*, 12 June 1965; information officer to governor, 27 September 1965, in PCC O/REP 7; Doolan memo, 1 April 1970, board of directors meeting of 17 April 1970, and Doolan to lieutenant governor, 15 May 1970, in PCC O/PER 5-9.

7. *Panama Tribune*, 16, 23 April, 16 July, 6 August, and 22 October 1966.

8. Ibid., 15 July 1967; Johnson, quoted in the National Labor Relations Board decision of 10 June 1966, in PCC PER 4-5.

9. Congresswoman Leonor Sullivan, cited in *Panama Tribune*, 24 June 1967, and 13, 20 May 1967.

10. Maugé to Leber, 18 April 1967, in PCC PER 4-5; *Panama Tribune*,

22 April, 22 July 1967; Canel to file, 17 April 1967, and 1967, *passim*, in PCC REP 7.

11. *Panama Tribune*, 23 December 1967; *Panama Election Factbook* (Washington, D.C.: Operations and Policy Research, 1968), *passim;* LaFeber, *The Panama Canal*, p. 148.

12. "Conventions, 1967–68," Westerman papers; *Star and Herald*, 25 December 1967.

13. Westerman interviews, 1 February and 8 May 1981.

14. Steve C. Ropp, *Panamanian Politics* (New York: Praeger, 1982) is the best source on Torrijos and the post-1968 regime.

15. LaFeber, *The Panama Canal*, ch. 6.

16. Alfredo Castillero Calvo, *La sociedad panameña* (Panamá: Dirección de Planificación, 1970), pp. 106–09; Westerman interviews, 11 and 12 May 1981; *Panama Tribune*, 27 March 1971, and 8 August 1970; Castillero Calvo interview, 16 March 1983.

17. Conley to governor, 4 April 1972, Koren to Parker, 3 May 1972, in PCC O/PER 4-9; Robert F. Jeffrey, "Latin American Communities Study," 19 June 1979, in PCC O/BLD 6, pp. 114–16 and annex c.

18. Talk by Aquilino Boyd, 20 March 1973, cited in Jeffrey, "Latin American Communities Study"; *Estrella de Panama*, 28 September 1973; Jorden, *Panama Odyssey*, chs. 8–9.

19. See the Jeffrey study cited in note 17.

20. For example, during a 1971 visit to the Canal Zone, Congresswoman Leonor Sullivan was given a packet of materials, including "The Problems of the Latin American Communities," in Johnson to Civic Councils, 20 January 1971, Webster papers; Jeffrey, "Latin American Communities Study," p. 1.

21. Jeffrey, "Latin American Communities Study," p. 135.

22. Transcript of Civic Councils meeting with Ellsworth Bunker, 27 November 1973, in PCC REP 7.

23. Leber to Secretary of Housing Weaver, 28 June 1969, in PCC SER 3-1; report of 28 December 1970, in minutes of board of directors, 19–20 January 1971, unnumbered file, PCC.

24. Steve Ropp, "Panama's Blacks: A U.S. Responsibility," *New Leader*, 7 November 1977, pp. 7–8; John P. Augelli, "The Panama Canal Area in Transition," *American Universities Field Staff Reports* 3–4 (1981), pt. 1, pp. 11–13.

25. Congressional Research Service, *Senate Debate on the Panama Canal Treaties* (Washington, D.C.: Government Printing Office, 1979); Jorden, *Panama Odyssey*, chs. 12–20 and epilogue.

26. Interviews with Silvestri, 30 July, and Henry, 7 July 1981.

27. Augelli, "The Panama Canal Area,". 1, pp. 9–10.

28. Anderson interview, 24 July 1981; "Problemática laboral panameña frente a los nuevos tratados," Local 907 pamphlet, May 1978.

29. Doolan to governor, 7 February 1968, in PCC PER 4-5. Cf. the discussion above in ch. 6.

30. Frick memo, 5 January 1970, and 1968–72, *passim*, in PCC PER 4-5; Mark Tartar, "Position paper of Canal Zone labor presented to . . . Subcommittee on the Panama Canal," 15 January 1970, in PC.

31. The previous year the National Labor Relations Board declined jurisdiction over a canal labor dispute on the grounds that international relations might be affected: Cooper to governor, 18 April 1973, in PCC PER 4-5; 1975–76, *passim*, in PCC PER 4 and PER 4-5; Russell (president of Local 907) to Foreign Minister Tack, 7 March 1974, in PCC PER 5-9; Simoneau interview, 12 August 1981.

32. U.S. Congress, Senate, 26 July 1979, *Congressional Record*, pp. 10603–10; Simoneau interview, 12 August 1981; "Statement of Kenneth Blaylock . . . House Committee on Merchant Marine," 24 February 1979, in Gittens papers.

33. Interviews with Lioeanjie, 1 May, and 5 August, and Maugé, 7 July 1981; *Estrella de Panama*, 29 March 1981.

34. Westerman speech, "Panama Canal Policy Changes . . . 1914–1974," McAllister College, September 1973, Westerman papers; Raymond Allan Davis, "West Indian Workers on the Panama Canal: A Split Labor Market Interpretation," Ph.D. diss., Stanford University, 1981, table 13.

35. For example, see the letter by former Peace Corps volunteer Michael Lang in McKabney (general counsel) to Deputy Undersecretary of the Army Siena, 11 August 1969, in PCC SER 3-1.

36. *Panama Tribune*, 28 February, 7 March, 7 November 1970; "Congressman Augustus Hawkins," Westerman papers.

37. *Panama Tribune*, 12 December 1970, and 1971, *passim;* "Discrimination-Elks 1971–73," Westerman papers.

38. *Panama Tribune*, 22 May 1971, 29 July 1972; Caroll interview, 12 June 1981.

39. Ernest Frazier to deputy chief of staff for personnel, 5 July 1973, in PCC O/PUB 6; McGinnis to file, 8 June 1973, in PCC O/PER 5-9.

40. Leggett to Elmer Staats, comptroller general, 30 August 1974, in PCC PUB 2-1; Leggett-Parker exchange, July 1973–April 1974, in PCC O/PUB 6.

41. Minton Francis to William Brehm, 15 April 1974, McGinnis to file, 1 March 1974, and Walton to file, 1 April 1974, in PCC O/PUB 6; Constant (Washington office) to file, 28 March 1974, in PCC PER 5-9. Leggett's investigation was printed as U.S. Congress, House Subcommittee on the Panama Canal, *Hearings before the Subcommittee on . . . Latin American Communities in the Canal Zone* (Washington, D.C.: Government Printing Office, 1975).

42. Pestillo report, July 1974, in PCC PER 4. On the 1973 pilots' sickout, see Anthony Ingrassia to Constant, 26 June 1975, in PCC PER 4; Simoneau interview, 12 August 1981.

43. Constant to file, 21 March 1975, summary of meeting of 3 April 1975, in PCC PUB 2-1; "Panamerican Games 1959—Ralph Metcalfe," Westerman papers; Westerman interview, 31 May 1981.

44. U.S. Comptroller General, *Report to the Subcommittee on the Panama Canal* (Washington, D.C.: Government Printing Office, 1975); "Governor Parfitt's Opening Statement to the Panama Canal Subcommittee . . . 16 June 1975," in PCC PUB 2-1.

45. Superintendent Speir, "Report to Mr. Veysey on possible consolidation of schools," 29 September 1975, and Kenneth Hannah (AFT Local 29) to Albert Shanker (AFT/New York), 3 November 1975, in Webster papers; Simoneau interview, 12 August 1981.

46. Parfitt circular letter to congressmen, 6 February 1976, in PCC PUB 1-2-1. I am grateful to Audley Webster for loaning me the papers collected by Superintendent David Speir for use in a doctoral dissertation.

47. "File 9.2, Analysis of LA Schools," Webster papers; Jeffrey, "Latin American Communities Study," pp. 56–74; 1970–71, *passim*, in PCC SCH 1-2; 1972–73, *passim*, in PCC O/SCH 1-2.

48. Speir to governor, 5 December 1973, Speir to GAO, 30 September 1974, Speir report to Mr. Veysey, 29 September 1975, in Webster papers.

49. Hannah to Shanker, 3 November 1975, in PCC SCH 1.

50. Speir to civil affairs chief, 8 March 1976, in PCC O/SCH 1-2.

51. Webster interview, 30 July 1981.

52. "Principal address . . . 15 August 1979," in Gaskin papers.
53. Jorge R. Arosemena, "Los panameños negros descendientes de antillanos: ¿Un caso de marginalidad social?" *Estudios sociales centroamericanos* 5 (1976): 9–34; interviews with Hayes, 6 August, and Lewis, 8 August 1981.
54. Two files entitled "The *Panama Tribune*," Westerman papers; interviews with Westerman, 31 May, and Harrison, 14 July 1981.
55. *Panama Tribune*, 29 June 1958, 4 February 1961, 6 May 1961, 4 November, and 16 December 1967; Barton interview, 11 August 1981.
56. Ibid., 23 September 1961; Jeffrey, "Latin American Communities Study," pp. 75–81, 88–89; 1962–65, *passim*, in PCC LAW 15.
57. "Youth Study Committee Report," 16 August 1966, "Professional Counseling Services," 17 April 1968, in PCC LAW 15; cf. Dunsmoor to governor, 26 August 1963, in PCC SER 3-1; and Jeffrey, "Latin American Communities Study," annex e.
58. Jeffrey, "Latin American Communities Study," pp. 118–31; *Panama Tribune*, 12 July 1969, 17 January 1970, and 27 March 1971.
59. Interviews with Anderson, 24 July, and Welsh, 16 July 1981; *Panama Tribune*, 24 April, 11 September 1971.
60. Interviews with Gadpaille, 20 July, Gittens, 5 July, Hutchinson, 21 July, and Smith, 5 August 1981. Cf. Hector Gadpaille, "Memorias de la Junta Comunal de Rio Abajo, 1972–78," pamphlet published by author, 1978.
61. Alberto Smith Fernández, "El Afropanameño antillano frente al concepto de la panameñidad," *Revista nacional de cultura* 5 (September–December 1976): 45–59.
62. Melva Lowe Ocran, "El idioma inglés y la integración social de los panameños de origen afro-antillano al carácter nacional panameño," *Revista nacional de cultura* 5 (September–December 1976); 22–43.
63. Juan Materno Vásquez, "La nacionalidad panameña," *Revista nacional de cultura* 9–10 (August 1977–January 1978): 83–93.
64. *Estrella de Panama*, 21 January 1979. Cf. Clarence King's reply in ibid., 12 February 1979.
65. "Afro-Panamanians in the United States," in *Panama: Sovereignty for a Land Divided* (Washington: Epica Task Force, 1976), pp. 116–18.
66. Gittens interview, 5 July 1981.
67. Ibid.; Brathwaite speech, mimeographed, Webster papers.
68. Interviews with Smith, 5 and 7 August, and Harrison, 5 July 1981; "Comunicado del ARENEP," 1980, in Gittens papers.
69. *República*, 29 August 1977, 9 and 10 March 1980.
70. Alberto Smith Fernández, "Documento Central del Primer Congreso del Negro Panameño," *Memorias del Primer Congreso del Negro Panameño* (Panamá: Instituto Nacional de Cultura, 1981). Cf. Smith's November 1980 paper presented at the University of Panama.
71. *Panama Tribune*, 14 August 1971.

Chapter 8: Conclusion

1. *República*, 14 and 21 October 1979; Carlos Guillermo Wilson, "Aspectos de la prosa panameña contemporanea," Ph.D. diss., UCLA, 1975; Mirna Miriam Pérez-Venero, "Raza, color, y prejuicios en la novelística panameña contemporanea de tema canalero," Ph.D. diss., Louisiana State University, 1973, chs. 2, 3, 5, 6.
2. La Llorona, in *Estrella de Panamá*, 25 August 1978; Roberto de la Guar-

dia, "Mecos—Chombos—Afros West Indians—Blacks—Latinamericans," unpublished manuscript, January, 1980.

3. *Estrella de Panamá*, 12 June 1977, in file entitled "Discrimination 1970, case of Roberto Morgan," Westerman papers.

4. Pérez, in *República*, 21 September 1977; Gittens to Pérez, 25 September 1977, Gittens papers; *Crítica*, 24 August 1978; cf. Alberto Smith Fernández, "Dominio y comercialización de los prejuicios raciales en Panamá," *Memorias del Primer Congreso del Negro Panameño* (Panamá: Instituto Nacional de Cultura, 1981), pp. 94–103.

5. George W. Westerman, *Los inmigrantes antillanos* (Panamá: Impresora de la Nación, 1980).

6. Mitil interview, 11 August 1981.

7. Panama Task Force, *One Task Completed Towards One Cause: The Unification of Panama* (New York: n.p., 1978); "Afro-Panamanians in the United States," in *Panama: Sovereignty for a Land Divided* (Washington, D.C.: Epica Task Force, 1976).

8. Interviews with Hayes, 6 August, Welsh, 16 July, Giscome, 15 July, and Harrison, 5 July 1981.

9. Consular official Frank Silvestri, letter to author, 22 April 1983.

10. Lawrence O. Ealy, *Yanqui Politics and the Isthmian Canal* (University Park: Pennsylvania State University Press, 1971), p. 84.

11. John Biesanz and Luke M. Smith, "Race Relations in Panama and the Canal Zone," *American Journal of Sociology* 45 (July 1941): 11–12.

Selected Bibliography

Essay on Sources

The best annotated bibliography is Eleanor Langstaff, *Panama*. Walter La-Feber, *The Panama Canal*, pp. 287–99, provides a good guide to the literature in English on U.S.-Panamanian relations. The standard bibliographical source is the *Handbook of Latin American Studies* (1936–   ). David McCullough's *The Path Between the Seas* offers the most entertaining account of the construction of the canal, as well as the best guide to the sources for that era.

In researching this book, I sought documentation that would represent the points of view of the several ethnic and national groups of twentieth-century Panama. George Westerman's papers were the richest source for first generation Panamanians of West Indian descent. His newspaper clippings, back files of the *Panama Tribune*, and private correspondence were a record of a people and of one man's attempt to help them make a home in a new land. Other community leaders loaned or gave me papers that filled gaps in the record. Several dozen people spoke with me about their careers and experiences. These interviews, though largely open-ended, covered a few key points regarding political participation, education, perceptions of race relations, the debate over black identity in the 1970s, and the Canal Zone. The interviews, together with information gleaned from newspapers, also allowed me to assemble a prosopographical file useful for generational analysis. Information on West Indian descendants living in the United States came largely from the press and interviews.

The canal experience of the West Indian community is thoroughly documented in the Panama Canal Commission records, RG 185, stored in the National Archives Record Center, Suitland, Md., and in the Diablo Record Center, Panama Canal Area. Richard Giroux's "Textual Records of the Panama Canal," *Preliminary Inventories*, no. 153, Washington, D.C., USNA, 1963, provides an overview. The earliest PCC filing system utilized a number-letter-number combination (e.g., 2-P-71); after 1960 it was replaced by one utilizing three letters and several numbers. Confidential files used the same codes but were preceded by a *C* or an *O*. I saw very little secret material. The single best document in this huge collection is Robert Jeffrey, "Latin American Communities Study."

Official publications of the Panama Canal, though less candid, were essential for fitting labor and race policies into an administrative framework. The *Annual Reports* of the Isthmian Canal Commission (later the Panama Canal) covered major decisions and provided statistics. The *Canal Record* (1907–), published by the ICC and PC, yielded some information about the construction days but less after 1920. Surprisingly, no official history has been done since Goethals's two-volume edited work, *The Panama Canal*, published in 1916.

State Department and military records at the USNA supplemented RG 185 but were neither as complete nor as well organized. Records of diplomatic relations with Panama are contained in RG 59; various intelligence and military files are located in RGs 38, 94, 98, 165, and 395. John Major kindly indicated those files relevant to the West Indians and shared his notes. I am also grateful to him for references to documents in the FDR Library, Hyde Park. Finally, Almon Wright's "The United States and Panama" provides a solid account of diplomacy from 1933 to 1949.

Congress generated many good studies of the canal, especially in construction years, the early 1920s, the mid- and late 1930s, the 1950s, and the mid-1970s. The papers of George Goethals, Robert Taft, and Joseph Mehaffey in the Library of Congress Manuscript Collection yielded some information on the West Indians.

Latin Panamanian views of the West Indian community came from several sources. The press carried stories of and about the immigrants, as well as Latin American reactions to them. About a dozen people spoke frankly with me about their attitudes toward West Indians. Some secondary works deal with the subject, especially John Biesanz's and Mavis Biesanz's fine *People of Panama* and Jorge Arosemena's "Los panameños negros." The dissertations by Carlos Wilson and Mirna Pérez-Venero examined racial attitudes and behavior as revealed in Panamanian literature.

The West Indian community has generated a surprising number of self-portraits. Foremost among them are George Westerman's "Fifty Years of West Indian Life in Panama" and Charles Barton's "Towards the Development of Panama: The Afro-Panamanian Contribution." Raymond Davis's dissertation, "West Indian Workers on the Panama Canal," Alda Harper's study of colored schools in the Canal Zone, Allan Morton's "The Private Schools of the British West Indians," and Lancelot Lewis's *The West Indian in Panama* are fine studies. The 1963 Isthmian Historical Society's compilation of stories by West Indian old-timers ("Reminiscences of Life and Work") affords glimpses of the construction era. I am grateful to David McCullough for sharing it.

Secondary works on United States-Panamanian relations that must be consulted include LaFeber, *The Panama Canal*, already noted; John Major's several articles; Larry Pippin, *The Remon Era;* William D. McCain, *The United States and Panama;* Sheldon Liss, *The Canal;* Norman Padelford, *The Panama Canal in Peace and War*, Eduardo Lemaitre's *Panamá y su separación de Colombia;* and David Farnsworth and James McKenney's *U.S.-Panama Relations.* An early assessment of the Carter-Torrijos Treaty is John Augelli's "The Panama Canal Area in Transition."

The West Indian background is covered in Velma Newton's "British West Indian Emigration," Olive Senior's two articles, and the study by G. W. Roberts. The British *Parliamentary Papers* contain Colonial Office reports that deal with the West Indies. For the period 1904–1950, the Foreign Office papers, located in the Public Record Office in London, offered an intimate and trustworthy view of the West Indian community in Panama. Many fine books available on Antillean society and culture proved less useful than I expected, because migrants to Panama quickly created their own immigrant subculture, drawing on Panamanian and North American traditions as well as those of the islands.

Interviews

Between 1979 and 1981 I interviewed the following persons: Luis Anderson, Teresita de Appin, Wilfred Barrows, Charles Barton, José Dominador Bazán, Ana Bennett, Harold Caroll, Alfredo Castillero Calvo, Ernesto Castillero Pimentel, Carlos Castro, Félix Figueroa, Terry Ford, Hector Gadpaille, Edward Gaskin, Carlos Manuel Gasteazoro, Ivor Giscome, Leroy Gittens, John J. Harrison, Clarence Hayes, Philip Henry, Margot Hutchinson, Pablo Kirven, Carlos Lewis, Rene Lioeanjie, Philip Malcolm, Eunice Mason, Saturnín Maugé, Chesney McDonald, Juanita Mitil, Alfred Osborne, Gaspar Pacheco, Sadith Paz, Silvanns Scarlett, Frank Silvestri, Paul Simoneau, George Simpson, William Sinclair, Alberto Smith Fernández, Egbert Weatherborne, Audley Webster, Winston Welsh, George Westerman, Harold Williams, Leslie Williams, Hugo Wood-Lyder.

Archival Materials

CO	Colonial Office Papers (Britain), Public Record Office, London
FDR	Franklin Delano Roosevelt Library, Hyde Park, N.Y.
FO	Foreign Office Papers (Britain), Public Record Office, London
ICC	Isthmian Canal Commission records (*see* Panama Canal Commission)
LCMC	Library of Congress Manuscript Collection, Washington, D.C. (papers of George W. Goethals, William H. Taft, and Joseph Mehaffey)
PC	Panama Canal Collection, Panama Canal Area Library and Library of Congress, Washington, D.C. (includes the *Canal Record*, Isthmian Historical Society [IHS] materials, and annual reports of the ICC, the Panama Canal Company and Commission, and the PCWIEA)
PCC	Panama Canal Commission (Isthmian Canal Commission, 1902–1914; Panama Canal Company, 1914–1979) records, RG 185, U.S. National Archives Record Center, Suitland, Md., and Diablo Record Center, Panama Canal Area
USNA	U.S. National Archives, State Department and Military records, RGs 38, 59, 94, 98, 165, 395, Washington, D.C.

Private Collections

Edward Gaskin papers
Leroy Gittens papers
Audley Webster papers
George Westerman papers

Selected Bibliography

Periodicals

Crítica
Estrella de Panamá/Star and Herald
Independent
Nation
Panama American
Panama Tribune
República
Workman

Secondary Works

Arosemena, Jorge R. "Los panameños negros descendientes de antillanos: ¿Un caso de marginalidad social?" *Estudios sociales centroamericanos* 5 (1976): 9–34.

Augelli, John P. "The Panama Canal Area in Transition," 2 pts. *American Universities Field Staff Reports* 3–4 (1981).

Barton, Charles. "Towards the Development of Panama: The Afro-Panamanian Contribution." Unpublished manuscript in author's possession.

Biesanz, John. "Cultural and Economic Factors in Panamanian Race Relations." *American Sociological Review* 14 (1949):772–79.

Biesanz, John, and Mavis Biesanz. *The People of Panama*. New York: Columbia University Press, 1955.

Bray, Wayne D., ed. *The Controversy Over a New Canal Treaty Between the United States and Panama*. Washington, D.C., 1976.

Davis, Raymond Allan. "West Indian Workers on the Panama Canal: A Split Labor Market Interpretation." Ph.D. diss., Stanford University, 1981.

Farnsworth, David N., and James W. McKenney. *U.S.-Panama Relations, 1903–1978*. Boulder, Colo.: Westview Press, 1983.

Franck, Harry A. *Zone Policeman 88: A Close Range Study of the Panama Canal and its Workers*. 2d ed. New York: Arno Press, 1970.

Giroux, Richard. "Textual Records of the Panama Canal," *Preliminary Inventories*, no. 153. Washington, D.C.: U.S. National Archives, 1963.

Goethals, George W., ed. *The Panama Canal*. 2 vols. New York: McGraw-Hill, 1916.

Goldsberry, Kenneth E. "The Strike of 1920: A Study of the Black Labor Movement in the Canal Zone." Unpublished paper, Panama Canal Collection.

Harper, Alda. *Tracing the Course of Growth and Development in Educational Policy for the Canal Zone Colored Schools, 1905–1955*. Ann Arbor: University of Michigan School of Education, 1979.

Hoetink, Harry. *Slavery and Race Relations*. New York: Harper and Row, 1973.

Isthmian Historical Society. "Reminiscences of Life and Work During the Construction of the Panama Canal." Unpublished papers, Panama Canal Collection, 1963.

Jeffrey, Robert F. "Latin American Communities Study," 19 June 1979, in PCC O/BLD 6, RG 185, USNA.

Jorden, William J. *Panama Odyssey*. Austin: University of Texas Press, 1984.

LaFeber, Walter. *The Panama Canal: The Crisis in Historical Perspective*. 2d ed., rev. New York: Oxford University Press, 1979.

Langstaff, Eleanor. *Panama*. Oxford and Santa Barbara, Calif.: CLIO Press, 1982.

Selected Bibliography

Lemaitre, Eduardo. *Panamá y su separación de Colombia*. Bogota: Biblioteca Banco Popular, 1972.

Lewis, Lancelot S. *The West Indian in Panama: Black Labor in Panama, 1850–1914*. Washington, D.C.: University Press of America, 1980.

Liss, Sheldon B. *The Canal: Aspects of United States–Panamanian Relations*. Notre Dame, Ind.: University of Notre Dame Press, 1967.

Major, John. "Wasting Asset: The U.S. Re-Assessment of the Panama Canal, 1945–1949." *Journal of Strategic Studies* 3 (1980): 123–46.

———. " '*Pro Mundi Beneficio*'? The Panama Canal as an International Issue, 1943–8." *Review of International Studies* 9 (1983): 17–34.

———. "FDR and Panama." *Historical Journal*, forthcoming.

McCain, William D. *The United States and the Republic of Panama*. Durham, N.C.: Duke University Press, 1937.

McCullough, David. *The Path Between the Seas: The Creation of the Panama Canal, 1870–1914*. New York: Simon and Schuster, 1977.

Morton, Allen Glenn. "The Private Schools of the British West Indians in Panama." Ph.D. diss., George Peabody College for Teachers, 1966.

Newton, Velma Eudora. "British West Indian Emigration to the Isthmus of Panama, 1850–1914." M.A. thesis, University of the West Indies, 1973.

Padelford, Norman J. *The Panama Canal in Peace and War*. New York: Macmillan, 1942.

Paz, Sadith Esther. "The Status of West Indian Immigrants in Panama from 1850–1941." M.A. thesis, University of Massachusetts, Amherst, 1977.

Pérez-Venero, Mirna Miriam. "Raza, color, y prejuicios en la novelística panameña contemporanea de tema canalero." Ph.D. diss., Louisiana State University, 1973.

Pippin, Larry LaRae. *The Remon Era: An Analysis of a Decade of Events in Panama, 1947–1957*. Stanford University Institute of Hispanic American and Luso-Brazilian Studies, 1964.

Roberts, G. W. "Emigration from the Island of Barbados." *Social and Economic Studies* 4 (1955): 245–88.

Senior, Olive. "The Colon People," 2 pts. *Jamaica Journal* 11–12 (1978): 62–71, 87–103.

———. "The Panama Railway." *Jamaica Journal* 14 (1980): 66–77.

U.S. Adjutant General's Office. *History of the Panama Canal Department*. 4 vols. Microfilm copy of typescript in PC, 1947.

Westerman, George W. "Fifty Years of West Indian Life on the Isthmus of Panama, 1903–1953." Unpublished, Westerman papers.

———. *Los inmigrantes antillanos en Panamá*. Panamá: Impresora de la Nación, 1980.

Wilson, Carlos Guillermo. "Aspectos de la prosa panameña contemporanea." Ph.D. diss., UCLA, 1975.

Wood, Robert E. "The Working Force of the Panama Canal." In *The Panama Canal: An Engineering Treatise*. 2 vols., ed. George W. Goethals. New York: McGraw-Hill, 1916.

Wright, Almon. "The United States and Panama, 1933–1949." U.S. Department of State, Research Report 499, August 1952. Mimeographed.

Index

Index

PITT LATIN AMERICAN SERIES

Cole Blasier, Editor

The Hovering Giant: U.S. Responses to Revolutionary Change in Latin America
Cole Blasier

Illusions of Conflict: Anglo-American Diplomacy Toward Latin America
Joseph Smith

Puerto Rico and the United States, 1917–1933
Truman R. Clark

The United States and Cuba: Hegemony and Dependent Development, 1880–1934
Jules Robert Benjamin

USSR Policies

Discreet Partners: Argentina and the USSR Since 1917
Aldo César Vacs

The Giant's Rival: The USSR and Latin America
Cole Blasier

Other National Studies

Barrios in Arms: Revolution in Santo Domingo
José A. Mareno

Beyond the Revolution: Bolivia Since 1952
James M. Malloy and Richard S. Thorn, Editors

Black Labor on a White Canal: Panama, 1904–1981
Michael L. Conniff

The Origins of the Peruvian Labor Movement, 1883–1919
Peter Blanchard

The Overthrow of Allende and the Politics of Chile, 1964–1976
Paul E. Sigmund

Panajachel: A Guatemalan Town in Thirty-Year Perspective
Robert E. Hinshaw

Rebirth of the Paraguayan Republic: The First Colorado Era, 1878–1904
Harris G. Warren

Social Security

The Politics of Social Security in Brazil
James M. Malloy

Social Security in Latin America: Pressure Groups, Stratification, and Inequality
Carmelo Mesa-Lago

Other Studies

Adventurers and Proletarians: The Story of Migrants in Latin America
Magnus Mörner, with the collaboration of Harold Sims

Authoritarianism and Corporatism in Latin America
James M. Malloy, Editor

Constructive Change in Latin America
Cole Blasier, Editor

Female and Male in Latin American: Essays
Ann Pescatello, Editor